PETER ANGUS
LOCOMOTIVE BUILDER

NARROW GAUGE STEAM IN THE GARDEN

I would like to dedicate this book to my wife Patricia who, for the past 40 odd years has patiently suffered, without complaining, my life devoted initially to model steam boats, then motor bikes, then Land Rovers and finally to the subject of this book.

© **Peter Angus 2015**

British Library Cataloguing-in Publication-Data:
a catalogue record of this book is held by the British Library.

First Printing 2015
ISBN No. 978-1-909358-20-1

Published in Great Britain by:
CAMDEN MINIATURE STEAM SERVICES
Barrow Farm, Rode, Frome, Somerset BA11 6PS
www.camdenmin.co.uk

Camden stock one of the widest selections of fine engineering, technical and transportation books to be found. Write to the above address, or see the website, to request a copy of their latest Booklist.

Layout and Design by Andrew Luckhurst, Trowbridge, Wilts.
Printed and Bound by Amber Book Print.

PLEASE NOTE!

In this book the author and publisher are only passing on knowledge; your safety, and that of others, is your responsibility, both in the workshop and when running the locomotive.

The brazing of locomotive boilers and gas tanks carry special risks, and should only be undertaken either under the supervision of someone experienced in such assembly operations, or by them. Additionally, such pressure vessels should always be hydraulically and steam tested before use, as required by current legislation, and annually thereafter.

CONTENTS

PREFACE

BY TAG GORTON

Steam powered garden railways have existed almost since the very early days of the prototype. Taking a look around the Ffestiniog museum, one would find Topsy, a narrow gauge locomotive that technically, was the first steam locomotive to be built at Boston Lodge, actually in 1869. She is a 3 1/8in gauge working model, based on, but not identical to, the George England engines as they appeared at the time. She was built on the orders of Charles Easton Spooner and ran on a figure-of-eight track built in the garden of Bron-y-Garth, Spooner's home.

Later years saw gauge 3 and gauge one railways running in very large gardens (perhaps in a paddock behind the west wing) and while these were very few, there were such lines around in the 1930s and certainly, with the birth of the Gauge 1 Model Railway Association after the second world war, the garden railway tended to use primarily gauge 1 standard gauge trains, some of which were steam powered rather than electric or clockwork.

Perhaps the modern renaissance of garden railways began with the commercial products of LGB, which being narrow gauge, could fit into the sort of real estate provided by the modern garden. Certainly this attracted a growing interest, but in the United Kingdom, narrow gauge trains tended to run on rails that were around two feet apart, designed to fit into the odd or awkward corners of these islands where the heavy engineering and high cost standard gauge could not be attempted. Parallel therefore, with the commercial growth of LGB, there were those who modelled 2ft gauge trains on 0 gauge track, producing the mixed designation of 16mm/ft or 1:19 scale. Early example of this sort of modelling were entirely amateur and motive power generally consisted of home built bodies on old Gauge 0 chassis.

RAISING THE PRESSURE

In the 70s and early eighties, several things happened. First of all Stuart Browne of Archangel Models designed a 16mm scale narrow gauge live steam locomotive whose fire did not go out if the wind was such that it prevented cigarette smoke rising vertically from the Air Ministry roof. Others followed and Roger Marsh (later to become the proprietor of Minimum Gauge Railways) experimented with 16mm and Robin Gosling also moved into this market place. Others followed, but Archangel actually produced a significant range of locomotives at this time, ranging from the cheap and simple 'Brick' to models of prototype locos such as Snowdon Ranger. Jack Wheldon wrote a ground-breaking series of articles in the sadly defunct Model Railway Constructor and, under the generic title Raising the Pressure, introduced so many of us (including me) to the possibilities and pleasures of working narrow gauge steam in the garden.

The early eighties also saw the beginnings of Roundhouse Engineering and Merlin Locomotive Works, while kits for rolling stock also made their appearance. The Association of 16mm Narrow Gauge Modellers had been formed and the hobby began to grow.

During this period, an electrical engineer in the North-East of England was at the time building model steamboats but was excited at the idea of running real steam trains in the garden. Now Peter Angus, like myself, was brought up in an era when comics such as The Eagle featured cutaway coloured drawings of all the exciting engineering of the period for the delectation of small boys. Most of us had Meccano sets and many happy hours were spent constructing, well – anything we could, from massive working Meccano cranes to delicate balsawood Spitfires that actually flew. We were therefore inclined to build and modify.

Once Peter had discovered working narrow gauge steam in the garden scales, he tried building a Lindale kit of the IoM Caledonia that, it seems, was never completed. This was quickly followed by a conversion of the simple four-coupled internally gas fired Beck based Merlin, which was rebuilt into an 0-4-2. Now the idea of this modification was to help the locomotive stay on the very indifferent trackwork systems then available. Who else remembers the Merlin 'bent tin' rail that slotted into itself? Certainly the standard gauge 0 trackwork was not suitable for narrow gauge although if one could find some old 'coarse scale' that was an improvement…

Odd, Unusual and Bizarre

It was the process of hunting out locomotive types that would run safely and at a scale speed on the indifferent track of the period that led Peter Angus into his search for the odd, unusual and sometimes downright bizarre prototype examples of narrow gauge motive power for modelling purposes. Peter discovered that what really interested him was not producing an absolutely rivet perfect model of a popular steam locomotive from the bare metal, but building a properly working model from old photographs, hard sought prototype information and patient acquisition of facts. It should be remembered that, almost by definition, these working items of narrow gauge motive power were not the sort of thing sought out by railway enthusiasts, who generally in the early days, preferred the iconic and often highly polished main line steam locomotives. Narrow gauge locomotives, certainly in the far-flung corners of the world, tended to be utilitarian bits of machinery, cared for and documented only in as much as was required to keep them working economically and they were scrapped without a thought when no longer required.

Peter Angus did not try to re-invent the wheel when producing his first models of unusual prototypes. For instance, excellent cylinders and running gear were available from Roundhouse Engineering and these were used in many of the models produced. Other model locomotives were more suitable for marine plant with geared oscillating cylinders, allowing scale speed running over indifferent track, with the bonus of a particularly impressive plume of steam from the chimney. The attraction for Peter was always the new model of a rare or unusual prototype and after building more than fifty locomotives, selling many on to fund new builds, he discovered something I think has always been a significant part of our hobby. You see, one of the main reasons for moving into both live steam and garden operation is that many of us look for something a bit different from yet another 00 gauge GWR branch line. The garden railfarer has always been a bit of a maverick and we all like our line (and our locomotives) to be particular to ourselves. Peter Angus therefore, found that his locomotives were very much sought after, partly it must be said, because they were very well built and performed impeccably, but also I believe, because most of these locomotives were so very different to their stablemates from the larger manufacturers of narrow gauge garden steam.

Comparative Singularity

Peter Angus Locomotives was formed in 1996 after the production of around fifty models, and this new business specialised (then as now) in producing single or very short runs of hand built locomotives. To date there has been more than three hundred locomotives produced and the overwhelming majority of these have been 'one off' models of unusual prototypes. Now, this actually provides something of an archive, both for the rare and unusual prototypes and the locomotive models that are the result of the research. Certainly this marque of live steam models, partly because of their comparative singularity, but also because of their build quality, are very much sought after and it is therefore not very often that one is seen on the secondhand market.

In view of the above, Peter was asked to document and share these superb models, together with their prototype information, by means of this book. What he has produced will, I believe, be on the shelves of all those who love both attractive working steam models and the narrow gauge steam locomotive in all its diversity. Certainly it will be on mine…

Tag Gorton
Editor GardenRail magazine

INTRODUCTION

This is a book about model steam locomotives or more accurately, narrow gauge locomotives in all their considerable variety and complexity – as applied to garden railways. It is not a book specifically about garden railways, or for that matter, an accurate specification of the full size locomotive. Unlike standard gauge locomotives and in particular those of British Railways, many narrow gauge locomotives spent their working lives out of sight of the general public and very often toiled away in far-off lands. In addition the owners of mines, quarries and plantations where these locomotives worked actively discouraged any interest from the general public and in particular steam enthusiasts. It is not surprising therefore to find that many of these narrow gauge locomotives carried out their working lives unrecorded and are remembered only by the works photographs. For information on these locomotives we can only rely on these images, although there may be works drawings from the more recognisable builders.

For some, this is one of the attractions in building what may be the first and only model of a particular locomotive. If this model is then developed from only a single picture with no drawings available, then who can criticise or demand a recount of the number of rivets? It is along these lines that the production of Peter Angus Locomotives has developed. As the number of models produced has increased so also has the availability of extra information and thus repeat models have become more accurate and more detailed. Another consequence is that the increasing number of models, and the demands of the garden rail fraternity, have tended to steer the Peter Angus building programme towards more conventional locomotives from the more well-known manufacturers. Despite this there will always be room for the odd, the rare or the downright unusual. This book is about all these locomotives in all their magnificent variety and strangeness...

Perhaps we should start by following the numerical list of Works Numbers but this would lead to one very long and tedious chapter. The opportunity has therefore been taken for locomotives that form a special class or type to

(Right) **VALVE GEAR ON JACK**

A left hand side view of the model of the 18in gauge Hunslet Jack, showing the Roundhouse Engineering cylinders and Walschaerts valve gear, including the lifting links for reversing. With this simplified valve gear, the non-functioning combination lever, union link and drop link are supplied as an extra to the main package. The crosshead on this locomotive has been changed from the one supplied by Roundhouse. The description 'simplified' is used because the valve gear does not include a functioning combination lever/union link/ drop link, although it does offer forward and reverse running but not variable cut off. It should be noted that the crosshead is for show only and does not support the piston rod. This does not affect the running of the cylinders and Roundhouse Engineering products are renowned for their long life.

(Author)

(Left) **VALVE GEAR ON JACK**
Detail view of the Roundhouse cylinders and valve gear on the completed Jack. The cylinder covers have been added to the original, which finishes things off nicely and also simplifies the painting and lining.
(Author)

(Right) **GEARED LOCOMOTIVE**
This is an example of a geared locomotive – in this case the first model of one of the Avonside Engine Co geared articulated locomotives based on the only four cylinder locomotive Works Number 2059 named Blackburn. This model was WN5 of 1984 finished originally in works grey/black and named Renishaw No 2. The twin cylinders in this view are the Caton marine engine with the cylinders on the far side the dummy ones.
(Chris Webster)

be included in separate chapters, and I shall be starting with a particular favourite – the Avonside Geared Articulated Tank locomotives. The remaining locomotives from the works list have been contained within the two chapters, Early Days and Consolidation. The list is not complete, for you will note that there are some blank spaces where, for one reason or another, the model was not built.

Many of the narrow gauge models could come under more than one chapter and are therefore placed within whichever chapter is convenient. For instance, the chain driven Sentinel Industrial locomotive appears in the industrial chapter, but is also an important model in the very beginning of Peter Angus production. The first example, WN008, has a mention in the Early Years chapter. This provides relief from slavishly following the previously mentioned Works List. It may also be noticed that as the list progresses, the number of 'one-off' or 'peculiar' designs diminishes and the models tend to be a repeat of previous models or variations on the same class.

PHOTOGRAPHS AND MUSEUM ARCHIVES

A book of this nature relies heavily on the provision of suitable photographs covering the span of model locomotive production, from the early 1980s to the present day. This period of time however has seen a huge change in photographic equipment and associated technology. Initially, the models could only be suitably photographed using expensive cameras that required considerable

expertise and there are many examples of these photographs in the book. These pictures were originally in large format, often in black and white and supplied by Ken Johnson and the late 'Dougie' Kirkbride. Eventually and far more conveniently, there followed the photographs taken on 35mm SLR cameras – in particular the large number of photographs supplied by Geoff Lumsdon. Unfortunately, there are many other photographs that failed to reach the standards of reproduction required by the publisher.

The advent of the digital camera has transformed the photographic scene and there is now little difficulty in recording models built in the last few years. For those locomotives where the photographs are of poor quality or do not exist, it has been necessary to obtain photographs from their present owners or their fellow garden railway enthusiasts. It is important to say that I am very grateful indeed to these owners/ photographers because without them, this book would have been next to impossible.

In addition, there are a large number of photographs of the full size locomotives, which have been provided by visitors to preserved railways and museums. For all of these photographs and the permission to reproduce them, I am very grateful and this book would be poorer without them. One of the joys of reading articles on railways and their locomotives is the availability and reproduction of archive material. This has been provided from individual collections, in particular from the large number of photographs taken from the collection of Andrew Neale. Finally, there are the official

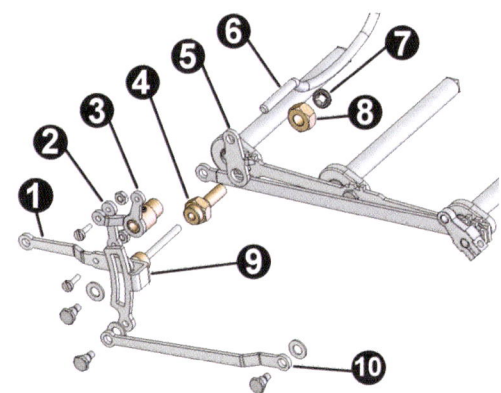

sources of archive material available from museums. These hold the works photographs and drawings of the locomotive manufacturers and have been clearly acknowledged alongside this material. In particular, I must thank the Museum of Science and Industry at Manchester (MOSI) and their Archivist Jan Shearsmith for providing and allowing reproduction of the large number of Works Photographs and General Arrangement Drawings from the Beyer Peacock collection.

MODEL BASICS

Before launching into the locomotives it is perhaps an appropriate time to look at the main components of the models, namely engines, boilers and gas tanks. The model locomotives featured in this book fall into four main categories. Firstly, those with direct drive cylinders, which provide the power and therefore are truly representative of the full size locomotive such as the larger Garratt models and the Eva class Hunslet locomotive. Secondly, there are those models that use a hidden geared engine as the source of power but are based on a direct drive locomotive – an example being the small Garratt models or the early Fowler plantation locomotives. Thirdly, there are the full size locomotives that actually had a geared drive, for instance the Robey geared saddle tank and the Avonside geared articulated tank locomotives. Finally, there are some model locomotives where, in full size the locomotive, was direct coupled but their layout can easily be converted to a geared drive, such as the De Winton type and several of the

tram locomotives. For instance, many of the tram locomotives, by definition, had all-over protective plating, which hid the cylinders and motion and even where this was not the case, as with many continental tramway engines, the direct drive cylinders and valve gear were hidden inside the frames.

SIMPLIFIED WALSCHAERTS VALVE GEAR

For all of the locomotives using direct drive cylinders, the excellent products of the Roundhouse Engineering Co have been used exclusively. The items are supplied as a cylinder pair ready assembled and a simplified Walschaerts valve gear kit sealed in a clear

Assembly of Walschaerts type valve-gear
1). Radius Rod. 2). Lifting Link. 3). Lifting Arm. 4). Expansion Link Bush.
5). Weigh Shaft Bracket (Penguin). 6). Weigh Shaft. 7). Starlock Washer.
8). 2BA Nut. 9). Expansion Link. 10). Eccentric Rod.

SIMPLIFIED WALSCHAERTS VALVE GEAR
(Courtesy Roundhouse Engineering)

PETER ANGUS – LOCOMOTIVE BUILDER

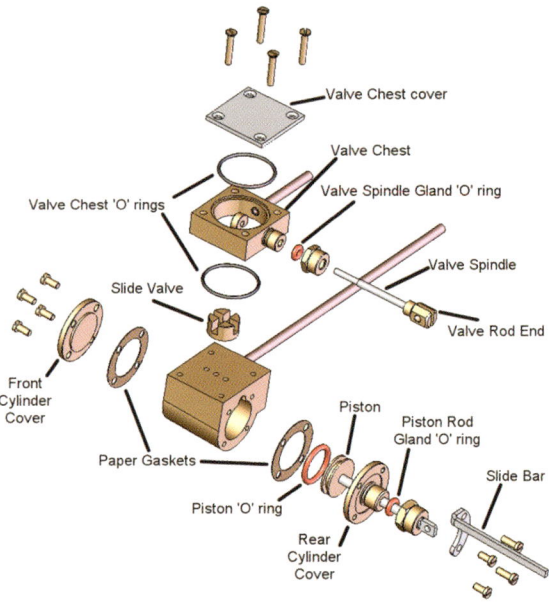

ROUNDHOUSE CYLINDERS AND VALVE GEAR
(Courtesy Roundhouse Engineering)

plastic sausage-like tube. Along with the components is a clear set of instructions and a dimensioned drawing for fitting the parts to custom built frames.

GEARED LOCOMOTIVES

Many of the locomotives use some form of geared engine drive and these have varied over the years as the availability of ready-made engines has changed. The first engine to be used was the excellent piston-valve twin cylinder 8mmx12mm Caton marine unit, originally marketed by Maxwell Hemmens. A long stroke, slow running and compact engine, it was ideally suited for adoption to locomotive applications and first appeared in 1984 with the Avonside Articulated Tank locomotive model Renishaw No 2, which is still running today. It was even produced with the bedplate inverted to effectively reduce the overall height. Several

(Below) **CATON ENGINE**
This 'end on' view shows just how neat this engine design is. The reversing piston type valve is located on the right side of the cylinder casting behind the exhaust pipe with the operating arm extended over the top of the cylinders. The steam inlet to the engine is on the left hand side shown as the ¼in x40 brass insert at the lower centre of the cylinder block.

(Brian Clarke)

(Above) **CATON ENGINE**
The original Caton engine was designed by Brian Caton and manufactured by Maxwell Hemmens as a marine engine for model boats. This engine was unusual in having piston valves. This simplified the method of reversing, but required very accurate machining of the piston valves and bores. As with an oscillating engine, reversing required only that the inlet and exhaust be changed over – a process carried out within the cylinder block using a third piston valve. The example shown was removed from the Garratt locomotive Christina, WN34, and still has the transfer gearbox attached. Notice how the engine bedplate has been inverted to reduce the overall height.

(Brian Clarke)

other locomotives used this marine engine until Maxwell Hemmens decided to completely redesign the unit to be compatible with CNC production, the new engine being renamed the Max11.

From the locomotive point of view, this was a much larger engine, although it had the advantage of ball race bearings on the crankshaft and a generally heavier construction. Unfortunately, the larger size reduced the possible range of applications to the bigger locomotives where it could be used as the hidden geared engine in such models as the Brazilian Sugar Garratt WN46, Carla's Court and the Kitson Meyer Strathfarrer, WN42. The Max11 engine did however find favour when applied to the geared articulated Shay locomotive. In this case the four steel pillars supporting the cylinders were removed and the bedplate rotated through 90degrees and held in place by a special bracket. The use of ball race bearings and the heavier construction of the Max11 engine resulted in these locomotives having a long and successful life with very little engine wear.

GEARED LOCOMOTIVE APPLICATIONS

The size of the Max11 engine continued to be a problem until the advent of the geared SVS engine. This twin-cylinder (8x12mm) oscillating engine had been produced for several years as a direct drive to the propeller shaft of model boats, but was eventually expanded to include a geared version for paddle steamers. Either way, it was a very compact unit that could be adapted for use in geared locomotive applications, including some quite small engines. By shortening one side of the output shaft (short shaft engine), it was possible to fit the lower part of the engine between the wheels to gain a further 2:1 gear

(Left) CATON ENGINE

This shows how the Caton engine is used on the Mayumbe Garratt Christina. The gearbox transfers the drive to the centre of the unit; then provides a double-sided drive via Carden shafts to the bogies. Notice how the square drive shaft is located between the trunk guide and the support columns.

(Brian Clarke)

(Below) MAXWELL HEMMENS MAX 11 ENGINE

The engine that followed the Caton was the larger 'CNC friendly' Max 11, seen here attached to the frame of the Michigan California No2 Shay. Originally supplied as a marine engine, the columns have been removed and the bedplate rotated through 90° with a suitable support bracket. Unlike the previous engine the crankshaft has ball race bearings and is of a more solid construction.

(Geoff Lumsdon)

(Left) The SVS Short Shaft Engine

The original arrangement of the 8x12mm twin cylinder double acting oscillating engine designed for use in paddle boats with the integral 4:1 reduction gearing. As originally supplied, the output shaft was double ended but would not fit between the 32mm gauge wheels and so one side of the shaft was discarded. The next improvement was to include ball race bearings on the output shaft and engine crankshaft. The method of attaching the 4:1 reduction gears was also improved. This engine is used vertically in locomotives such as the De Winton or horizontally between the axles as in the Graffenstaden Tram.

(Author)

(Right) The SVS Overtype Engine

The engine was designed solely for the Stephen Lewin overtype locomotives but has also found a use in the later Sentinel 80hp Industrial chain driven locomotive, where it is mounted by the outrigger bearing. The engine differs from the standard unit by having longer double output shafts and a supporting third ball race bearing corresponding to the output gear.

(Author)

(Left) The SVS Boxer Engine

Again, a variation on the original design with the object of making a very compact unit that could be mounted across the frames with its double output shaft driving along the longitudinal length of the locomotive. The idea was to drive carden shafts to front and rear bogies as in the Avonside Geared Articulated tank locomotive. By using only one output shaft, the engine found use as a hidden drive on the Single Fairlie. The engine has even found use fitted under the horizontal part of the 'Lumpy Tom' boiler in the compact 0-4-0 Lumpy Tom locomotive.

(Author)

reduction, although this meant the engine was slightly offset to the locomotive centre line.

The engine could be mounted vertically for tramway locomotives or De Winton types. It could also be laid flat between the frames and in some cases between the axles, as in the case of the George England locomotives. Further applications produced variations on the basic layout, for instance the addition of an outrigger bearing (Overtype engine) for the Stephen Lewin locomotives or the compact boxer arrangement for the Lumpy Tom and SLM tram locomotives. There was even a Shay version with the original double output shaft. For larger locomotives the engine could be supplied with increased 10mm bore cylinders and sometimes the final gearing was changed to 1.5:1, giving an overall reduction of 6:1 with a slight increase in speed.

As early experience in the operation of locomotives was gained, it became obvious that the application to locomotives placed a different set of stresses on the engine to that of driving a propeller shaft. Consequently, the original plain bearings of the output shaft and engine crankshaft were replaced with ball race bearings. The extra torque associated with the geared engine could, under certain conditions, defeat the 'Loctite' fitting of the crankshaft spur gear, so it was replaced with a composite gear and shaft. This is where the shaft and gear are machined as one, termed a double-ended pinion shaft. The gear on the output shaft was also pinned to the shaft. 8ba tapped holes were added so a stop could be attached to the forward/reverse lever. In this form, the engine has continued to be used without further modification.

PORCUPINE COPPER STUDS

At the beginning of the present garden railway movement, the type of boilers adopted by the emerging locomotive builders carried on with the simple plain potboiler that had been around for years, although sometimes they were improved by the addition of water tubes or porcupine copper studs. These boilers used methylated spirits as the source of heating and without some form of fireguard, these locomotives could only operate in very calm weather. With an external firebox however, these locomotives were effective and tractable little beasts in most weather conditions.

One of the earliest and most successful of this type of narrow gauge garden locomotive was Charles Pooter, an externally fired 0-4-0, developed by Jack Wheldon. Jack was not interested in supplying the demand that his locomotive generated and therefore passed on the design to Roger Loxley at Roundhouse Engineering, who was prepared to manufacture them alongside their Lady Anne and Dylan engines. What the Charles Pooter class locomotive demonstrated very effectively was that a correctly designed externally fired model, with a suitable firebox, could operate satisfactorily outdoors, even in fairly inclement conditions. This model was available from 1982 until 1994, by which time the problem of obtaining good quality methylated spirits, safety considerations and the difficult art of setting the wicks, made them uneconomic to continue in commercial production. In fact, Ron Grant of Gratech Services could, at the time, replace the wick burner with an external gas-fired type, which did make life easier for the many new people then trying live steam in the garden for the first time. This type of firing however largely fell out of favour, primarily because of the requirement for dummy sidetanks to hide this external firebox – and this severely attenuated the list of prototypes that could be modelled.

Thirty years on, Lupin at Bishops Amble. Jack Weldon's methylated spirits fired 'Pooter', one of the first really successful externally fired narrow gauge garden railway locomotives.

(Dave Pinniger)

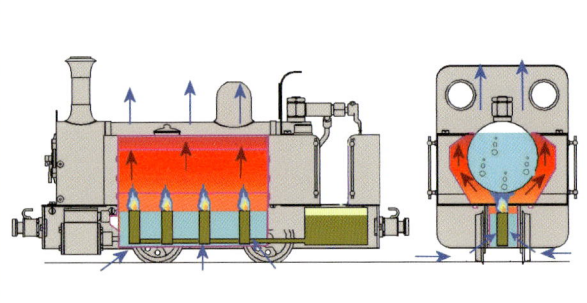

15. Diagram illustrating the arrangement of a simple external spirit fired potboiler locomotive as used on the Roundhouse Engineering 'Charles Pooter'.

(Courtesy Roundhouse Engineering)

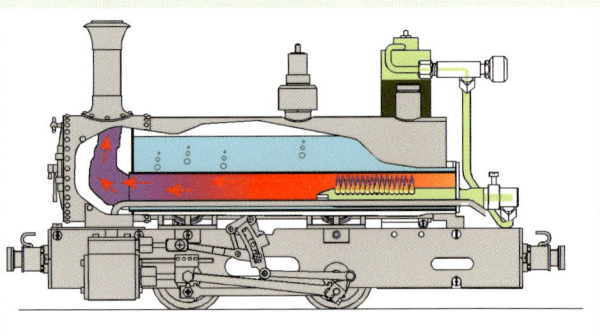

16. Single closed flue gas system as used on internally fired Roundhouse model steam locomotives.

(Courtesy Roundhouse Engineering)

As interest in steam powered narrow gauge garden railways continued to grow, the demand for a boiler system free of these constraints resulted in the appearance of the centre flue gas fired boiler onto the 16mm garden railway scene. Roundhouse Engineering introduced their own internally gas fired plain centre flue boiler models in 1994/5 in the form of the Fowler 0-6-2 locomotive which did not have side tanks and was therefore unsuitable for spirit firing. The basic system is illustrated in the diagram courtesy of Roundhouse Engineering. It is interesting to note that internally spirit fired boilers have never been particularly popular in the world of 16mm scale garden railways, whereas this type of spirit-fired boiler is still the mainstay of garden steam in Gauge One standard gauge.

THE VISIBLE GLOW

As can be seen in the locomotives covered in this book, plain centre flue gas fired boilers have been the mainstay of locomotive production with merely dimensional variations to accommodate a particular prototype – including of course the position of domes, sandboxes and the like. With some models, the barrel was brought forward of the front tube plate to act as a smokebox, as in the case of the Sentinel and Stephen Lewin engines. Where a faster steaming boiler was required, the centre flue can have the addition of water tubes but these can effect the operation of the burner and in some cases, may cause howling. The other popular boiler used is the vertical centre flue type fitted with water tubes and a ceramic burner. Whereas the setting of

17. (Top left) This Hohenzollern Conical boiler is an example of a plain centre flue boiler for use with a poker type gas burner. The boiler is very unusual in having a conical outer shell, which in full size practice was designed to have the greater mass of water around the firebox to give rapid steaming. The main source of heat transfer takes place around the firebox with the fire tubes becoming less and less effective as they travel further from the firebox. The boiler also has a large steam dome typical of locomotives operating on gradients and rough undulating track; this locomotive was intended for military use.
(Author)

18. (Top right) Here we have a short horizontal plain centre flue boiler with a larger diameter vertical element developed for the 'Lumpy Tom' class locomotives and used correctly on the SLM tramway locomotives (Brown Patent). As with the Hohenzollern type, these boilers have good steam space for difficult conditions and both give excellent steaming. Both boilers use the 2¼in Finescale Engineering poker type burners.
(Author)

19. (Left) The project boiler is a much more sophisticated type of boiler generally preferred by the Gauge 1 fraternity but in this case fitted with a wet backhead to provide a conventional water gauge. Water tubes are fitted to the firebox and also to the centre flue to increase the heating surface. Steam is taken from the centre dome to the regulator located on the backhead. This boiler is fitted with a large firebox and 2½in barrel for a Garratt locomotive with four working cylinders. In this case a blower is fitted to the smokebox to draw the fire through the boiler, otherwise the burner tends to choke and will not give its full output. For this boiler a rectangular ceramic burner is used.
(Mike Lax)

a poker type burner can be difficult in noisy conditions, these boilers have the advantage of the ceramic burner being visible down the flue, enabling the burner to be set from the visible glow. In general, these boilers are not as efficient as their horizontal counterparts and in practice there was, in any case, a very limited number of locomotives that used them. With the exception of the Sentinel type, full size locomotives fitted with a vertical boiler were limited to short journeys with frequent stops, as in civil engineering contracts.

In order to supply steam to larger and more demanding locomotives, other types of boiler have been used, including the Project type boiler often used by the Gauge 1 Association members. The addition of water tubes into the flue and the firebox however can stifle the burner by preventing the hot gasses from escaping without introducing a backpressure. In these circumstances, it is necessary to add a blower to the smokebox to draw out the hot gasses. Finally, the ultimate boiler is the Belpaire coal fired locomotive boiler (with or without superheating), which is a miniature of the full size unit. Apart from the high cost of this type of locomotive boiler (which can be many times more than a simple centre flue type), locomotives so fitted require a degree of experience to fire them reliably.

RECTANGULAR BRASS TUBE

Despite being a pressure vessel, the gas tank has not always been treated with the same

20. The ultimate model locomotive boiler for coal firing with a Belpaire wet firebox. This superb boiler built by Brian Nicholls for a model of the Burma Mines No 9 locomotive, (built by the North British Locomotive Company as their wn18674), has the advantage of a wide firebox made possible by the full size engine having the frames widened at the rear, (see WN216).

(Brian Nicholls)

21. (Far left) Two views of a standard gas tank which can be mounted between or on top of the locomotive frames more usually at the rear in the cab area or, in the case of some tramway locomotives, in front of the boiler on top of the frames. This front/rear view shows the modular construction using two vertical tubes alongside each other.

(Author)

22. (Left) End view showing the 1in square tube and the heavy end plates with the bottom one acting as the mounting plate. Notice the fillet of silver solder around the end plate joints and the identification information on the base.

(Author)

23. This is type of gas tank used on the Sentinel, Robey and several other locomotives where the standard gas tank is not suitable. The boss on the side of the tank is for mounting to the locomotive frames using 6ba socket cap screws. The boss on the side of the turret is for the gas-regulating valve with the Ronson type filler valve in the top. Again, the construction is modular using two 1in square brass tubes this time in horizontal formation.

(Author)

24. Three examples of ready-made poker type gas burners. From left to right, Finescale Engineering Co, Roundhouse Engineering Co and finally, an early Maxwell Hemmens unit. The two former burners use a jet holder and separate gas jet that can be supplied in different jet hole sizes, which may have to be changed to tune the burner to the particular boiler and smokebox arrangement. The third burner used a fixed gas jet size that had been very accurately drilled and was a very efficient burner.

(Author)

respect as the steam boiler. Early gas tanks were sometimes built using rectangular brass tube of limited thickness and often without stays on the flatter faces. They could also be connected to the burner using flexible silicon tube without any reinforcement. Unlike steam boilers that operate within a set range of pressure and are protected by a safety valve, the gas tank pressure can be affected by the surrounding temperature and induced heat.

For instance a gas tank located close to a heat source such as the boiler would reach a pressure with pure butane of 60psi at 40° Celsius or 110psi at 60° Celsius. A 70/30 butane/propane mix will reach over 110psi at 40° Celsius. With such pressures as these, the design of gas tanks and their location in the locomotive is of considerable importance. The consideration of parameters for these pressure vessels should at least be equal to the respect given to steam boilers. Simple precautions require all gas pipe connections to be made with suitable copper pipe, brass unions should be silver soldered and due regard given to siting for adequate ventilation. The gas tank should be located away from a heat source such as the boiler, or if this is not possible as with a location in a side tank, there should be adequate insulation between the tank and the boiler.

Typical gas tanks are shown in the photographs and it will be noted that they are of a modular construction using square brass tube with end plates of sufficient thickness and silver soldered throughout. At present gas tanks are tested at 400psi, (originally 350psi).

Three examples of typical poker type gas burners are illustrated. They look fairly straightforward, but anyone who has ever built such a beast finds that in reality burners are something of a black art. Let the manufacturers do the hard work of providing a working unit and then time can be spent adjusting jets and air to fit the locomotive boiler and smokebox configuration.

We have spent long enough in the workshop looking at components and perhaps now we should look at the actual models...

SCALE AND GAUGES

Unlike other types of modelling, such as model boats, railway modelling is unique in being governed not only by scale but also by the track gauge. For obvious practical reasons, the gauge is set by the availability of ready-made track, which can be supplied in either coarse or fine scale. If the model railway is to be based on British railways standard gauge, using the readily available track to the gauge of 32mm or 45mm, then the 4ft 8½in standard gauge would give a scale of 7mm/ft on 32mm track and 10mm (3/8in)/ft on 45mm track, both of which would be on fine scale track. The complications arise when we consider the narrow gauge. Take for instance the common narrow gauges around the 3ft mark and we have 3ft gauge, metre gauge and 3ft 6in gauge. At the lower end we have 18in, 20in, 2ft and 600mm, 2ft 4¼in and 2ft 6in and a few 'one offs' in between, which is all very confusing. To overcome this difficult situation and produce some degree of consistency, the Association of 16mm modellers and the G scale society were formed. Narrow gauge track is usually of heavier section relative to the gauge and is termed coarse scale. This allows the wheels of narrow gauge locomotives and rolling stock to use deeper flanges, which are more appropriate to the tighter curves and uneven nature of the track bed.

Wolfgang and Eberhard Richter created G scale when their family firm, Ernst Paul Lehman Patentwerk, introduced their innovative indoor/outdoor LGB brand trains in 1968. A typical G scale model train is built to a scale of 22.5:1 and represents narrow gauge stock on metre gauge track operating on the traditional 45mm coarse scale track. This proportion allowed the Richters to model trains based on European narrow gauge and could also include American narrow gauge. The scale of such models was not only suitable for garden railways but was also a very handy and chunky size, which could be used for live steam locomotives. Despite this, the vast majority of G scale models, regardless of the prototype, stick to electric power, either from the track or with on-board batteries and radio control.

Whereas G scale was suitable for the metre gauge (with a degree of flexibility, the 3ft and 3ft 6in gauge), it was totally unsuitable for the smaller narrow gauges around the 2ft mark. Yet many narrow gauge railways, in particular industrial lines, used a smaller gauge. This included the narrow gauge railways of Wales, which mainly operated on the very popular 2ft and 600mm gauges. These railways could be modelled at 7/8th scale on 45mm track but the rolling stock and locomotives would become rather large. The obvious solution was to model at a scale of 16mm/ft for operation on 32mm gauge coarse scale track, which led to the formation of 'The Association of 16mm Narrow Gauge Modellers'. Unlike the previous scale, the balance of the locomotive power is live steam with some of the models being suitable (with a degree of tolerance) for G scale. To widen the scope of the 16mm Association, the group also includes operation on 45mm gauge at a scale of 16mm or thereabouts. This tolerance in scale is just as well, because some narrow gauge loading gauges can be larger than standard gauge, (the former Rhodesia Railways loading gauge width was 13ft 6in with a cab width on a class 14A being 10ft). This flexibility in scale allows us to accommodate not only the smaller locomotives at a slightly larger scale but also the larger locomotives at a smaller scale. There are many examples of this in the following chapters.

The model steam locomotives featured in this book are, in general, built to a scale of 16mm/ft or thereabouts for operation on 32mm/45mm gauge coarse scale track. In the case of some very small locomotives, such as the Stephen Lewin overtypes, this scale tolerance has been extended in the interests of producing a

1. (Left) A 2ft gauge Fowler plantation locomotive to the scale of 16mm/ft for operation on 32mm coarse scale track. This is the correct scale and gauge on which the Association of 16mm Narrow Gauge Modellers was founded and would be equally appropriate for any locomotive operating on the 2ft gauge such as in a Welsh slate quarry.

(WN188-3 – Mike Lax)

2. (Below) Standard gauge NER class M1 built to a scale of 10mm/ft for operation on LGB coarse scale 45mm track. A standard gauge locomotive built to a scale of 10mm/ft or 3/8in/ft would normally come under the accepted rules of the Gauge 1 Model Railways Association (G1MRA), but would be for operation on 45mm finescale track.

(WN195-1 – Mike Lax)

3. (Left) This model of the 2ft 6in gauge Buthidaung Maungdaw Tramway Beyer Garratt locomotive was built to a scale of 16mm/ft arranged to run on 32mm coarse scale track when the correct gauge would be a non-standard 40mm.

(WN032-2 – Ken Johnson)

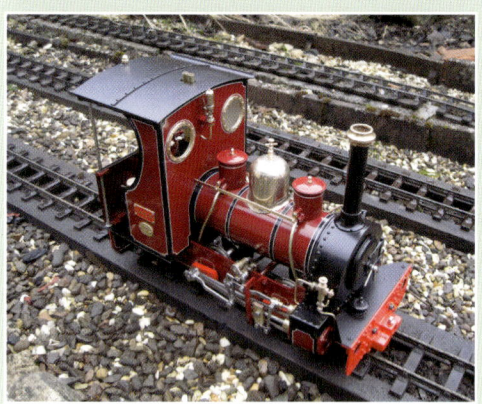

4. (Top) This is the same tramway Garratt as WN148 above but arranged for operation on 45mm coarse scale track.

(WN119-2 – Geoff Lumsdon)

5. (Above left) Jack, an 18in gauge locomotive built to a scale of 7/8in/ft for operation on 32mm track. The correct scale would be 21.3mm/ft.

(WN250-3 – Author)

6. (Above right) Eaton Railway 15in gauge locomotive built to a scale of 1in/ft – which would be correct on 32mm track. However, the model was built to operate on a garden railway that used 45mm track.

(WN233-8 – Author)

practical model for the, often difficult, conditions of a garden railway. The converse is also true, where the dimensions of the full size locomotive would cause problems with the loading gauge of typical garden railways, the scale has been reduced. For example, the model of the Rotterdamsche Tramweg Maatschappij No57, WN76, had to be reduced to a scale of 14.25mm/ft because these 1067mm gauge trams were indeed rather large and quite out of proportion to other 16mm stock. Even so, the length of the model is still one inch longer than a Roundhouse Lady Anne. So here are photographs of models built to several different scales to accommodate locomotives of different gauges on the commercially available track of 32/45mm gauge. All are within the 16mm or thereabouts criteria, as well as an example of a standard gauge locomotive on 45mm track.

7. (Above) Samuel Geoghegon designed locomotive for the 20in gauge Guinness Brewery railway in Dublin. The model is built to 22mm/ft scale for operation on 32mm track. This scale was adopted for practical reasons, whereas the correct scale should have been 19.2mm/ft.
(WN208 – Dave Pinniger)

8. (Left) The diminutive Stephen Lewin locomotive of the Guinness railway was even smaller than the Samuel Geoghegan locomotive on the same railway. In this case the model was built as small as considered practical using existing engine and boiler types. The scale is really academic but the model gives an excellent performance and does not look out of scale on 16mm layouts.
(WN209-2 – Dave Pinniger)

9. (Bottom left) An example of a large prototype modelled to a reduced scale of 14.25mm/ft to bring the size within acceptable limits and to be compatible with typical 16mm stock. Tramway locomotives are usually small but this continental engine is still longer than a Lady Anne, despite the scale reduction.
(WN076-2 – Michael Porter)

EARLY DAYS

This chapter deals with the early locomotives but excludes those that appear in the more specialised chapters, for example the first Garratt model, WN3, appears in the chapter on Garratt locomotives. It would seem logical to start this chapter with WN1 but there is a problem with this. WN1 was almost certainly a kit supplied by Lindale of the 2ft 6in gauge Isle of Man Caledonia. There are no details of this model (which was never completed) and its subsequent fate is not remembered.

The situation improves with the next model, which actually made it to the track. Remember, these really were the early days, with a very limited availability of locomotives, rolling stock and all the other items required for the budding garden railway enthusiast. One of the first suppliers and indeed the person credited with starting the present movement towards narrow gauge live steam in the garden was the late Tom Cooper. His German manufactured Beck 'Anna', introduced the gas fired centre flue boiler and piston valve cylinders to an emerging locomotive scene. Based on this design, Tom Cooper brought out the Merlin 'Maestro' 0-6-0 side-tank locomotive with reversing gear along with the simpler and cheaper Merlin 'Midas'. This was the same model but was fitted with slip-eccentric valve gear and was the basis for the second locomotive, WN2.

Now, even at this early stage yours truly was not one for following the ordinary line. The chassis was rebuilt to an 0-4-2 configuration, and a tender was added to carry the radio control. Apart from making the model that little bit different, it may have also been to improve the locomotives ability to stay on the indifferent track of this period. This modified Merlin Midas was given the name Juliet using a set of plates from a 3½in gauge locomotive.

The next alteration to an existing commercially available model does not even appear on the works list. The photograph is all that remains

and illustrates a Roundhouse Engineering 'Charles Pooter' suitably altered by replacing the entire bodywork with a pannier tank style, based on a photograph of a Hudswell Clarke locomotive supplied to South Africa. The model carried the name Princess Dawn.

GARRATT LOCOMOTIVE PIRACICABA WN3

Why the next model should be a giant leap from a simple commercially available engine suitably modified to the complicated articulated Garratt design is not clear, but was almost certainly a combination of three reasons. Firstly, the available garden railway tracks of the early 1980s often consisted of made up track laid directly on a minimum of ballast. Small locomotives, such as the Mamod, were very much in evidence, yet keeping even these simple four-coupled engines on the track, especially at the speeds they were capable of reaching, was not easy. Larger models made the situation even worse so why not adopt the solution used on full size railways of using a small articulated engine of the Garratt type with the greater flexibility of bogies to cope easily on this indifferent rail? Secondly, the extra size would make it easier to include radio control, which in those days simply did not have the miniaturisation available today.

Finally, and probably the main reason, was to produce a model that was so completely unusual and, at the time – unique in this gauge. This theme was to rule virtually all my subsequent choices of model prototypes in the early construction programme. WN3 was to be the beginning of a fascination with the incredible variety of narrow gauge engines and a reputation for building the unusual, however ugly. The black and white photograph shows WN3 which was based on the very small Garratt locomotives built by Société Anonyme St. Léonard for the metre gauge South American Porto Feliz Sugar Co. in 1927.

1. (Left) Juliet, a Merlin Midas 0-4-0 with the addition of a spring loaded trailing truck and a small four-wheel tender. Notice the slip-eccentric outside valve gear and the servo lead from the tender to operate the single servo controlling the steam regulator. Typically, a tender would be added to carry the larger radio control of this era, but room was still required to fit the servo into the locomotive. An interesting point regarding this early locomotive was the location of the oil lubricator in the front dome above the steam outlet valve. The top of the dome was unscrewed to fill the lubricator with oil.

(WN002 Juliet – N D Kirkbride)

2. (Above) Model of a Garratt locomotive based on the very small Brazilian sugar plantation locomotives built in 1927 by Société Anonyme St. Léonard of Liége, Belgium for the Porto Feliz Sugar Company. It was built on one powered and one unpowered 0-4-0 chassis supplied by Robyn Gosling. The chassis in fact was the standard type used for his Hunslet saddle tank locomotive. The rear unit was the powered version and due to the models very free running, a disc brake was fitted to one axle of the front non-powered unit. Radio control was accommodated in the rear bunker.

(WN003-1 Piracicaba – Author's collection)

3. (Left) For this model, which does not appear to have been issued with a works number, the original Roundhouse Engineering Charles Pooter had the body removed and scrapped. A new pannier tank style body was then constructed, based on a photograph of a Hudswell Clarke locomotive supplied to South Africa. It is similar to wn1485 of 1922 but without the four-wheeled tender.

(Princess Dawn – Author's collection)

4. (Below left) The Single Fairlie Patricia, which is described in the chapter on Festiniog locomotives.

(WN004-3 – Author's collection)

5. (Above) Based on redundant stock from the Roundhouse Engineering Plynlimon & Hafan 'Victoria' Tram, the model adopts the layout of a typical De Winton industrial locomotive. The vertical boiler had a single plain centre flue with heat provided from a two-wick methylated spirit burner and supplied steam to the single cylinder direct drive engine.

(WN006 Loxan – N D Kirkbride)

6. (Top left) The second model to use the Roundhouse chassis was constructed as a freelance tram type locomotive. The front tank contained water and was used to vacuum fill the boiler at the end of a run. Both models were great fun to play with but the direct drive single cylinder engine limited operation to a reasonably flat track.

(WN007-1 Goliath – N D Kirkbride)

7. (Middle left) Goliath is emerging from a tunnel on my first garden railway at Whitley Bay. The pipe leaving the front water tank runs to a valve on the bottom of the water gauge and was used to vacuum fill the boiler. Even at this early stage, the lubricator has a suitable drain valve rather than a drain screw. The lubricator is attached directly to the engine by the steam chest cover.

(WN007-2 Goliath – N D Kirkbride)

8. (Bottom left) Photographed with a rake of tipper wagons, WN8 is certainly not the most attractive of locomotives. The side skirts on the model, based on the photograph in the Hudson catalogue, do not seem to appear on any other pictures of the Sentinel 80hp industrial locomotives. No doubt they were intended to protect the chains from debris or to give protection to workers in a plantation or similar.

(WN008-2 Bulldog – N D Kirkbride)

Details of this model, the Garratt design and its application to modelling in 16mm scale are covered in the chapter on this type of locomotive. With the success of the Garratt, the first articulated model, enthusiasm for articulation continued with the next two locomotives, WN4, the Single Fairlie Taliesin, based on the locomotive built by the Vulcan Foundry of Newton le Willows in 1876. This was followed by WN5, the Avonside four cylinder articulated tank locomotive, Renishaw No 2. Again these models are dealt with in their respective chapters.

LOXAN & GOLIATH, WN6&7

After three complicated articulated locomotives, a return was made to the simplicity of the basic 0-4-0 type. At this time, Roundhouse Engineering, one of the earliest builders of garden railway engines, operating from the dismal and windowless Old Cold Store in Doncaster, had decided to end the production of one of their earliest models based on the Plynlimon & Hafan tram Victoria. This model used a ½in bore single cylinder engine with a simple plain centre flue boiler, several of which were left over at the end of production.

Never one to miss an opportunity, these leftover items, along with two sets of frames and boilers formed the basis of the next two engines. Incidentally, the plain flue vertical boilers were methylated spirit fired with two-wick burners. WN6 was to represent a typical De Winton locomotive and WN7 a freelance tram. The water tank on the tram could be filled with water and used to vacuum fill the boiler. These two locomotives were great fun but being direct drive with a single cylinder engine required a reasonably flat track to give consistent running.

THE SENTINEL 80HP INDUSTRIAL LOCOMOTIVE, WN8

By this time, the construction of the more unusual locomotives had not gone unnoticed. Whilst visiting the garden railway of the late Bob Farnsworth at Blanchland in Northumberland, the phrase was heard, "Got something for you – it is rather ugly so I thought you might be interested?" It was to be repeated on a regular basis over the years with suitable alternative, "Came across a picture of this weird locomotive so I thought you may be interested." WN8 was certainly different to any locomotive seen

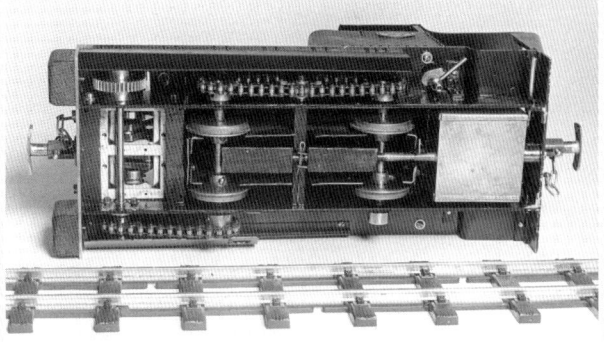

9. (Above left) Compare the model of the 80hp Sentinel Industrial locomotive with the photograph from the Andrew Neale collection of the full size engine. In almost all photographs, the chain drive is completely exposed and it is unfortunate that the one photograph on which WN8 is based is of insufficient quality to be reproduced. Note the very small but highly efficient vertical water tube boiler and the horizontal water tank.

(Sentinel 80hp – Andrew Neale collection)

10. (Above right) The underside view of Bulldog shows the methylated spirit burner and firebox, along with the chain drive. What is not so clear is the intermediate sprocket on the inter axle chain drive is mounted on an eccentric bearing to provide a degree of chain tensioning. The underside of the Caton marine engine can be seen along with the 2:1 reduction countershaft.

(WN008-3 – N D Kirkbride)

11. (Above) A very realistic B/W photograph of Bulldog with a suitable industrial background.

(WN008-5 – Author's collection)

previously and came under the title 'Hudson Light Railways.

This was a firm that specialised in supplying light railway equipment for plantations, quarries, horticultural systems or any situation where temporary or lightly laid track was required. The track could be supplied as prefabricated straight or curved lengths along with turnouts, turntables to connect track sections and various mechanical items to facilitate the loading and unloading of trucks. To complement this track, an extensive selection of rolling stock, such as tipper trucks was available. However, this would not have been complete without motive power. Whereas Hudson manufactured most of the previous items, locomotive builders Decauville and Sentinel supplied Hudson. Indeed it was the firm of Sentinel of Shrewsbury who were responsible for this unusual and rather ugly locomotive. Since building this particular model back in 1985, there have been several more, culminating in WN281. A description of the full size engines can wait until the section on industrial locomotives. The photograph on which WN8 was based was the only one to show side covers over the chain drive, whereas every photograph that has been seen since leaves the drive chains and sprockets exposed. Unfortunately, the photograph, taken from a Hudson catalogue is of very poor quality and cannot be reproduced here.

From the model point of view, the chain drive and the choice of engine are of interest. The smallest chain readily available at the time was 3/16in pitch and, along with the sprockets, was supplied by Ron Grant of Gratech Services, who was one of the earliest suppliers of garden railway items. The engine could have driven the wheels direct, but the advantage of an indirect drive is the ability to introduce gearing. It was found that a gear reduction of 2:1 was ideal – giving slow consistent running akin to the full size locomotive and narrow gauge railways in general. For garden railways of this era, this slow and consistent running resulted in operation without derailment, in contrast to the high-speed frolics associated with early direct drive models – and at a time when radio control was not very common. Now, to obtain a drive reduction of 2:1 between the engine and the front axle with such a large chain pitch was not really practical. This made it necessary to provide an idler shaft under the engine bedplate. The 2:1 reduction was therefore obtained by spur gears between the engine and idler shaft, leaving a 1:1 chain drive from the opposite end of the shaft to the to the front axle.

The drive layout, including the idler shaft, is illustrated in the photograph of the underside of WN8. Incidentally, what is not clear from the photograph is the idler sprocket between the axles to tension the chain. This was the first model to use the Maxwell Hemmens twin cylinder double-acting piston valve engine. It was to provide power for many more locomotives, until replaced by the larger and less suitable Max II. With a 3/8in bore and a long stroke of 5/8in, it was ideally suited to the slow running required for railway applications. Further examples of the Sentinel chain driven locomotive are covered in the chapter on

12. (Left) The first 0-6-0 model using a simple methylated spirit fired potboiler with the Caton marine engine mounted across the frame in front of the boiler and hidden by the smokebox. Looking at the photograph the engine cannot be seen. Despite being freelance the locomotive was quite attractive, the photograph having been taken before dummy cylinders were fitted. Once fitted the dummy cylinders effectively hide the gear drive from the engine to the front axle.
(WN011 – N D Kirkbride)

13. (Right) Renamed Tommy and now fitted with dummy outside cylinders, WN11 awaits a run on the Guildford Model Engineering Society 16mm outdoor layout at Stoke Park in July 2006. According to the owner, the locomotive may be in need of a little cosmetic attention but is still a regular performer and still running perfectly after 26 years. The forward/ reverse lever on the Caton Marine engine can be seen in the slot in the front of the smokebox. The location of the Caton engine across the frame under the smokebox is not apparent in this photograph. Unfortunately, the later version of the engine called the Max II was much larger and would not have fitted into this arrangement.
(WN011-3 – Chris Webster)

industrial locomotives. The picture also shows that this model was methylated spirits fired with a four wick burner and simple fuel tank supplied by Roundhouse Engineering from their Charles Pooter model range. The boiler was a simple potboiler.

WN10 & 09

WN10, named Atlas, was a freelance model built on a Robin Gosling chassis of which there is no record, whereas WN09, the second Garratt locomotive, is covered in the Garratt section.

FREELANCE 0-6-0 TOMMY (FORMALLY R W ROWLEY) WN11

WN11 was the second of the locomotive models to use the excellent Caton marine piston valve engine. As with the Sentinel locomotive, the engine was mounted across the frame at the front, a location that partly hid the engine under the dummy smokebox. Despite the cylinders being wider than the smokebox, they were still hidden by the side tanks. Geared 2:1, the engine drove the front axle using gears arranged along the inside of the RHS frame. Typical of these early locomotives, the boiler was of the plain pot type fired by methylated spirits. Although freelance, this model has attractive lines and the first photograph shows the model as built without the addition of dummy cylinders. These cylinders were added later and at some time the name was changed to Tommy and is shown some 20 years later at the Guildford Model

Engineering Society outdoor 16mm layout, still a regular performer.

> WN11, Tommy: Length over the buffer beams - 280mm. Width - 110mm. Height - 155mm.

IMPROVED MEYER KAKAVOS, WN12

Next on the list was WN 12 based on the articulated Meyer type locomotive built by Andrew Barclay & Sons as Works Number 960 of 1903 and supplied to the Anglo Greek Magnasite Co as their No 3. Now this is a particularly interesting model as it introduces the idea of a direct drive locomotive being driven by a geared hidden marine engine. There are two main problems with direct drive articulated locomotives such as the Meyer or the Garratt. The first problem, which also applied to the full size locomotives, was the provision of flexible steam connection to and from the bogies and the second was the supply of sufficient steam for the four cylinders. Even if these problems are resolved, the flexibility of the articulation makes it essential to fit radio control. On the other hand, dummy cylinders and valve gear with a hidden geared engine would remove these problems and the technology of the geared drive had already been proven with the Avonside four cylinder articulated tank locomotive WN5. Against this mechanical solution has to be weighed the extra complication of the geared drive and the provision of dummy cylinders and valve gear. However, the sight of a large articulated locomotive with two sets of moving

14. (Top left) A view of the finished Modified Meyer Kakavos based on Andrew Barclay wn960 of 1903. Note the correct Andrew Barclay works plates on the cab side panels. The model is interesting due to the double power bogies and associated valve gear, but the rather plain body offsets this. Several of the Kitson Meyer designs located the cylinders at the rear of the bogie including Kakavos, but cylinders could also be located leading or to the outside of the bogie. Early designs of Kitson Meyer directed the exhaust from the rear bogie through a chimney in the rear bunker slightly preheating the feed water.
(WN012-1 – N D Kirkbride)

15. (Left) The mechanical layout of the drive shafts for Kakavos is illustrated in this photograph, in particular the location of the Caton engine and the additional carden shaft to the splitter gearbox. Notice how the engine is cantilevered out over the rear bogie on beams attached to the rear bogie pivot mainframe stretcher. Another point to observe is how the rear bogie horizontal and vertical movement is limited using the bar located at the rear of the main frame cross member.
(WN012-2 – N D Kirkbride)

cylinder and valve gear parts moving slowly and realistically along the track is quite fascinating and goes a long way to justify this extra work.

The problem with the Meyer design was the location of the firebox relative to the rear articulated bogie. The wheels, axles and brake gear were under the firebox, which required the firebox to be shallow and thus reduced the ashpan capacity. Messrs Kitson of Leeds eliminated this situation by the simple expedient of moving the bogies further out to allow the firebox to be located between the bogies. A similar method was used by Andrew Barclay on their Meyer locomotives, including Kakavos, with their designs being referred to as an 'Improved Meyer'.

For the model, the location of a hidden geared engine in the firebox area of the 'Improved Meyer', design would have been ideal, but unfortunately there was not sufficient room to fit the rather long marine engine and the drive components. On the other hand, the rather large rear bunker would be large enough to fit and conceal the engine but a method had to be found to transfer the drive from the engine to a suitable position to pick up the carden shafts

to the bogies. The solution was to provide a further carden shaft from the engine to a splitter gearbox located in the area of the firebox. This arrangement is illustrated in the photograph of the uncompleted model.

The extra drive to the splitter gearbox is clearly shown along with the method of mounting the engine over the rear bogie and rear pivot. The engine mounting frames are bolted to the rear pivot frame cross stretcher and the engine itself is bolted to the underside of these bars. Incidentally, the dummy cylinders were almost certainly ex-Roundhouse. At this time the company itself constructed all components and, as with any manufacturing process there would be unusable items where, say, a tap was snapped. Though useless as live steam cylinders, they were supplied and used as dummy units on models such as Kakavos.

Now another unusual aspect of this design was the double chimney arrangement. This was a feature common to the earlier Kitson Meyer designs and was included in this Andrew Barclay locomotive. The exhaust from the rear bogie was routed through the rear bunker and in the case of the Kitson Meyer was used to

16. (Top right) Kakavos was photographed in 2006 after 20 years of use and still running well. By 2009 the only parts that required replacement were the plastic universal joints. There is a common failing with this type of plastic universal joint caused by the plastic splitting over the brass boss. Later models use the steel miniature universal joint, which are designed for far more exacting applications and are consequently quite expensive. In this view the rear chimney is clearly visible in the rear bunker, an unusual feature of locomotive design.

(WN012-3 – Ian Jones)

17. (Right) The right hand side view of WN42 based on the 'Improved Meyer' locomotives built by Andrew Barclay. The model is a combination of the dimensions taken from the drawings of Caledonia Works Number 1956 of 1928 with the addition of side tanks, illustrated in the photographs of Joan w Works Number 1299 of 1913. Joan had the advantage of side tanks, which provided a location for the gas tank and water filler system. From the photographs of WN42, it is not obvious that the model uses a geared drive from the engine located in the rear bunker, the engine being hidden by the dummy woodpile.

(WN042-1 – Peter Holland)

slightly pre-heat the feed water. In the model, the steam exhaust passes into a cylindrical tank and is then split to give exhaust steam to both chimneys, the front facing pipe being slightly restricted to even out the steam distribution. A valve was also fitted to blow down any initial condensate.

The end result was a model of a novel type of articulated locomotive, capable of powerful slow running for up to an hour on one fill of gas. Topping up of the boiler water was by a Goodall valve and check valve.

For anyone wondering about the practicality of this more complicated dummy cylinder/geared drive, Kakavos WN12 is shown still operating extremely well in 2008 on the layout of the then owner Ian Jones. The only casualties so far are the plastic 'Huco', universal couplings, which have had to be replaced due to the plastic splitting.

IMPROVED MEYER STRATHFARRER, WN42

Similar to Kakavos and built along the same lines, WN42 was a model based on the Andrew Barclay 'Improved Meyer' locomotive, Caledonia

(Works Number 1956 of 1928). A drawing of this locomotive appears in the original hard backed version of Kitson Meyer Articulated Locomotives by Donald Binns.

This locomotive was very similar to a previous engine, Joan, Works Number 1299 of 1913, which had the advantage of side tanks. WN42 was developed from the drawing of Caledonia and the photographs of Joan including the side tanks. The main external difference between the model and the full size engine was the use of outside framed bogies, whereas both Joan and Caledonia, (intended for 3ft gauge), used an inside frame arrangement. Notice how the cylinders are on the inside of the power bogies. The drive system and location of the engine on WN42 was identical to the previous model of Kakavos, although by now the Caton engine had been replaced by the larger Max11 unit. One of the interesting features of the earlier Improved Meyer designs was the second chimney located in the rear bunker. Later versions such as Joan and Caledonia returned to the conventional single chimney in the smokebox, thereby utilising all of the draught for the boiler.

As with all of these model locomotives with a

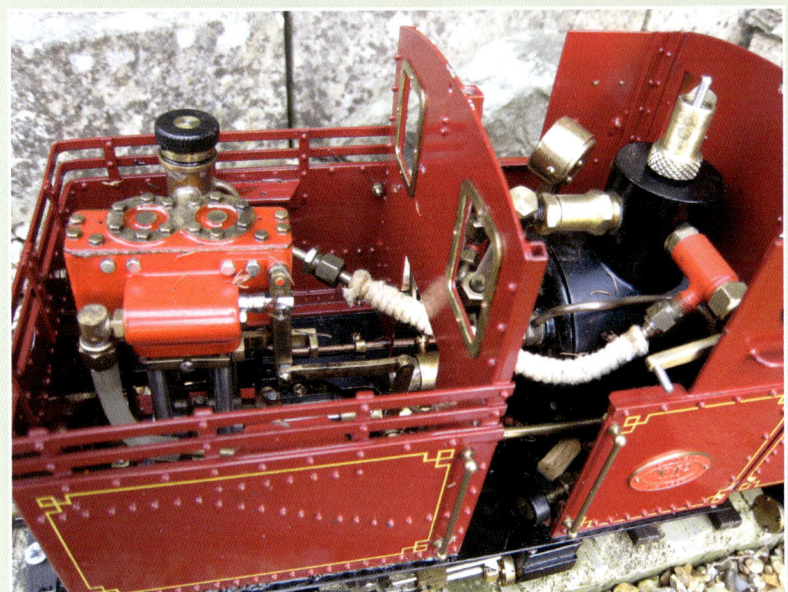

18. (Above) This is the opposite view of the 'Improved Meyer', Strathfarrer, which was taken on 12th December 2012 after 16 years of service. The top of the displacement lubricator can be seen in the rear bunker amongst dummy logs with the drain valve below the front of the cab. The adjacent 3/32in pipe is from the water gauge blow down valve. As with the Kitson Meyer Kakavos, the cylinders are located on the inside of the power bogie but in this design the rear bogie exhausts to the smokebox in the conventional way.

(WN042-3 – Peter Holland)

19. (Left) In this view of Strathfarrer, the dummy wood load in the bunker has been removed to expose the hidden MaxII marine piston valve engine. The mechanical layout is similar to that of the previous Kitson Meyer Kakavos but as can be seen, the engine is larger than the previously used Caton engine. In practical terms, the increase in size of the MaxII engine meant that this engine could only be used in the larger size of locomotives. The valve visible in the lower part of the cab entrance is the water level/blow-off valve. The lubricator drain valve is located away from the actual lubricator and the pipe between them is visible running along the bunker/cab floor.

(WN042-5 – Peter Holland)

20. (Bottom left) Bluebell is based on the Stephen Lewin Overtype locomotives Hops & Malt. The single cylinder engine uses redundant ½in bore Roundhouse cylinders but notice how the limited space on top of the boiler requires a short connecting rod. Part of the unpainted Roundhouse 'Charles Pooter' firebox is visible below the flywheel but is effectively covered by the side tanks.

(WN015-1 – Authors Collection)

[21. This picture of Bluebell shows the chain drive down to the idler shaft with a probable 4:1 reduction spur gear to the rear axle. The full size overtype locomotives used a large intermediate gear wheel to cover the distance between the engine spur gear and the spur gear mounted on the rear axle. Notice the oil cups on the crankshaft and the tank of the Roundhouse 'Charles Pooter' four-wick methylated spirit burner.

WN015-2 – Authors Collection)

hidden gear drive, the cylinders and valve gear are dummies, taking advantage of rejected cylinder parts from the same well-known manufacturer. The model was finished in burgundy with yellow lining and named Strathfarrer after a glen in the Scottish Highlands.

STEPHEN LEWIN OVERTYPE LOCOMOTIVES WN15, 19, 20 & 28

The next group of locomotives could not be further from the complications of the Meyer type. Again the availability of redundant stock from Roundhouse Engineering made it possible to build several small single cylinder models with the engine located on top of the boiler as per traction engine practice. Unlike the efforts of Aveling and Porter, (whose railway locomotives were simply traction engines on railway wheels), the company of Stephen Lewin of the Poole Foundry in Dorset produced several geared overtype locomotives, including Hops and Malt for Arthur Guinness & Co Ltd, the renowned brewers of Dublin. These were tiny engines built to run on the Guinness internal railway of 1ft 10in with a single 6¼ x 8in cylinder, mounted on the boiler and driving through steel gearing to the cast steel wheels. A large flywheel assisted the smooth running of the engine and a clutch was provided to release the drive so that the locomotive could be used to operate stationary plant.

For the models, several compromises had to be made, not least the fact that spirit firing with a potboiler was still the preferred method of steam production and would require side tanks to hide the firebox. In order to cover the distance from the engine to the rear wheels, it was decided to use a chain drive instead of the large middle wheel and smaller outer gear wheels of the original. This variation also required outside frames. At least the engine was in the right place. WN15 Bluebell illustrates the first of these models.

Despite being somewhat suspect as regards accuracy to the prototype, as a model, WN15 Bluebell performed rather well and always had an appreciative audience. The gearing provided slow consistent running in contrast to the high speed of the engine. Locating the engine on top did have the disadvantage of oil running down the boiler towards the burner and consequently a tray was provided to collect the oil and thereby reduce the mess. WN19 Petal and WN20 No 2 soon followed with some cosmetic alterations. Even this was not to be the end of either the methylated spirit fired overtype or the redundant cylinders, because a final model was produced as WN28 Heracles.

The end of the Roundhouse redundant cylinders did not signal the end of the Overtype locomotive, but further production would require a new engine and by this time the preferred method of firing would be by gas in a centre flue boiler. These locomotives will be discussed in the chapter on industrial locomotives.

The next models, W/N 16 and 21 were based on the John Fowler plantation locomotives built for sugar plantation work in Queensland, Australia. This firm was established at Bristol in 1850 to manufacture traction engines, steam rollers and agricultural machinery with

22. (Top) Petal, the second of the Overtype locomotives using the Roundhouse redundant cylinders and a methylated spirit fired pot boiler.
(WN019-2 – N D Kirkbride)

23. (Above left) No2, another overtype locomotive but now fitted with a cab and full length side tanks. Notice the tray under the engine to reduce oil spill onto the boiler. This model was exported too and now runs in America.
(WN020-1 – N D Kirkbride)

24. (Above right) No2, the opposite side view of the overtype locomotive which has retained the long chain drive and cover.
(WN020-2 – N D Kirkbride)

25. (Left) Gear side view of Heracles, another variation on the overtype theme with the chain drive more exposed but less conspicuous than the overall chain cover. This was the last of the methylated spirit fired potboiler overtype models using the redundant Roundhouse Engineering ½in cylinders. Notice the large 6mm pitch chain, which would eventually be replaced in later chain driven models by the rather expensive 4mm pitch stainless steel pre-stretched chain.
(WN028-2 – N D Kirkbride)

John Fowler devoting his life to the design and production of steam ploughs and other farming equipment. By 1860, John Fowler had set up a new factory at Leeds, not surprisingly called The Steam Plough Works, for the manufacture of ploughing engines. It was not, however, until two years after the early death of John Fowler in 1864 at the age of 38 in a riding accident, that steam locomotives were manufactured, including six 0-6-0s for the Chatham & Dover Railway. Further orders for the manufacture of standard gauge and main line locomotives continued until 1885/86, with subsequent orders in 1890 and 1897, but from 1871 the emphasis had changed to industrial and narrow gauge engines.

It was in this field that Fowlers gained a reputation for high standards, particularly in the supply of equipment for overseas sugar plantations, quarries, forestry etc. The first of the John Fowler plantation models was WN16, named Hercules, based on Fowler Works Number 16036 Coolum, supplied in 1923 to the Moreton Central Sugar Mill of the Colonial Sugar Refining Co. Ltd., Queensland, Australia. It is interesting that the John Fowler Catalogue No 2 of 1926, (reprinted by the Industrial Railway Society in 1972), shows this locomotive with the caption, 'an engine to be proud of'. At this point, there is somewhat of a mystery as the model as built was photographed with a four-wheel tender complete with a methylated spirit chicken feed to the locomotive burner. At some time, this tender was transferred to the second locomotive WN21 and careful observation of the photographs of both models confirms this is the same tender. Recent photographs of Hercules, which are unsuitable for publication, show the model without the tender.

The second John Fowler locomotive, WN21 named Vulcan, was based on Fowler (16030?), an 0-6-0 locomotive with 8½ x 12in cylinders and a four-wheel tender (Fowler 16031?), apparently supplied to India. Both of these models used a simple pot type boiler fired by a Roundhouse Engineering wick type methylated spirit burner. The burner was altered to take the extra supply of spirits from the tender, including the air feed to the airtight tender tank. The advantage of the chicken feed system is that the burner can have a minimal size fuel tank with the main supply located elsewhere, in this case in the tender. The arrangement extends the endurance of the fuel supply but only works safely if the supplying tank is airtight and of course higher than the burner tank. Unfortunately, failure of the air feed system will result in flooding the burner with excess fuel with obvious fire implications. Consequently, this feature has not been repeated in any methylated spirit fired models. The motive power, namely a Caton marine engine, was located at the front between the frames under the dummy smokebox. The engine in turn was coupled to the leading axle by 2:1 spur gears, including an intermediate gear to cover the distance from the crankshaft to the axle. The gears, painted black, run down the outside of the LH frame behind the dummy cylinder and behind the axle crank. In this location the gears are virtually hidden from sight and only careful observation betrays their presence. The photographs illustrate these locomotives, which gave slow, powerful and consistent running that amply repaid the extra involvement of fitting a hidden geared engine drive system and dummy cylinders/valve gear.

> **WN21, Vulcan with tender: Length locomotive and tender over the buffer beams – 455mm. Width –110mm. Height –155mm.**

26. Hercules based on the John Fowler plantation locomotive Works Number 16036 Coolum, built for the Moreton Central Sugar Mill of the Colonial Sugar Refining Co Ltd, Queensland, Australia. The model was constructed from a photograph on page one in the John Fowler Catalogue No 2 of 1926, (reprinted by the Industrial Railway Society in 1972).

(WN016-1 – N D Kirkbride)

27. (Opposite) Attractive photograph of Hercules on one of the rather basic bridges at my original garden railway in Whitley Bay showing the tender which was transferred to WN21 at a later date. Coolum, on which the model was based, does not have a tender in the Fowler Catalogue photograph, so why this tender was built and originally fitted to WN16 is a mystery. The filler at the rear of the tender was for the tank feeding methylated spirits to the wick type burner. As with many of the early models, the brass domes and sandboxes were left highly polished, although in reality they would have been painted.

(WN016-2 – N D Kirkbride)

28. Vulcan, based on the John Fowler plantation locomotive Works Number 16030 with a four wheel tender (16031?) supplied to India. On the original locomotive the tender included a small canopy arranged slightly below the locomotive roof canopy.

(WN021-1 – Chris Webster)

29. Vulcan is seen here on the heritage stand at the 16mm AGM at Stoneleigh – probably in 2010. Careful observation below the smokebox reveals part of the Caton marine engine, which is lying across the frames in front of the potboiler. The lever sticking out forward below the smokebox is connected to the forward reverse lever on the engine. Between the locomotive and the tender can be seen the connecting pipes for the chicken feed from the tender meths tank to the wick burner below the boiler. One pipe feeds the burner tank while the other regulates that supply to maintain a constant level in the burner tank.

(WN021-2 – Ian Bunch)

30. This is another view of Vulcan at Guildford in October 2010. At the time of the photograph, and now 32 years old, the engine was out of service pending a trip to the workshop for the replacement of worn gears and the layshaft bearings.

(WN021-4 – Chris Webster)

SANDY RIVER & RANGELEY LAKES 0-4-4 FORNEY LOCOMOTIVES, WN23 & 29

The next locomotive in this chapter comes from America and represents the 0-4-4 'Forney' locomotives of the 2ft gauge Sandy River & Rangeley Lakes Railway. Over a hundred years ago the American Government granted Matthias Nace Forney a patent for a locomotive, which he considered to be the perfect solution to short haul operations. Basically, this was an 0-4-0 tank locomotive with the frames extended back-over to incorporate the tender which was supported underneath by a four wheel bogie. This arrangement kept the weight on the driving wheels almost constant, whilst the weight on the rear bogie varied depending on the water and fuel consumed. To Forney, this was the preferred situation and he described his engines as 'Four-coupled Back-tank with swivel truck'. To everyone else they were just Forneys. They became the standard engine of the elevated railways of New York and Chicago including the suburban lines radiating from New York. They also appeared by 1880 on the narrow gauge railways of Maine with the last one being built in 1919. There was a pictorial book by Gary Kohler entitled, Main Two Foot Pictorial-SR & RL Locomotives, which gave a wealth of photographs on these 0-4-4 engines

31. (Above) This side view of the 0-4-4 Forney Colorado Star indicates the size and length of the locomotive, which would have great difficulty negotiating the tight curves of the average garden railway. The locomotive is built with radiating axles on the driven wheels to provide a degree of flexibility that in practice made this model a very smooth runner. The model is driven by a geared marine engine in the position of the boiler firebox with the engine crankshaft just visible behind the rear driven axle. A rather nice touch is the brass lettering on the side of the bunker indicating Sandy River and Rangeley Lakes Railway. Notice also the No.5 on the cab side and the smokebox front.

(WN023-1 – N D Kirkbride)

32. In this right hand side view of Colorado Star, the gear drive to the radiating axle is visible behind the rear driven axle. Again typical of early models, the large dome on the model has been left unpainted, very unlikely on an American locomotive where the dome was often painted and intricately lined.

(WN023-2 – N D Kirkbride)

33. The first photograph (right) shows the radiating axle bogie in the straight-ahead position. The most important point is that the wheelbase of the bogie and the distance between the driving axles has to be the same and the bogie must be pivoted centrally. Notice also the drive from the Caton marine engine to the rear driven axle with the base of the engine visible behind the bogie.

(WN023-3 – Joy Seymour)

34. The second photograph (left) shows the bogie displaced as if negotiating a curve. In both pictures the drive pins between the fixed axle and the hollow axle can be seen and notice that they are in synchronization with each other. Built in 1988 the flexible drive was photographed in 2009 still in full working order after 21 years of service, a testament to the basic design.

(WN023-4 – Joy Seymour)

along with the other locomotives used on the line.

Many of the photographs illustrate the 'Forneys' in a state of distress, having derailed and lying forlornly on their side or in some cases upside down at the side of the track. This is not surprising, when it is considered that the driving wheels were rigid relative to the chassis with the rear trailing wheels located on a swivelling bogie. Such an arrangement on a narrow gauge of 2ft must have resulted in considerable stresses on the wheelbase tending to destabilise the engine on tight curves. Considering the very tight curves of a typical garden railway this situation would be even more critical.

One way of overcoming this would be to adopt the Single Fairlie principal and this was done with WN 29 but for WN23 a more novel solution was envisaged and would make this model unique in the collection. To provide flexibility, the two driven axles remained with fixed axle bushes within the frame but the wheels were not rigidly attached to these axles. Imagine a frame with two independent bogies. The non-driven rear bogie was conventionally mounted on a pivot with a degree of flexible vertical movement around the pivot.

From the outside, the front parts of the frames seem conventional with fixed cylinders driving via coupling and connecting rods the four driving wheels. However, further investigation reveals that these wheels are not attached to driven axles. In fact the wheels are mounted on hollow axles supported by an independent bogie contained within the frames. Now with the wheelbase of the bogie being that of the solid driven axles and the pivot at the centre, the driven axles will be central inside the tubular wheel axles in the straight ahead position and the flexibility of the bogie will depend on the relative diameter of the central and the inside dimension of the tubular axle.

By providing sufficient internal bore to the hollow axles, the required flexibility can be provided. To provide a drive to the hollow axles and thence the wheels, it is necessary to machine a slot in the hollow axles and a drive pin in the centre of the inside axles with the axles being reinforced accordingly. The pins for the two axles have to be in synchronization to prevent a tendency for vertical oscillation of the bogie. Despite the novel nature of the flexible drive, the system worked extremely well with the locomotive being flexible and free running. The arrangement of the wheels being mounted on a hollow axle with a fixed driving axle inside can be recognised as the Klien-Lindner system, which was also used on the Duffield Bank railway.

However, what is not often realised with either of these systems is that it cannot accommodate a reverse or 'S' curve without a straight stretch of track equal to the wheelbase of the locomotive. A reverse curve without a tangent would lock the flexible drive into a rigid wheelbase. In the case of model railways, this would be a severe handicap. The arrangement on WN23 has no such restraint and will happily negotiate any curvature within the limit of the bogie movement. Before leaving this unusual model, it should be pointed out that the outside cylinders are dummy with the power being supplied from a Caton marine engine located between the two

35. (Above) This is the second Forney type locomotive, having a similar 0-4-4 wheel-arrangement. Unlike the previous example the front driving wheels operate on the Single Fairlie principle. The model has been photographed before a dummy fuel load has been added which exposes the rear cylindrical gas tank located behind the cab. Behind the gas tank, the bunker contains a small water tank with a hand force pump. In this photograph, the driving Caton engine can just be seen under the cab behind the dummy firebox plate. This engine lying across the frame drives the outer bogie axle via a carden shaft with an overall gear ratio of 2:1. The front headlight operates from rechargeable batteries in the rear bunker. The SR&RL lettering and the number 22 are separate etchings riveted to the sides
(WN029-2 – N D Kirkbride)

36. (Left) View of WN29 from the other side. The valve below the cab is the displacement lubricator drain valve and the pipe running under the air receiver is the steam exhaust from the hidden Caton marine engine. The smokebox is attached directly to the boiler without any supporting frame, indicating that driving wheels are part of a swivel bogie and that this is a model based on the Single Fairlie type of articulation
(WN029-3 – N D Kirkbride)

bogies and lying on its side across the frame. Spur gears transmit the drive to the rear fixed driven axle and provide a 2:1 reduction.

The photographs show the model named Colorado Star along with the unusual drive arrangement of the powered bogie. The latter photographs, having been taken in 2009, show that the radiating axle method of providing a free and flexible drive has also stood the test of time.

The next Forney type locomotive named Evelyn A, again with the 0-4-4 wheel arrangement, was built on the much simpler Single Fairlie principle and was WN29 in the works list. As with the previous model,

Evelyn A is based on a typical Sandy River and Rangely Lakes locomotive but in this case the front driving wheels are located in a bogie arrangement that was pivoted to give the necessary flexibility horizontally and longitudinally but not laterally. Again the cylinders are dummy with the power provided by a Caton marine engine located between the bogies in the area of the dummy firebox. The rear unpowered bogie or truck has a horizontal bearing mounted in a rubber bush to give all round limited movement. The rear bunker contains the cylindrical gas tank and also a hand operated water pump. Both models are finished with SR&RL etched brass lettering riveted to the rear bunker sides, etched brass numbers and smokebox number plates.

TRAMWAY CANTARIERA 0-6-2 TENDER LOCOMOTIVE, WN36

Following on from the two Forney engines, there were two further American locomotives built during the early days of model production. The first was WN36, based on Baldwin Works

Number 37398 of 1911, a 2-6-0 tender locomotive built for the 600mm gauge Tramway Cantariera Railway, located in the state of Sao Paulo, South America. The model uses the Roundhouse Engineering Sandy River No 24 chassis, suitably altered along with their cylinders and valve gear. The original locomotive was unusual in having the valve gear driven from the rear axle, whereas the connecting rods drove to the middle axle, a feature not repeated on the model. Rather than fitting the gas tank in the tender, with the attendant problems of isolation and a flexible coupling, the tank is located up in the roof of the cab. This does limit the gas capacity. The locomotive was built to run as No 10 on the Penlan & Cascade Railway of Colin & Joy Seymour.

BUCYRUS FOUNDRY AND MANUFACTURING COMPANY DIXIE, WN41.

The final American locomotive dates from the turn of the previous century and is not only unique in appearance but it was also the only engine built by the Bucyrus Foundry and Manufacturing Company. Named Dixie, it ran on the 3ft gauge Navarro Railroad in North America. There is no further information on this locomotive, such scant information given having been obtained from the book Articulated Locomotives of North America which included a rather poor photograph from which the model was built. The model, WN41, named Bucyrus, was articulated with only the front bogie driven, as was the case with the prototype.

However, looking at the photograph it may be possible that the power bogie may have been rigid. This point noted, the main difference between the model and the prototype is the location and type of steam engine. The original had tiny cylinders mounted horizontally above the driven rear axle driving to a countershaft

37. Photograph of WN36 Maine Star based on the Baldwin locomotive Works Number 37398 of 1911 and supplied to the Tramway Cantareira. The full size locomotive was unusual in having the valve gear driven from the rear axle, whereas the connecting rods drove the middle axle, a feature not repeated on the model.

(WN036-2 – Joy Seymour)

38. (Top left) Model based on a photograph of the most unusual and only locomotive built by the Bucyrus Foundry and Manufacturing Company named Dixie built for the 3ft gauge Navarro Railroad. There does not seem to be any further information on the locomotive and approaches to various American sources have not produced any information on the railroad or even its location. This B/W photograph really shows the excellent lining by Geoff Munday, surely justified for such an odd locomotive and just notice the added brass fleur-de-lys badges on the side of the cab. The Cheddar Models V-twin oscillating engine is attached to the main frame and drives the front bogie axle.
(WN041-1 Bucyrus – N D Kirkbride)

39. (Left) This is the opposite side view with the rather large but effective water/oil separator at the side of the vertical boiler. To reduce the overall height, the boiler has been dropped between the frames. This Cheddar Models vertical boiler has a 'J' flue typical of marine practice.
(WN041-2 Bucyrus – N D Kirkbride)

40. (Below) Colour photograph of the model based on the Bucyrus Foundry and Manufacturing Company BFM1 locomotive Dixie. There was no indication of the colour of the original locomotive and the lining was far simpler than that of the model.
(WN041-3 Bucyrus – N D Kirkbride)

above and between the driven wheels. One must therefore assume that the countershaft was geared to the two axles without connecting rods. For the model, the problem of very small cylinders, steam connections to the articulated bogie and the availability of a 'V' twin-oscillating engine suggested a different approach. The engine was mounted between the water tank and the vertical boiler, driving underneath to a carden shaft and then to 3:1 crossed helical gears on the leading axle of the front powered bogie, with a toothed belt then transmitting power to the rear axle.

Cheddar Models supplied the engine and boiler as their 'Pintail' unit. The finishing touches to the model are the superb lining by Geoff Munday and the polished brass fleur-de-lys on the cab sides. As for running, the single powered bogie easily slips on greasy track and when this situation combines with

an incline then the locomotive will often come to an ignominious halt. The gearing is a little high but these problems are a small price to pay for such a unique model. Not surprisingly, Bucyrus, who were noted more for their steam shovels and self propelled cranes, produced no further locomotives.

OTAVI MINEN UND EISENBAHN GESSELLSCHAFT 0-6-2 LOCOMOTIVE WN31

With the American locomotives dealt with a return can be made to the works list. WN31 was taken from a photograph out of the facsimile reprint of the Arthur Koppel locomotive catalogue No. 786 of 1905. The locomotive in question appears on page 44 with the reference V1.7669 and was one of twenty five supplied in 1904 by Arthur Koppel, of Berlin, to the 2ft (600mm) gauge Otavi Minen und Eisenbahn Gessellschaft, (Otavi Mine and Railway Company), located in the then German South West Africa. The line started at a point some forty feet above sea level at the port of Swakopmund and travelled some 300 miles to the north east to the town of Otavi and thence to the copper mines at Tsumeb, a total distance of 565km, and was opened to traffic in 1906 after three years of construction.

To give some idea of the terrain and the difficulties of building in such an arid area the following points are of interest. For a distance of 68 miles, the line climbed steadily at 1 in 66 to Ebony, 3500ft above sea level, then dropped to Usakos at 2640ft before continuing to Kalkfield at the highest altitude on the railway of 5200ft. The first 140 miles out of Swakamund, the railway crossed the Namib Desert. To provide water for the locomotives, an auxiliary tender was required which contained 2,200 gallons of water and 7,700 pounds of coal. Despite the terrain of stone, desert and severe lack of water, the railway continued to operate until it was taken over by the Tsumeb Corporation in 1947 with the average copper ore transported per week increasing to 1350 tons and a future assessment of 2000tons. In addition, the overall economic picture of South West Africa indicated that the narrow gauge line would have to be replaced by a standard gauge line, which would be built alongside the existing railway to minimise interruption. The last narrow gauge train left Tsumeb on the 27th November 1960.

Although the contract for the construction of the railway and the supply of all equipment used on it was given to Arthur Koppel, the locomotive illustrated in the catalogue was not built by them but by the company of Arn Jung of Jungenthal, Germany. The first consignment of locomotives were delivered in 1904 and numbered 1 to 10, construction numbers 707-716 and were soon followed by a further five locomotives to the same design and from the same builder. With a wheel arrangement of 0-6-2, they carried 37,770 pounds of their 48,880 pounds total weight on the driven wheels, giving a tractive effort of 6000 pounds. Concurrently with the order placed with Jung, an order was placed with Henschel & Sohn for ten locomotives of the same design. Of the 25 locomotives built only 23 were delivered as two were lost when the steamer Edith Heyne sank on the 3rd November 1904 after hitting a rock off the mouth of the river Cess on the Liberian coast.

The model was based purely on the illustration in the catalogue and influenced by the requirement to use the Roundhouse Lady Anne chassis suitably altered to provide the trailing wheels. There were no drawings available or useful dimensions, until a sketch was found after construction, in the book Namib Narrow Gauge by Sidney M Moir and H T Crittenden. This out of print book is highly recommended for anyone interested in the history of colonial railways built in difficult geographical locations and affected by the tribulations of war. Although the model appears to be conventional, in fact the construction follows the previous layout of a Caton marine engine located under the dummy smokebox lying across the frames and geared 2:1 to the front axle. The giveaway to this arrangement is the reversing lever at the

41. This model is based on the ten locomotives supplied by Arthur Koppel to the Otavi Minen und Eisenbahn Gessellschaft in 1904. They were built by the German company of Arn Jung, Jungenthal as their wn707 to 716. The valve in the cab entrance controls the supply of methylated spirit from the rear bunker tank to the burner tank using the chicken feed principle. The silicon pipe behind this valve is the air supply to the tank, which maintains the spirit level - and just in front of the valve and below the side tank is a sight tube indicating the level in the burner tank. The chicken feed system is very effective in locating the spirit tank away from the burner, in this case in the rear bunker, the integrity of the air pipe is essential to the safe operation – otherwise disaster strikes!
(WN031-1 – N D Kirkbride)

42. Opposite side view showing the displacement lubricator in the side tank and the drain valve below it. In the rear bunker can be seen the methylated spirit tank filler with 'O' ring essential to maintaining an airtight seal to the tank. Typical of locomotives designed for very hot climates, there was a roof vent fitted to the cab roof along with sliding side louvers to the cab window openings.
(WN031-2 – N D Kirkbride)

43. *Very attractive front three-quarter view showing the bar type cowcatcher and the unusual pipe connections to the side watertanks. From these photographs it can be seen that only the forward/reverse lever at the front of the smokebox indicates that this model has a geared engine drive. Notice the ventilation holes in the cab front sheet, they are also on the rear sheet, and that the full size locomotive would have had a double roof as indicated on the model.*
(WN031-3 – N D Kirkbride)

44. *The locomotive was photographed during construction and is typical of that era. The chassis is fitted with dummy cylinders and valve gear from Roundhouse Engineering. It can be seen that the motive power comes from the Caton marine engine located at the front of and across the frames with gearing to the front axle. The boiler is a plain potboiler with a methylated spirit wick type burner and firebox.*
(WN031-5 – N D Kirkbride)

45. *This is an indirect drive jackshaft locomotive based on Orenstein & Koppel Works Number 8090 of 1916. The full size locomotive was in fact eight coupled with a Klien-Linder hollow axle system, which was thought to be too complicated for the model. The engine crankshaft drove to the jackshaft (located between the 2nd and 3rd axle) giving the impression of the locomotive being ten-coupled. The locomotive was geared to increase the power to the axles and provide a smoother drive without increasing the engine weight. For the model the engine crankshaft is geared to the centre axle using reduction spur gears.*
(WN038 – Geoff Munday)

left hand side of the smokebox. More clearly, the photograph taken during construction shows the position of the engine. It is to be assumed that the boiler was of the pot type with a methylated spirits wick burner fed from a chicken feed tank in the bunker. Roundhouse Engineering supplied the dummy outside cylinders and valve gear, the cylinders having been rejects unsuitable for steam working. From the photographs it can be seen that there is a lot of detail on this very attractive locomotive, including the unusual arrangement of pipe work connected to the side tanks.

WN31 was the last methylated spirit fired locomotive to be built.

ORENSTEIN & KOPPEL JACKSHAFT DRIVE PLANTATION LOCOMOTIVE, WN038

The Javanese sugar industry had more than its fair share of unusual locomotives, where continental builders used their ingenuity to address the problem of maximising adhesion weight without raising axle loads. There were many articulated and semi-articulated locomotives, for example the 0-8-0 sidetank

46. A final photograph for the 'Early Days' chapter of Renishaw No 2, Tommy and Vulcan with a combined age of 72 years, pictured at the Guildford Model Engineering Society 16mm group's outdoor layout at the club grounds at Stoke Park, Guildford in 2010.

(WN005-011-021 – Chris Webster)

engines with Klien-Lindner 'hollow axle' systems and 0-10-0 tank engines with Luttermoller geared end axles. This model was based on a very unusual 0-8-0T locomotive driven by an indirect jackshaft. This was built by Orensticn & Koppel in 1916 as their Works Number 8090 and supplied to the 700mm gauge Rejosari Mill as their No 10. A photograph of this locomotive appeared on page 8 of Locomotives International No 4. At first glance the position of the cylinders above the wheels makes No 10 look like a rack locomotive with ten coupled wheels. However on closer inspection, it can be seen that the centre axle is the jackshaft, which one would assume was driven from the engine crankshaft by reduction gearing to provide a smoother drive with increased power. In order to simplify the model, the eight-coupled arrangement was replaced with the 0-6-2 wheel layout, otherwise the outer axles would have required the equivalent of the Klien-Lindner hollow axle to negotiate the curves of a typical garden railway. As originally built, the model had problems with the valve gear but Roger Loxley of Roundhouse, using their Walschaert's valve gear, solved this difficulty. The engine crankshaft drives through reduction gearing to the centre axle and rotates in the opposite direction to the wheels. The oval tank on the tender indicates that the original

locomotive was oil burning, but this was later changed over to bagasse. Bagasse is dried and bundled sugar cane waste of low calorific value and considerable bulk, which usually requires a large tender.

This very unusual locomotive is a fitting end to this chapter.

REFERENCES:
- Stephen Lewin and the Poole Foundry by Russell Wear & Eric Lees.
- Kitson Meyer Articulated Locomotives by Donald Binns.
- John Fowler & Co Ltd catalogue No 2 of 1926. Reprinted by the Industrial Railway Society in 1972.
- Maine Two Foot Pictorial SR&RL Locomotives by Gary Kohler.
- Namib Narrow Gauge by Sydney M Moir & H T Crittenden.
- Locomotives International No 4 Editor Donald Binns.

THE AVONSIDE GEARED ARTICULATED TANK LOCOMOTIVES

This first chapter to deal with a specific type of locomotive introduces the specialised articulated tank engines produced by the Avonside Engine Company of Bristol. By the middle of the 19th century, the standard arrangement of direct drive horizontal cylinders, arranged below the smokebox, had become the standard throughout all parts of the world. British locomotive manufacturers could not see any need to depart from the general characteristic of a design which had proved suitable for almost all railway conditions.

When locomotives were required for overseas railways, they simply modified their existing designs to suit the particular situation. However, when it came to the specific problems associated with the adverse conditions of lumber and mining operations with their rough track, severe gradients and sharp curves, the often heavy and almost rigid standard design locomotives were not well suited. It was this challenge of lightly laid, uneven track, tight curves and the ever increasing demand for more power, that forced locomotive builders and their customers to consider some form of articulation and, for the more demanding situation of steep inclines, the use of gearing. This incorporation of gearing into the articulated locomotive was to lead in America to the development of the Shay, Climax and Heisler type of locomotives and in New Zealand to the Bush Tram. Whereas most articulated locomotives of British origin were of direct drive, there was a particular British company that produced one of the most innovative designs of geared articulated locomotive. This was the Avonside Engine Company of Bristol, even though the basic concept had been that of the American Heisler. These unique locomotives are illustrated in this chapter.

During the 1920s, the Avonside Engine Company Ltd of Bristol proposed a novel form of articulated locomotive aimed at the 2ft gauge

sugar plantation railways of South Africa. Their sales brochure was entitled A Novel Type of Articulated Locomotive for Operation on Badly-Laid Track of Light Section for Plantation, Forestry and Similar Duties. The locomotives were to be available in two sizes of 40 & 50hp and would be able to negotiate curves down to 50ft radius and have a maximum speed of 12mph. Two four wheel bogies supported the locomotive type boiler, cab and side water tanks with a twin cylinder 'V' type engine which was mounted under the boiler in a similar way to the American Heisler locomotive. Drive to the bogies was through Carden shafts to bevel gears on a lay shaft mounted on each bogie and thence by chains to the axles. Mounting the engine on the main frame removed the need for complicated flexible steam joints, which in turn simplified and reduced maintenance when compared with a locomotive having the cylinders on the bogies.

The design failed to generate any interest at a time when locomotive orders were few and the project was shelved. However by 1928, things began to happen with the appointment of a new Chief Draughtsman, Mr L T Grime. He realised that articulated locomotives would be of benefit to Avonside's sugar estate customers by providing them with a more powerful locomotive able to negotiate the lightly laid and often badly maintained track to be found on the average estate. He was also conscious of the development of the diesel engine for locomotive traction, examples of which were already being built by Hudswell Clarke and Kerr Stewart.

In 1930 Messrs. Frank Theakston Ltd, agents for various sugar plantations in South Africa, gave an order to the Avonside Engine Company to produce a design of locomotive to replace the smaller steam locomotives on the Ellingham Sugar Estate in South Africa. The design required a tractive effort, equivalent to the larger 'main line' engines then operating on 30lb rail, yet would be capable of running on 16lb rail with a minimum radius of 40ft. This was the type of application ideally suited to a geared articulated locomotive of the type proposed by Avonside in the 1920s. L T Grimes set to work and designed a double bogie 0-4-4-0 articulated locomotive, but (unlike the previous Avonside Engine Co design) decided to replace the steam plant with a diesel engine. The locomotive would use a Gardner 6L2 six-cylinder diesel engine, which was coupled to a three-speed gearbox by a Wigglesworth disc type friction clutch. From the front and rear output shafts of the gearbox, two universally jointed carden shafts drove to worm gears on the outer axle of each bogie. Side coupling rods then connected the inner axle of each bogie. This gear and drive shaft arrangement can be compared with that of the Shay and Heisler. The Shay locomotive had bevel gears on all axles, with the drive shaft on one side of the trucks. The effect was to have very short drive shafts with considerable longitudinal displacement. The Heisler on the other hand, located the drive shafts in the centre line of the locomotive and drove over the inner axle of

the truck to the bevel gears on the outer axle. The central location minimised the longitudinal displacement and the longer shafts resulted in smaller angular displacement. The use of bevel gears still required the final drive shaft to be angled down to the centre of the outer axle. This was not required in the Climax design, due to the use of skewed bevel gears – but these gears were very difficult to produce. By the 1930s, gear manufacturers could guarantee a 97% efficiency using enclosed worm gears running in oil and therefore by replacing the bevel gears with enclosed worm gears and mounting the worm above the axle, the drive shaft could be arranged to run horizontally over the inner axle. Locating the outer universal joint below the bogie pivot also reduced displacement of the Carden drive shaft. So there it is – a drive system with minimum displacement on curves, a virtually straight horizontal layout and enclosed gears running in oil. The locomotive built to the design of L T Grime became Works Number 2046 of 1930, was named Ellingham Estates and supplied to the cane estate of the same name. Fortunately Ellingham Estates has not only been preserved but still resides in South Africa.

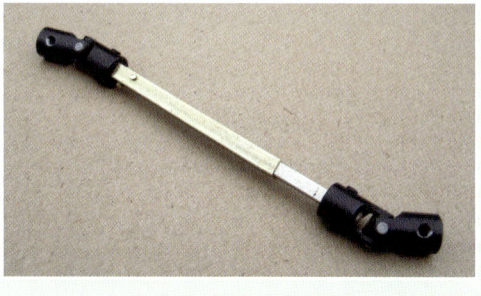

1. (Above) This is an example of Carden shafts as used on WN300.

(Carden Shaft – Author)

2. (Top right) This is the Avonside 2 cylinder Articulated Geared Locomotive Works Number 2057 of 1931. One of the initial three two-cylinder steam locomotives built after the diesel engine driven articulated bogie locomotive supplied in 1930 for the Ellingham Sugar Estate in South Africa. These locomotives had a tractive effort of 6438lbs at 80% boiler pressure and weighed 14 tons.

(Andrew Neale collection)

3. (Right) This is the Avonside Four-Cylinder Articulated Geared Locomotive Works Number 2059 of 1931. Named Blackburn, it was the only four-cylinder version built by Avonside and was supplied to the Natal Estates under Order No.10400. Built after the three two-cylinder locomotives, it utilised many of the drawings produced for the two-cylinder version, including the same size cylinders and bogie details. Both designs of locomotive were far more attractive than the later engines produced by the Hunslet Engine Co. in 1939.

(Andrew Neale collection)

Originally, the universal joints were the type used on model boats with the body made of plastic as WN005 and Kakavos, which lasted remarkably well but eventually the plastic split. The neatest plastic units are those made by Huco as 'Miniature Acetal Fork Universal Joint', obtainable from RS with a 5mm bore. Although relatively cheap, they are nevertheless quite large in both diameter and length. WN037 on the other hand was fitted with homemade units. The universal joints shown are now used as standard and were supplied again by RS and described as 'Miniature Universal Joints-Steel' (ref.689-221). They are rather expensive, but as well as being all metal are only 8mm diameter and 24mm long. The sliding part of the Carden shaft consists of 1/8in square nickel silver bar sliding inside 5/32in square brass tube. To locate the square bar in the 4mm bore of the universal joint the square edges have to be slightly reduced. The square tube is attached

to the other universal joint using a short length of the same bar and held in position by Loctite and two brass rivets. Incidentally, the universal joints have to be tapped for 3mm grub screws as they are supplied plain only.

The next order in 1931 was again from Francis Theakston but this time it was for three steam engine versions, one each for the Illova, Sezela and the Renishaw Estates in South Africa. The design used a 6½x8in twin cylinder 'V' type engine with Marshal type valve gear and 'Wota' type piston valves, the whole unit being totally enclosed to protect the motion and provide a constant supply of oil. The piston valves were of large diameter relative to the cylinders, a necessary condition to allow the engines to run at the high speed of 600-800rpm with 600rpm equating to 15mph. The drive system followed that of the previous locomotive, with the drive from the enclosed worm gearbox to

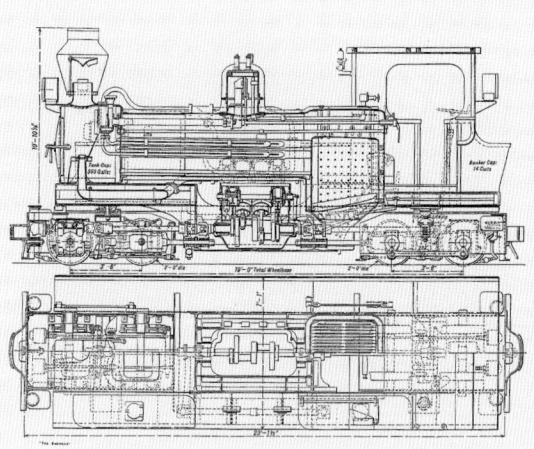

4. (Left) Four-cylinder Avonside Geared Articulated Locomotive.

A general arrangement of the four-cylinder locomotive. Reproduced by kind permission of Donald Binns and originally copied from an Avonside reprint of an article from The Engineer 6th November 1931. This drawing regularly appears in any article on the Avonside geared articulated locomotives and in this case was reproduced from a definitive article by F W Harman in Locomotives International No.9 – a must for anyone interested in these unusual engines.

(The Engineer)

5. (Below) Engine four-cylinder Avonside.

A Section through the four cylinder engine reproduced by kind permission of Donald Binns, originally copied from an Avonside reprint of an article from The Engineer 6th November 1931. Notice how the crankshaft is arranged with the cylinders together and the valve gear on the outside and the cylinder blocks are offset. This allows opposite front and rear cylinders to occupy the same bearing on the crankshaft.

(The Engineer)

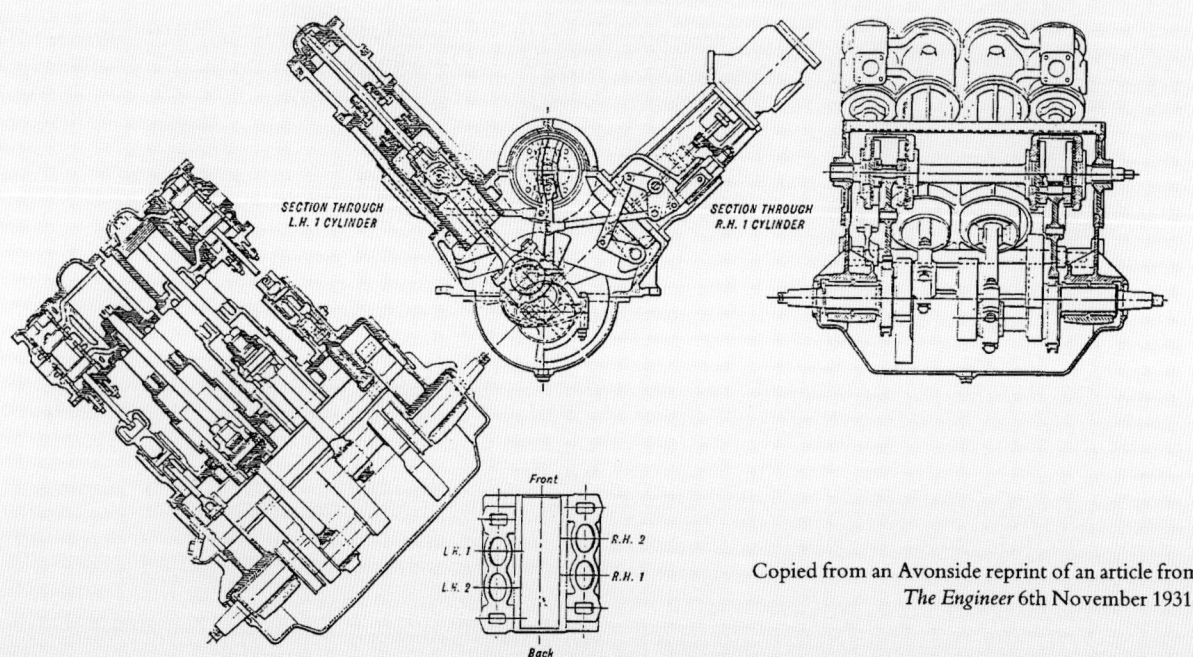

Copied from an Avonside reprint of an article from
The Engineer 6th November 1931.

b) Section through 4-cylinder steam engine.

6. (Top left) An interesting photograph of the drive train showing both Carden shafts utilising the marine type plastic universal joints. One of them has obviously had one of the half units replaced using a black insert. Although these parts are not normally subject to heat, the plastic will eventually split over the knurled brass boss. Unusually, the Caton marine engine has retained its marine flywheel. The rather short carden shafts using the plastic universal joints can be compared to the longer units of the later models that use the shorter and much more expensive steel versions. The curved brass pipe around the engine is the conduit containing the wires for the working headlights. A silicon pipe attaches the exhaust pipe of the engine to the smokebox connection.
WN005 bogie detail 1 – Chris Webster)

7. (Left) This shows front bogie detail with the cover over the 2:1 bevel gears and the Carden shaft drive using plastic universal joints. Unlike later models, the bogies are single gauge only, equivalent to the original 2ft gauge locomotive and providing the locomotive with a better appearance, but dual gauge bogies are more suitable nowadays due to the increase in 45mm garden railways.

(WN005 bogie detail 2 – Chris Webster)

the crankshaft of the steam engine being in a straight line. The engine was placed centrally on the steel girder frames and underneath the Belpair type boiler. Water tanks were fitted either side of the smokebox at the front of the frames, with a conventional cab and rear coalbunker at the rear. The photograph of Works Number 2057 taken from the Andrew Neale collection best illustrates the layout.

The final order for an articulated locomotive was again received from Francis Theakston Ltd. but this time for the Natal Sugar Plantation Estates in South Africa. This design was for a larger version using a four-cylinder engine with a superheated boiler and increased water and coal capacity that increased the weight in working order to 21tons. Otherwise, it followed a similar design to the previous two-cylinder version and utilised many of the drawings from this design, with the four-cylinder engine using the same cylinder sizes of 6½ x 8in and almost the same bogie details. The Worm drive ratio was changed from the 7:20 ratio of the two-cylinder engine to that of 6:17 for the four-cylinder version. Again, from the Andrew Neale collection of photographs, the larger four-cylinder version is illustrated (Avonside Works Number 2059 of 1931). A subtle point to note is that the cylinders are offset between sides, due to the common crankshaft. In the case of the two-cylinder version, the piston valve/cylinder arrangement is inverted between sides. Thus, the crankshaft layout is No 1 valve gear, No 2 cylinder, No 1 cylinder, and finally No 2 valve gear. With the four-cylinder version, the valve gear is to the outside with the cylinders together to give from the front, RH cyl No 2 valve gear – LH cyl No 1valve gear – No 2 RH cylinder – No 1 LH cylinder – No 1 RH cylinder – No 2 LH

cylinder – No1 RH cyl valve gear – No 2 LH cyl valvegear. Now is that clear? If not, then refer to the drawing of the four-cylinder locomotive with the section drawing of the 'V' engine.

The story of these interesting locomotives does not end here, for even after the Avonside Engine Company went out of business, the Hunslet Engine Co. produced three further locomotives in 1939 based on the Avonside design. The order comprised two of the four-cylinder design and one of the two-cylinder design with the drive to the axles using bevel gears in place of the original worm drive.

THE AVONSIDE 4 CYLINDER MODELS BASED ON AVONSIDE ENGINE CO. WORKS NUMBER 2059 OF 1931

From the model point of view, the first locomotive to be built was Renishaw No 2 based on the four-cylinder version and was WN005 of 1984. The decision to go for the larger version was based on the availability of a suitable engine. At this time, the Maxwell Hemmens Caton two-cylinder marine piston valve engine could be used due to its small size and easy reversing. It had already been decided that a four-cylinder engine, even if it were available, would be beyond the steaming capacity of a simple centre flue boiler. In fact, this was later proven using a Saito four-cylinder engine which, when tested, soon flattened the boiler pressure despite this engine being single acting. To give the correct impression of four cylinders, a dummy cylinder body and head was fitted to the left hand side. Few people noticed this minor deception, especially on seeing this very unusual model for the first time. The next important point concerns the gearing on the outer axles. To give

8. *(Top left) This was the first model of the Avonside Engine Co Geared Articulated locomotives and was based on the only four-cylinder locomotive Works Number 2059 named Blackburn. The model was WN005 of 1984, finished in works grey/black and named Renishaw No 2. The twin cylinders on this view are in fact the dummy ones with the twin cylinder Caton marine engine on the other side. Maxwell Hemmens supplied the dummy cylinder castings and cylinder head. An interesting point on this model is the use of a silicon tube reinforced by a stainless steel braid for the connection from the gas tank to the burner and this is just visible in the entrance to the cab. Such a method nowadays would be totally unsatisfactory on safety grounds, but was accepted then and usually without the reinforcing braid. This flexible pipe has been replaced by solid copper tube. Another point of interest is the rectangular gas tank in the left hand side of the cab. The position of choice would now be the rear bunker away from the heat source of the boiler.*

(WN005-1 – N D Kirkbride)

9. *(Centre left) A right hand side view of Renishaw No 2, still in splendid condition despite its twenty six years of age. Notice how the displacement lubricator has been transferred to the right hand side front tank from the original position in the cab. The exhaust pipe into the smokebox can be seen in the bottom of the smokebox.*

(WN005-5 Renishaw No 2 – Chris Webster)

10. *(Left) Four-cylinder Avonside Geared Renishaw No 4. A later model of the four-cylinder version built in 1988 and named Renishaw No 4, still using the Caton marine engine on the RH side and dummy cylinders on the LH side. This view shows the steam pipes to the live engine, the reversing lever and the displacement lubricator clearly visible. At this time the colour of the full size locomotive was not known but green turned out to be correct – although this shade is too dark. Note that counterbalanced cranks were only fitted to the later Hunslet locomotives and were not of the shape indicated on the model.*

(WN025 – N D Kirkbride)

11. *(Below) A rather atmospheric shot of the four-cylinder Avonside Geared Articulated locomotive Renishaw No 2 with a suitable train of cane wagons crossing the bridge of Bob Griffiths' Ystweth Valley Railway in 2008.*

(WN005-6 – Chris Webster)

12. Blackburn based on Avonside Works Number 2059 and correctly named. Unlike the previous locomotive, the engine uses the Maxwell Hemmens Max11 unit, which is slightly larger and therefore more difficult to fit into the main frame. The photograph shows the dummy engine on the left hand side. The side tank houses the Goodall water filler valve along with the boiler check valve and also provides a location for the rechargeable batteries for the headlamp. The displacement lubricator is fitted inside the cab with the drain valve below the cab floor. The two 6ba socket cap screws in the reinforcing plate below the frames hold the wedge shaped brackets on which the engine bedplate is mounted.

(WN050-2 – Geoff Lumsdon)

a practical performance in a garden railway setting, a gear ratio on the outer axle of 2:1 was all that was required, which ruled out using the worm gears of the full size locomotive. Instead, the choice was to use bevel gears of 2:1 ratio, which can be seen on the photograph of the bogies.

The disadvantage of a bevel drive is that the final drive shaft has to incline downwards towards the centre of the driven axle. At some point this arrangement was replaced in later models with crossed helical gears, where the drive shafts can remain almost horizontal, driving over the inner axle to the gears on the outer axle. Incidentally, none of the model locomotives fitted with gears have had the gearing enclosed and this has not been found to be detrimental either to the gears or the performance of the model. The sizeable boiler was of the plain centre flue type fitted with a water gauge and fired with a poker type burner. The original location of the displacement lubricator was in the right hand side of the cab but at some time was transferred to the right hand side tank. The Goodall water filler was located in the right hand extension to the cab. The design of the articulation allows the locomotive to negotiate Mamod track on 2ft 6in radius.

An interesting point regarding the full size four-cylinder locomotive is that the main frames were plate frames with the engine sitting in a recess in the centre. From there, the frames were arched up and over to provide a location for the bogie pivots and the bodywork – what I would call a cantilever frame. Cross plates with riveted angles spaced the frames apart. With the models, using ¼ x 3/8in brass bar

stock and ¼in square frame spacers made for a simpler approach. Reinforcing plates were then riveted to the central part of the frame. Only WN150 had the correct cantilever plate frames with cross plates and riveted angles. The locomotive was finished in works grey/black and lined in black with black edging on the tank tops and carried across the cab sides, the same layout as the works photographs. At this time, there was no indication of the colour scheme used on the full size engines. The name Renishaw No 2 was not used by any of the Avonside or subsequent Hunslet locomotives.

At some time in the intervening years WN005 was repainted in black and a description of this model appeared on the 16mm Web site as 'Model of the Month June 2011' and included the following:

'Despite its 26 years of age, it still runs like the proverbial sewing machine and is a regular performer at garden meets, Guildford group open afternoons and on our portable layout Mwch Grumblyn... In fact it's the perfect manually controlled loco for garden meets and shows, as its steady running means its pretty much 'gradient proof' but, if required, it does have an adequate turn of speed so as to not hold up other traffic.'

The photograph of WN025 illustrates the second of the four-cylinder locomotives.

After WN025, the next four-cylinder locomotive to be built was WN050, now correctly named Blackburn and representing Avonside Works Number 2059 of 1931. By this time, the excellent Maxwell Hemmens Caton engine had been replaced by the slightly larger Max11.

13. (Above) The final model of the four-cylinder version of the Avonside locomotive but this time painted in a dark red. The other differences are the location of the gas tank in the rear bunker and the lubricator in the front extension to the cab. What is not obvious in the photographs is that the main frames are cut out of flat plate in the same shape as the full size locomotive and braced by cross plates with riveted angle. Previous models have used ¼ x 3/8in bar frames with a central reinforcing plate and ¼in square frame spacers.
(WN150-1 – Geoff Lumsdon)

14. (Top left) The opposite side view of the four-cylinder Avonside showing the dummy cylinder side. This engine uses a cylinder casting machined on the top and bottom faces with a machined cylinder head bolted on, the lack of a reversing piston valve the main clue to the false nature of the engine. The unusual cylindrical gas tank can be seen in the rear of the cab.
(WN150-2 – John Cam)

15. (Left) The locomotive photographed in 2011 on curved track. The small knurled knob in the main frame reinforcing plate operates the water separator drain valve in the steam exhaust circuit, a useful addition for reducing condensate from being ejected from the chimney, especially when starting up. Its effectiveness is limited by the size of the reservoir that is possible in a 16mm locomotive model. In comparison the oil/water separator used in model boats would typically be 1½in in diameter and 2-3in tall.
(WN150-5 – John Cam)

WN150 was to be the final four-cylinder model, since by this time even the Max II marine engine was no longer available and Maxwell Hemmens no longer existed. The model could only be built using up an engine that had been in stock for several years. WN150 was again correctly named Blackburn and fitted with the appropriate Avonside Works Number 2059 works plates.

The Avonside 2 Cylinder locomotives Works Number 2055 Ntinyana, Works Number 2057 Renishaw No 4 and Works Number 2058 Sezela No 7.

From the four-cylinder locomotive, we can now move to the two-cylinder version of the Avonside Geared Articulated locomotive. The first model was WN037 built in 1985 to represent

Avonside Works Number 2055 of 1931, named Ntinyana and supplied to the Illovo Estate in Natal. This model used a specially made two-cylinder engine, which used ex-Roundhouse Engineering ½in bore cylinders, arranged in V formation and utilising slip eccentric valve gear. To reverse the engine, a spur gear was fitted to the crankshaft, which could engage with a lever operated quadrant gear. Moving the lever through ninety degrees caused the quadrant gear to engage with this spur gear and move the crankshaft sufficiently to change over the slip eccentric valve gear, before again disengaging. This arrangement can be seen on the photograph of the underside of the model.

Note the position of the outer universal joint, which is located under the bogie pivot to minimise the side displacement of the drive shaft. The inner universal joint and the sliding joint are thus reduced to the minimum of movement. Compare this with the misalignment of the drive shafts on a Shay or the only slightly better situation of the Climax, which is considered in the chapter on logging locomotives. It is sufficient to say that the model Avonside can operate down to a minimum radius of 3ft

without any appreciable slowing down. What is also clearly illustrated is that the limiting factor on the minimum radius is the drive shaft coming in contact with the inside of the wheels or the end of the frames. For this reason, it is necessary to limit the movement of the bogies in order that a derailment does not damage the drive shafts. Likewise, the vertical movement must be contained to prevent the bogies fouling the underside of the mainframes. The design of the pivots is covered in the chapter on the Garratt locomotive, and is illustrated with the photographs of the bogies on WN300. Notice also the 90° crossed helical gears with the smaller driving gear surrounded by a frame which is bolted to the front buffer beam.

With this type of layout it is difficult to set up the correct meshing of the gears and the supporting frame has to be particularly rigid to prevent any movement. An easier method is to use two cross frame stretchers, located either side of the front wheels, which act as bearings for the helical gear drive shaft. Spacers have to be fitted to the drive shaft, either side of the gear, to bring both gears into correct alignment. This arrangement increases the rigidity of the

16. (Left) This lovely photograph of WN037 Ntinyana rounding a tight curve illustrates the articulation, the model capable of negotiating curves down to 3ft radius.
(WN037-1 – Ken Johnson)

17. (Below) A photograph is worth a thousand words and this shows the underside view of Ntinyana, clearly showing the layout of the gear drive from the engine to the outer axles using Carden shafts. The bogies are lying hard over against their stops to illustrate the effect of curvature on the drive system. Notice how little the Carden shafts are displaced with the offset mainly accommodated by the outer universal joint and how this joint is located under the bogie pivot. Compare that with the agonising displacement on a Shay type locomotive on a similar curve. The bearings for the bogie end of the drive shaft are cantilevered from the front buffer beam. This arrangement is difficult to set up and a far more effective method is to have frame cross stretchers whose location can be accurately machined on the bogie side frames. Below the engine in the photograph can be seen the method of reversing the slip eccentric valve gear. To the left of the engine can be seen the water separator used to reduce condensate in the exhaust steam. The universal joints are homemade rather than commercially obtained units.
(WN037-2 – Ken Johnson)

18. (Left) WN200, Sezela No 7 photographed on Stuart Davidson's garden railway. The forward/reverse lever of the engine can be seen below the cylinder and below that is the disc handwheel that operates the drain valve of the exhaust steam water separator. The two red marks in front of the smokebox are the highlights on the re-railing jack. The safety valve is mounted on the boiler steam dome, which also includes the steam pick-up for the backhead mounted steam regulator.

(WN200-1 – Author)

19. (Above) WN200 based on the Avonside two-cylinder articulated locomotive Works Number 2058, Sezela No 7. What is clearly shown in this view is the girder main frame of the two-cylinder version as opposed to the cantilever main frame of the four-cylinder locomotive. With the model, this was achieved by cutting a ¼ x 1/16in groove in the 1/4 x 3/8in bar frame. Unfortunately this results in the bar adopting a slight curve away from the groove which is offset by mounting the frames opposite to each other and pulling the frames parallel using the frame spacers.

(WN200-2. Author}

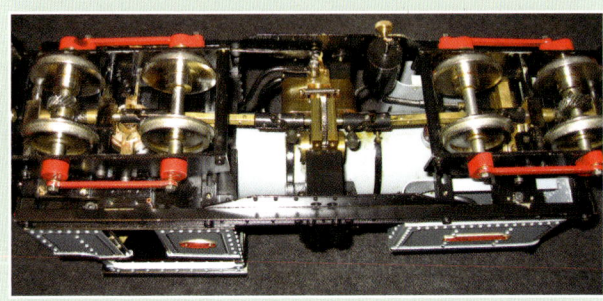

20. (Left) The underside of the SVS engined two-cylinder Avonside shown in the straight-ahead position. The support bearings for the driving crossed helical gear can be seen to be two frame stretchers rather than the cantilevered arrangement of WN037. This system can be set up very accurately using a digital readout on the milling machine when drilling the frame sides. Notice how a single lower one has replaced a full rear bogie frame stretcher in order to clear the drive shaft.

(WN200-5 – Peter Duckering)

21. (Right) The bogies are here at maximum displacement. From this photograph, it can be seen that the limit of displacement for 32mm gauge is governed by the drive shafts coming into contact with the rear flanges of the inner axle and therefore the bogie limit pins have to be set to prevent this happening. Compared to the drive shafts of the original WN005 the central sliding section is much longer due in part to the reduced size of the much more expensive steel universal joints. This in turn reduces the displacement of the drive on curves.

(WN200-6 – Peter Duckering)

frames and the stretcher holes can be accurately drilled at the correct distance from the axle bush position. The photograph of the underside of WN200 illustrates this arrangement, which has been used on nearly all subsequent articulated geared models.

Finally, the 2in diameter boiler uses a plain ¾in centre flue with a Finescale poker type burner. The working headlights operate from rechargeable batteries located in the right hand side tank.

The second two-cylinder version of the Avonside was to represent Avonside Works Number 2058, named Sezela No. 7 and was built as WN200 in 2007. With this model, the 'V' engine cylinders are dummy on both sides but are however correctly arranged as per the full size engine. Power comes from an SVS twin cylinder 'Boxer' type engine with an integral 4:1 reduction gearbox, which is located across the

frame directly under the dummy cylinders. This location of the engine gives the impression that the dummy cylinders are part of the engine with the double output shaft in the correct position to drive the carden shafts. As with the previous locomotives, the Carden shafts transmit power to the outer axles using 2:1 crossed helical gears. The helical gear driving-shaft uses the previously mentioned cross frame stretchers as bearings.

The construction of a further two-cylinder Avonside, namely WN300, gives the opportunity to illustrate the construction of the bogies on this articulated model. In this case the front bogie uses a plain spherical bearing to provide the full articulation. This bearing is then suitably enclosed to limit the movement, sufficient to cover minor fluctuations of the track. The rear bogie uses a flat disc bearing mounted on side pivots to give horizontal and longitudinal movement. All is revealed in the photographs of WN300.

22. (Top left) This shows the rear bogie in the construction stage before the addition of the semi universal pivot. The crossed helical gear drive and the frame spacer mounted bearings are clearly illustrated but it should be realised that although the driving helical gear appears at first to have teeth over its full length, in fact only one part has the full tooth profile. It is this section that engages with the driven axle gear. Purists may object to the use of socket cap screws but once tightened the bogie is very rigid and will retain its alignment. The wheels are set for 32mm gauge track and located in dimples in the axle using 3mm socket cap screws.
(WN300 Rear 1 – Author)

23. The bogie pivot arrangement with the large diameter horizontal bearing, essential to reduce any rocking caused by the torque reaction of the longitudinal drive from the engine. In this situation the mainframe pivot plate uses gauge plate direct onto the brass bearing with minimal clearance between them. A 4ba countersunk socket cap screw holds the whole unit together. The 6ba socket cap screw engages through a slot in the main frame pivot plate (gauge plate) to limit the horizontal movement whilst the other end goes through a pillar mounted on the bogie side frame to limit the longitudinal movement.
(WN300 Rear 2 – Author)

24. This illustrates the completed rear bogie with pivot ready to attach to the main frame. There should only be two holes at the ends of the mainframe pivot plate, the two extra outer holes were drilled in error. Although the main bearing is held up against this plate, the steel insert seen on the top centre of the plate maintains its central location. An oil cup is included to lubricate the bearings.
(WN300 Rear 3 – Author)

25. (Right) This shows the front universal bearing using a plain spherical bearing with limited movement. The plain spherical bearing is housed in a retaining ring screwed down onto the bogie frame pivot plate to hold the outer ring of the bearing. A 4ba countersunk socket cap screw goes through the centre of the inner spherical race and attaches it to the mainframe pivot plate with the gap between this plate and the outer race retaining-ring deciding the amount of movement allowed for lateral and longitudinal displacement. This gap is very critical and is only about 0.005in to give a displacement of 1/16in at the wheelbase.

(WN300 Front 1 – Author)

26. (Left) The assembled front bogie is here ready for fitting to the main frame. Again, the mainframe pivot plate includes a slot controlling the horizontal movement of the bogie.

(WN300 Front 2 – Author)

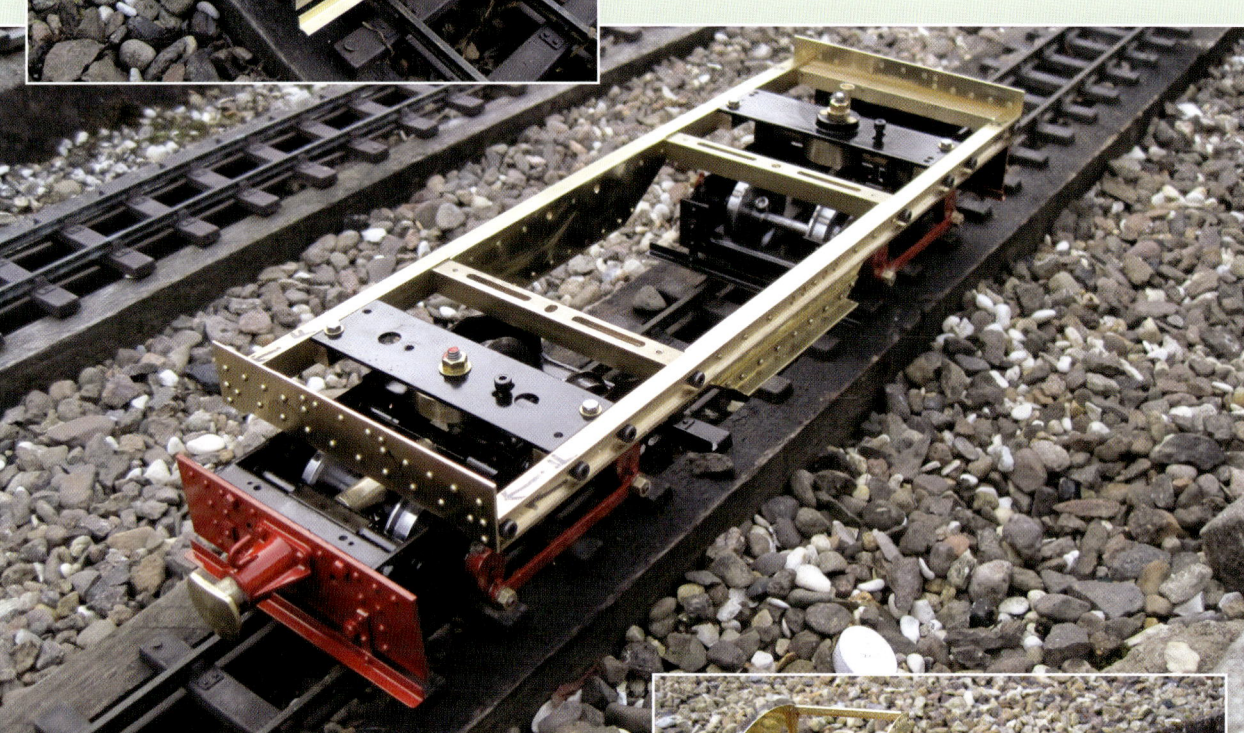

27. (Above) The two bogies mounted under the mainframes of WN300. Notice how the mainframes have been machined to resemble the girder construction of the full-size locomotive. Pulling the frames together using the frame spacers removes the curvature of the bar stock caused by the machining process.

(WN300-1 – Author)

28. (Right) Although the model of the Avonside geared engine is not the first one to be constructed, the building procedure has still been adhered to. The first part was to make the bogies and then to mount them on the frames. Next, the engine and transmission have been added, followed by the dummy cylinders. After the engine, the most important item is the mounting of the boiler and then the gas tank. The dome on the boiler is not just for the safety valve but also contains the steam pickup pipe to the boiler backhead steam regulator bush. However, before the gas tank can be mounted, the cab has to be in place

to ensure that the gas tank is accessible through the cab openings, in this case the rear bunker. Note how the gas tank has been sloped slightly outwards so that the filler valve is clear of the rear cab sheet for filling and the whole tank has been lowered to again clear the same rear cab sheet.

(WN300-4 – Author)

29. (Right) An interesting photograph that shows the construction of the cab. In a similar manner to that of the full size locomotive, the cab sides front and rear are attached to each other using rivets and 5/32in square brass tube. Using imperial brass tube allows the square tube to be reinforced by 1/8in round tube, otherwise the rivets would tend to collapse the square tube when peined over. It is normal practice to stagger the rivets on each side of the joint when using 6x6mm milled brass angle but this is absolutely essential with the small square tube. This can be seen on the photograph along with the ends of the square tube reinforced by the internal round tube. Observing the works photograph, it can be seen that the base of the handrails are located in the cab footplate, whereas with the model a bottom bracket is used. The advantage of this is that the cab assembly is self-contained making it easier to fit and remove. Attached to the bottom 1/4x1/4 x1/16in brass angle are four outriggers in the corner of the cab which allow the cab to be screwed to the frame cross members. Direct attachment to the cab floor using the heavy angle is not possible with this type of locomotive due to the position of the main side frames.
(WN300 Cab-2 –Author)

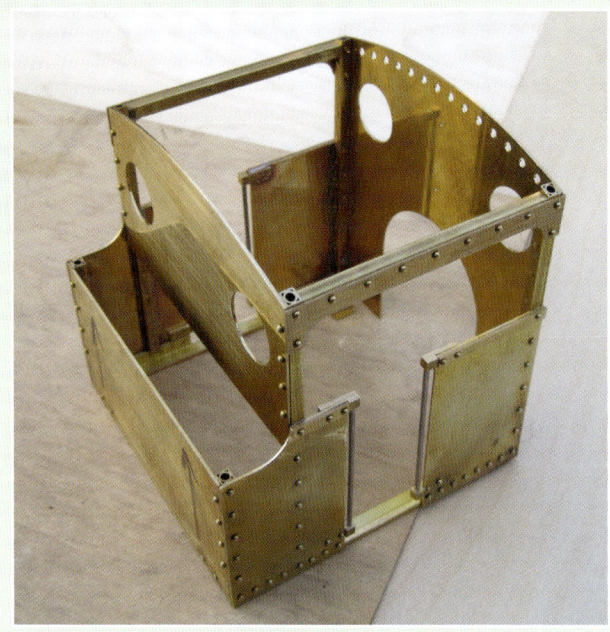

30. (Below) This photograph shows the model starting to look the part. The side tanks have been added along with the smokebox. Another feature is the spark-arresting chimney machined in two halves from solid brass bar stock. The alternative involves fabricating the chimney from rolled brass sheet requiring a return to schooldays geometry and the truncated cone. Drawing out the expanded shape and subsequent cutting is not the main problem, it is the seam required to join up the cone that is difficult to hide. Even then, the conical tubes still require to be fitted to brass rings, which still absorb valuable bar stock. Machining the bottom half from the correct length

of solid brass bar starts with the cylindrical base and a pilot hole. Mounting the solid base in the chuck, the outside taper is carefully machined with support from the tailstock and then the centre is drilled out further leaving adequate thickness for support in the chuck. Using the same setting of taper, the inside of the cone is carefully machined out, including the mid joining ring followed by the final centre drilling. A similar method machines the top cone and the finished parts are then silver soldered together.
(WN300-5 – Author)

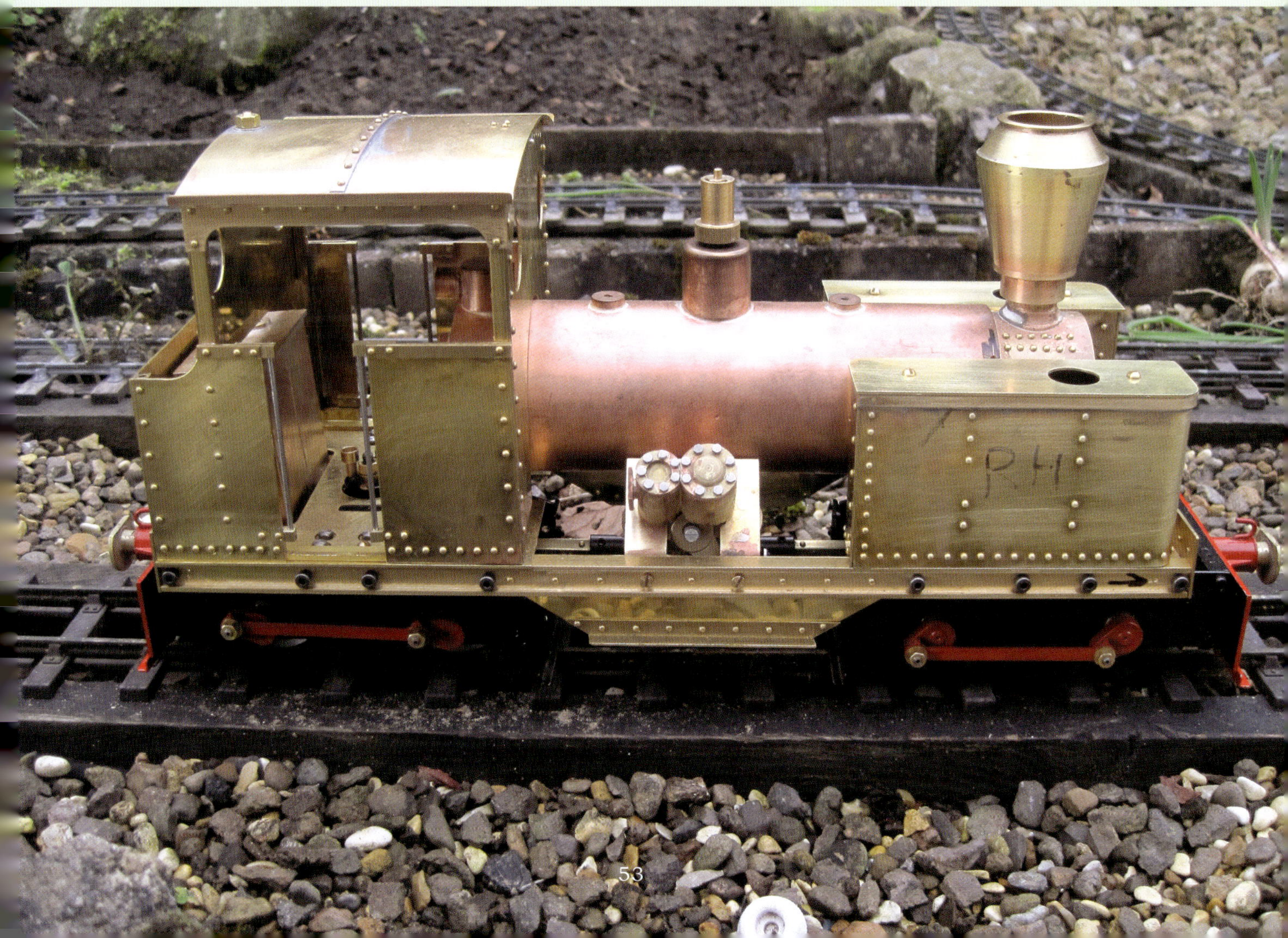

31. (Above) New Years Day 2010 provided a light settling of snow, lit by occasional shafts of early afternoon golden sunlight as Renishaw No 4 hauls a logging train past Great Scree on Mike Bew's Tillingbourne Light Railway, before being dispatched to Durban, South Africa.

(WN176-3 – Michael Bew)

32. (Top left) A Mike Lax built model of Avonside wn2057, Renishaw No 4, using the same design as WN200. Note the correct colour scheme of the locomotive in its final year of operation on the Renishaw Estates in 1968, including the yellow/black zig-zag lining of the side tanks and buffer beams. By this time, the Avonside boiler had been replaced with a Hunslet boiler, which accounts for the different pipe arrangement. The rear bunker had also been modified.

(WN176-2 – Mike Lax)

33. (Middle left) Another Renishaw No 4 in its original Hunslet form and painted in works grey and black.

(WN224-1 – Author)

34. (Bottom left) When WN005 reappeared on the heritage stand at the AGM of the 16mm Association in 2010, the model had acquired an overall black livery and looked splendid despite its 26 years of operation.

(WN005-2 – Ian Bunch)

35. A rare photograph of a two-cylinder Avonside Geared locomotive at work in the sugar plantation. In this photograph, the locomotive is Sezela No 8, one of the later Hunslet Engine Co built engines, Works Number 2005 of 1939 working for the Reynolds Bros. on the Sezela Estates.

(Sezela No8 collection of Jim Hawkesworth)

Following the construction of this model, photographs of the two-cylinder locomotives in South Africa were supplied by Jim Hawkesworth and for the first time we were aware of the actual colour finish of the full size engines. Two photographs were of these locomotives in derelict condition but the third showed Sezela No 8, one of the later Hunslet locomotives, still working and not withdrawn from service until 1967. At a later date, further information was provided showing Renishaw No 4, one of the original Avonside locomotives (Works Number 2057), still in use on the Renishaw Estates until its last journey in 1968 when the sugar mill turned over to road transport. The colour scheme was green with red frames and the reinforcing on the cab and water tanks were highlighted in red. The bogies were black with red cranks and coupling rods and the buffer beams and side tanks had diagonal yellow and black stripes.

Several further models of the Avonside two-cylinder locomotives have been built to the design of WN200 but this time constructed by Mike Lax. WN176 was finished in the correct green with red highlighting and included the jazzy yellow/black stripes on the side tanks and buffer beams.

As mentioned previously, the original diesel locomotive, Ellingham Estate, Works Number 2046 of 1930, is not only preserved but still resides in South Africa. Even more importantly, Renishaw No 4, Works Number 2057 of 1931, one of the original Avonside locomotives, which was still operating in 1968, was acquired by the Phyllis Rampton Trust and returned to England during December 1969. This is a private collection and the present condition of the locomotive is not known. Sadly all the other South African Heislers have been scrapped.

REFERENCES:

- The Engineer, 6th November, 1931. Article on Narrow Gauge Geared Articulated Locomotives.
- Locomotives International No 9. Article by F W Harman.
- Articulated Locomotives of the World by Donald Binns. Article on Avonside Geared Locomotives.
- Sugarcane Locomotives. Where Are They Now? Renishaw No 4. A small handout article from South Africa.

TRAMWAY LOCOMOTIVES

TRAMWAY LOCOMOTIVES IN BRITAIN

The steam tram has long since had its day. It really only flourished for about twenty years, roughly from 1880 to 1900, with a few tramways lasting into the early 1900s. In Britain, these tramways tended to be located in suburban areas, towns and cities such as Birmingham or they interconnected closely situated towns to give magnificent company titles, for instance, Manchester, Bury, Rochdale and Oldham Tramways Co Ltd. (MBR&O). It was this location in densely populated areas that made them vulnerable to the introduction of electric traction in the early 1900s. Some rural systems lingered on, with the last steam tramway in England running between Wolverhampton and Stony Stratford in Buckinghamshire, entering the General Strike in 1926 from which it failed to emerge. Yet the change to electric traction was not universal, particularly in Europe with many tramways in Holland, Belgium and Italy running for over fifty years. These lines were often extensive and inter urban and connected with rural areas along their way, which made them far less attractive in later years, given the high cost of electrification. Many of these lines soldiered on up until the Second World War and probably the last city in the world to have a steam tram service was Surabaya in Java. Here a Beyer Peacock tram, supplied in 1900, was still at work in 1973 with the line eventually closing in 1978.

So far, the demise of the steam tram has been discussed but what about the beginnings in Britain? Primitive tramways have been around for hundreds of years, promoted by the need to transfer heavy or bulky objects over rough tracks and un-metalled ways. By the middle of the 17th century they were well established in colliery districts, especially on the banks of the river Tyne. Initially, these tramways would have been of wood but their rapid wear was costly in both labour and materials. With the advent of iron, the wooden beams would be reinforced by capping with iron bars or plates held by nails. The first wooden tramway to be replaced by cast iron rails was at the Coalbrookdale Iron Works in Shropshire in 1767. This was soon followed by the introduction of iron rails to the mining areas of Northern England, Cornwall, South Wales and the Midlands. By the early 1800s there was the first stirrings of passenger carrying tramways, for example in 1809 a horse drawn tramway was proposed between Gloucester and Cheltenham, which was opened in 1821 for the conveyance of passengers and goods. By the middle of the 19th century the great railway boom was taking place and steam ships were familiar to most people. However, the application of steam technology had yet to have any real impact on road transport where the horse still reigned supreme. Certainly, there had been attempts to mechanise street traction, including mechanical assistance to the horse drawn tramway carriage, but it was the steam tram that would win the freedom of the road from the horse.

Very little of practical value appears to have been achieved before 1870, with the next ten years seeing the experimental introduction of steam tramway locomotives to existing and new tramways. The firm of Messrs' Kitson and Co of Leeds with their horizontal boiler engines (six of which were supplied to New Zealand in 1879) reached the practical perfection of the steam tramway locomotive in this country. These engines continued to give sterling service for over fifty years. Kitson went on to produce over 300 tramway locomotives, mainly for tramways in Britain, including Leeds, Bradford, Burnley, Edinburgh and Belfast. Other companies were also engaged in this enterprise with over 200 locomotives supplied by Beyer Peacock, along with such firms as Black Hawthorn & Co, Thomas Green & Sons, Falcon and Merryweather.

The development of the steam tram however, was not without its problems, one of them being the regulations of the Board of Trade, acting under the provisions of the Tramways Act of 1870, which stated that no visible smoke or steam must be emitted from the engine. It must also be free from noise produced by blast or machinery and that all working parts should be concealed from view at all points above 4in from rail level. Apart from the stringent requirements of the Tramways Act of 1870, the builders and operators of tramways had to contend with a public biased towards the horse and with conditions brought about by not having a dedicated rail track. If the track was incorporated in a road, it had to follow the camber of the road, resulting in uneven wear of the track and wheel tread. Curves could be very tight and gradients severe by rail standards and there was always the problem of dirt and grit getting into mechanical parts, as well as traction on a track covered in horse muck, market refuse and other noxious waste. In addition, overloaded un-sprung steel rimmed carts and wagons could damage the track. Despite being faced with this almost impossible, task hundreds of tramway locomotives were built and there were some very large tramway undertakings, such as the Birmingham Tramways covering some 67 continuous route miles and operated by about 200 locomotives.

Now the models, starting with the early freelance designs based on typical British tramway locomotives.

FREELANCE TRAMWAY LOCOMOTIVES

The first tramway locomotive models were basically freelance making use of the power plants then available. In the case of WN27 & WN33 the engine was the Caton Marine unit with the former locomotive having a horizontal spirit fired potboiler. The boiler had the same dimensions as the Roundhouse 'Charles Pooter' model and also made use of the Roundhouse methylated spirits burner and firebox. The arrangement of the Caton Engine at the front, the 6¼in long boiler along with the burner reservoir located at the rear, required a 10¼in long locomotive. Adding methylated spirits to the tank was facilitated through the side openings in the rather square body with a tell-tale fuel level gauge fed through and located in front of the buffer beam. A 6mm chain coupled the axles and the miniature jack plug located on the side of the body indicates that the headlights were working units.

1. The first freelance design of tram based around a standard methylated spirit fired potboiler and Caton marine engine. The boiler has a Roundhouse Engineering firebox and a four-wick burner with the boiler dimensions similar to their 'Charles Pooter' engine. The Caton engine was mounted at the front of the boiler across the frames and geared to the front axle by 2:1 spur gears. Transmission to the rear axle was by 6mm chain. The headlights are working with the battery just visible in this photograph. As with all of these models, the body is removable without interference to the chassis, including in this case the front and rear centre buffers.

(WN027-1 – N D Kirkbride)

2. *(Top left)* With this freelance locomotive, the body has been built around a full Maxwell Hemmens marine steam plant. The Caton marine engine can be seen at the front of the chassis, again laid across the frame and geared to the front axle. The vertical boiler is rather large and of the 'J' flue type, as can be seen by the position of the gas burner. At the rear is the cylindrical gas tank. The steam take-off point on this type of boiler is on the top and hence the regulator lever has been arranged to stick out from under the roof ventilation top cover. The red handwheel is probably the drain on the condensate separator with the other valve to the left the gauge glass blow-down.

(WN033-1 – Author's collection]

4. *(Left)* This photograph is shown purely to illustrate WN33 running in 2011, still operating after 21 years.

(WN033-3 – Mike Lowe)

5. *(Below)* Photograph of WN033 and possibly WN035 on the late Bob Farnsworth's line at Blanchland in Northumberland.

(WN033 & possibly WN035 – Author's collection]

6. (Above) Freelance tramway locomotive using the vertical boiler arrangement of other vertical boiler trams, such as the Beyer Peacock MBR&O Wilkinson Patent tram but with a cab based on a photograph of a freelance tram that appeared in an early issue of Tom Cooper's Steamlines magazine.

(WN081-1 – Geoff Lumsdon)

7. (Left) An opposite side view. The two front headlights are working units with the rechargeable batteries concealed in the dummy front water tank. The wiring is run through the external conduit and painted black for effect. Notice the hooks on the buffer beam to store the unused link chain. As with all the full cab tramway locomotives, the entire roof is removable.

(WN081-2 – Geoff Lumsdon)

For the second freelance tram, a complete Maxwell Hemmens vertical boiler marine plant was used (including the Caton engine) and was shoe-horned into a 10in frame to produce a locomotive similar in appearance to the previous model. However, the tram body corners have been curved round to eliminate a square riveted angle joint. The oval brass hooded front window apertures are particularly attractive and the tubular cowcatcher looks very well. In fact, the tram looks similar to the later models of the Backer & Rueb Dutch trams. One of the photographs shows a third horizontal boiler tram alongside WN33 on the track of the late Bob Farnsworth at Blanchland in Northumberland. It has a very similar shaped body and must have been built around the same time. There is no record or information on the tram, although it may be assumed to be WN35.

Finally, there were two freelance tram type locomotives WN81 and WN165 based on a photograph in an early Steamlines magazine and photographs of WN 81 illustrate these. The mechanical layout is the standard vertical boiler layout used on other trams and also on the De Winton locomotives.

THE WILKINSON PATENT STEAM TRAM

Many early tramway engines were built with vertical boilers but the horizontal locomotive boiler (which was far more efficient and could be used on more powerful units) quickly succeeded these. The exception was the special tram locomotives built by William Wilkinson and patented soon after the introduction of the Kitson engine. The construction of steam trams with vertical boilers was confined to very early experimental locomotives, with manufacturers rapidly adopting the conventional horizontal boiler. Wilkinson on the other hand designed his locomotive with a vertical boiler and a twin cylinder engine having small-bore cylinders and a geared drive to one axle. Tram locomotives were at a definite disadvantage when attempting to pull away on wet or greasy track but the gearing on the Wilkinson tram gave a more even torque and they were generally good starters. Further, the gearing improved the ability of the tram to negotiate steep inclines. Side rods connected the second axle. The tram locomotive was both compact and light and featured a means of superheating the exhaust steam, which then escaped through

Beyer Peacock & Co. Tram Engine 6336

8. *(Above) A works photograph of the Wilkinson Patent Tram built by Beyer Peacock (Works Number 2377) in 1883 for the MBR&O Steam Tramway as their No.21.*

(CD1222 IMG0075 3-A-51 – MOSI, Manchester)

9. *(Opposite) A General Arrangement drawing of the Wilkinson Patent Tram. Note the vertical boiler with field tubes and a cast iron superheating vessel fitted in the firebox, a device intended to reduce the emission of steam*

nuisance in public streets. Also, the vertical twin cylinder steam engine can be seen to be geared to the adjacent axle. This improved the ability of the tram to start and negotiate steep inclines. The drawing, kindly provided by the Museum of Science and Industry in Manchester, is unusual in that various parts are coloured in a way more associated with modern computer illustrations.

(34447-6336 – Museum of Science and Industry (MOSI), Manchester)

the chimney. This was an attempt to satisfy the Board of Trade requirement that no smoke or steam should be emitted from the engine but was not very successful and later locomotives featured a roof-mounted condenser. The early popularity of the engine soon outstripped the manufacturing capacity of the patentee and so production rights were given to Thomas Green & Son of Leeds who built 38, Black Hawthorn & Co of Gateshead built 32 and Beyer Peacock & Co of Manchester built a total of 71.

It was in the hands of Beyer Peacock that the Wilkinson tram was to become a very serviceable machine. The final consignment of Wilkinson engines supplied by Beyer Peacock to the MBR&O in 1886 (order 6736 for twenty 3ft 6in and order 6737 for four standard gauge), were fitted with roof condensers and were described

as magnificent engines, continuing to run with the fullest satisfaction until the electrification of the system was completed in 1905. For Beyer Peacock, the construction of tramway locomotives came to an end in 1886/7 with the construction of three tramway engines supplied to the standard gauge system of the MBR&O (orders 6741& 6754). They were fitted with horizontal locomotive type boilers, the last one having compound cylinders and all three were fitted with roof-mounted condensers. However, despite its initial success the Wilkinson tramway locomotive failed to compete with the tramway locomotives of Messrs Kitson and Co and production of just over 200 engines practically ceased by 1886.

From the model point of view, the Wilkinson tram offered the attraction of a vertical boiler and

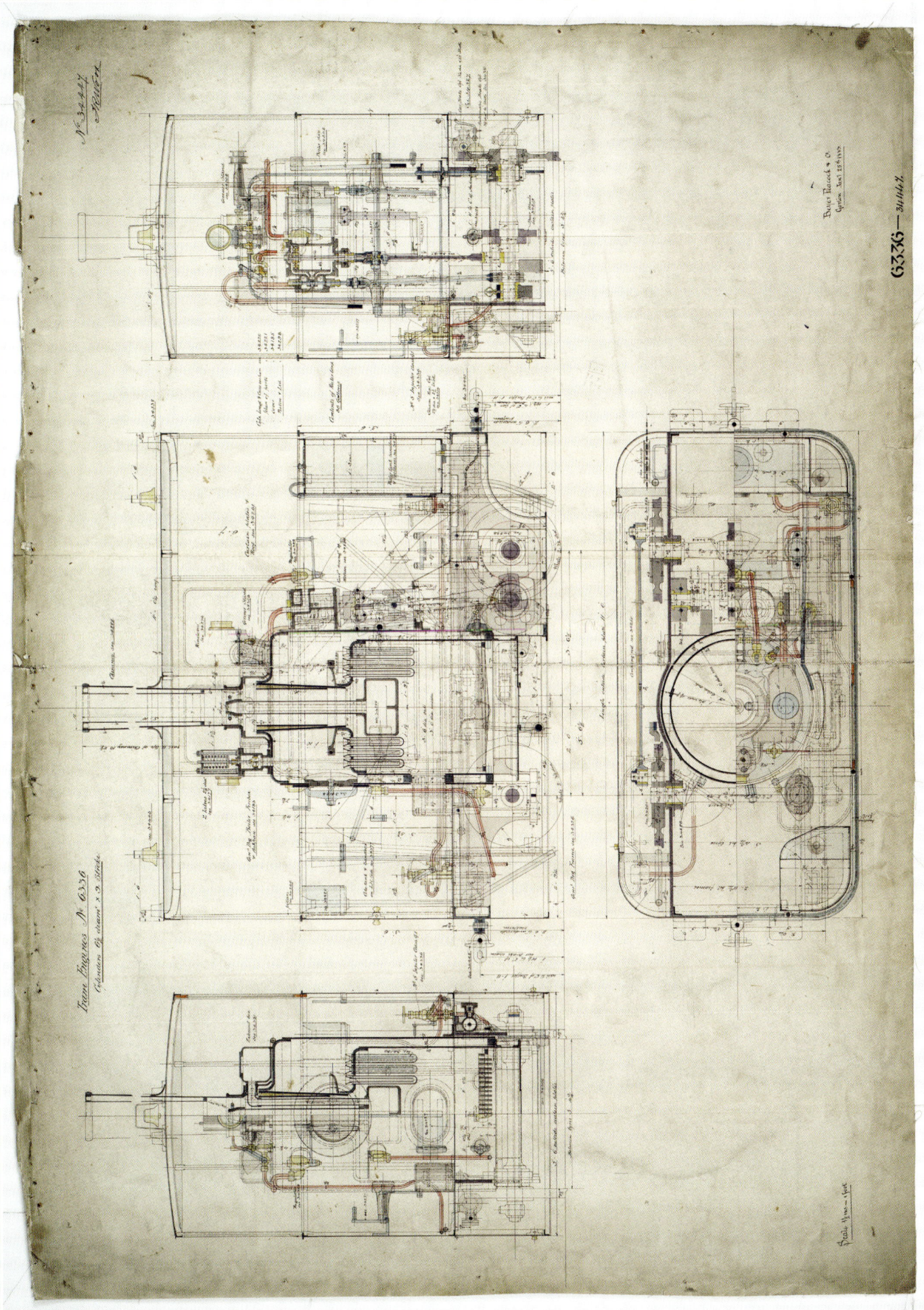

10. *(Top left) One of the Wilkinson Patent tramway locomotives, Works Number 375, built by Black, Hawthorn & Co Ltd. for the Alford & Sutton Steam Tramway as their locomotive No 1 and which forms the basis for the model WN51. The problem of the enclosed cab and the difficulty of access to controls are particularly illustrated by this tramway locomotive. With tramway locomotives, other than the Wilkinson type, the presence of side entry openings at least allows some access to controls, in particular the drain valve for the displacement lubricator.*

(WN051 – Geoff Munday)

11. *(Middle left) The second of the Alford & Sutton Wilkinson trams complete with hinged roof access. This model was still operating satisfactorily in 2010 when this photograph was taken, despite being over 20 years old.*

(WN052-3 – John Dunford)

12. *(Below left) Wilkinson Patent Tram based on the locomotives built by Beyer Peacock for the MBR&O Steam Tramway. The model is numbered 22 of the MBR&O and corresponds to Beyer Peacock Works Number 2378 of 1883. The model is finished with the correct plates including the Wilkinson Patent plates and has been lined by Geoff Munday of Lightline. This view shows the engine end of the tram with the displacement lubricator and engine visible. Access to the lubricator drain valve, normally located at the base, is not practical and hence a pipe has been run to a separate valve seen at the front of the locomotive.*

(WN60-1 – Geoff Munday)

13. *(Below right) This is No 22 from the opposite end showing the location of the gas tank and gas valve along with the operating side of the vertical boiler. The boiler is arranged with all the fittings at this end to best see the water gauge and pressure gauge - always a problem with enclosed tramway locomotives.*

(WN60-2 – Geoff Munday)

14. (Left) The final batch of MBR&O steam tram models, this time built by Mike Lax to the original design but more accurate in scale and detail. Note the frosted glass windows with a wooden frame, all neatly incorporated in this model. Notice how the inside of the tram cab is painted white and typical of later models, the body of the lubricator and Goodall valve holder are painted black.

(WN288-3 – Author)

geared drive. Cheddar Models had introduced ceramic burners to the marine modelling world with their vertical boiler marine steam plants and these burners were ideal for a vertical boiler tram. The vertical boiler offers a compact arrangement nestling between the axles with a vertically mounted engine driving the front axle. To reduce height, the boiler is dropped half way through the frame and sits on a steel plate bolted to the side frames, which also support the ceramic burner. To the rear, the vertical gas tank is located between the frames and can be of considerable capacity. The end result, without the body, is of a compact easily accessible steam plant that can be readily fitted into a chassis of only 8¼in long. The vertical boiler provides a clearly visible good length gauge glass and the burner can be set by observation down the flue, which is very handy in a noisy environment such as an exhibition layout.

The problem with any tramway model is the all-enclosing bodywork, which severely limits access to the controls as well as visibility of the gauge glass. There is no better example of these problems than that demonstrated by WN51 and WN52 based on locomotive No.1 of the Alford and Sutton Tramway – a Wilkinson Patent Tram supplied by Black Hawthorn in 1883. These models were produced specifically at the request of two customers and would for the reasons given not have been by choice. To improve access, one of these models had a section of the roof hinged.

A far more practical version of the Wilkinson Patent steam tram was based on the locomotives built in 1883 by Beyer Peacock for the 3ft 6in

MBR&O Tramways Ltd in 1883. A General Arrangement drawing supplied by MOSI, Manchester, illustrates the Beyer Peacock design and is particularly unusual in having been lined in colour. There were six locomotives in this order, Beyer Peacock Works Numbers 2377-82 and corresponded to the tramway companies numbers 21-26. The models, WN57, 60 and 61 were therefore numbered 21 to 23, with a much later model built in 2004 carrying the number 24.

Finally in 2010, Mike Lax produced two further models to exactly the same design but with more detail. By this time the previously mentioned drawings were available which allowed for a more accurate scale model. Further, the high resolution works photograph supplied at the same time by MOSI, Manchester, indicated that the side panels were in fact frosted glass in wooden frames, which in the model were carefully recreated by Mike and are shown in the photograph of WN288.

PLYNLIMON & HAFAN TRAMWAY

The next tramway locomotive is definitely not for the faint hearted, being ugly even by tramway standards. The situation was made worse with the failure of the full size locomotive to be of any use. Despite this, the engine named Victoria will always be associated with the 2ft 3in gauge Plynlimon and Hafan Tramway. Delivered on the 12th May 1897, its inaugural run to Talybont, eagerly awaited by an enthusiastic crowd, consisted of a distance of 22 chains. Next day, the engine did reach Talybont but it was a very poor runner and the company were forced to purchase another locomotive within

15. *(Left) Side view of the model based on the Plynlimon & Hafan tramway locomotive Victoria, the one and only locomotive built by J Slee & Co in 1897 and finished in dark red. This is surely one of the ugliest examples of a tramway locomotive and one that was also a total failure in use. Note the correct manufacturer's plates of J Slee & Co. This view also illustrates the problem of access to the enclosed cab where the steam regulator has been moved to the side of the boiler, making it more difficult to see the gauge glass. On the other hand the lubricator drain valve is accessible in the normal position.*

(WN118-1 – Geoff Lumsdon)

16. *(Below) The model seen attached to two Talyllyn coaches in which combination the locomotive looks almost attractive and is a considerable improvement on the lone engine.*

(WN118-3 – Geoff Lumsdon)

17. *(Right) This photograph of the second model of the Plynlimon & Hafan Railway Company, Victoria, still shows it as a very ugly duckling, even when finished in black with a superb grey and white outer lining by Lightline.*

(WN122-1 – Geoff Munday)

months. After this, it is doubtful if the engine ran again. The firm of John Slee & Co (who existed as general engineers located at Earlstown Engineering Works, Warrington) built the loco. John Slee had never made a locomotive before but was a director of the Plynlimon & Hafan Tramway, which may account for the choice of using his company to build the engine.

As with the full size engine, the model WN118 used a vertical boiler with a ceramic burner and vertically mounted SVS engine geared to one axle with coupling rods to the other axle.

It was built in much the same way as previous tramway models. As is the case with all enclosed tramway models, care had to be taken to arrange the best access to the controls by utilising the walk through gaps in the side panels. Finished in red and named Kay the model includes the correct J Slee works plates but when observed in isolation is unlikely to win a beauty contest. However, when connected to suitable carriages, the appearance is almost acceptable. A further model, WN122 was constructed and finished in black and was lined by Lightline. Both models are shown in the accompanying photographs.

THE GLYN VALLEY TRAMWAY

The Glyn Valley Tramway operated in the Ceriog valley, from Gledrid Wharf on the Shropshire Union Canal near Chirk, to the village of Glyn Ceriog some five miles into the valley. The area around the village was rich in slate, granite, limestone, lead and silicon, with slate having been quarried as early as the 1500s. The development of the valley was however hindered by the problem of transport, which was limited to the use of packhorse, there being no roads. The construction of the Ellesmere Canal in 1799 provided a connection to the areas of Shropshire and beyond but still left the difficulties of access up the valley. It was to remedy this that the 2ft 4¼ in gauge Glyn Valley Tramway was developed with work commencing in 1872. As with many tramways the line was initially operated with horses and despite the loss of slate traffic the line carried 10,000 tons of granite in its first year. However, it was not to last and very soon the limitations of horse drawn power coupled with an inadequate track layout, including at one point a very steep gradient, landed the company in financial trouble. To deal with this situation the company applied for conversion to steam operation in early 1885, which was to result in the Glyn Valley Tramway Act of the same year. This proved to be the spur to action on the line with the 1 in 19 gradient at Pontfaen replaced in 1888 by a 1 in 67 diversion to the GWR station at Chirk and on to the Shropshire canal basin at Blackpark. A two-mile extension at the Glyn end gave direct access to the granite quarries at Pandy and Hendre. In 1887 an order was given to Beyer Peacock to build two tramway type locomotives, the first Sir Theodore Works Number 2969, delivered in 1888 and the second Dennis Works Number 2970, delivered in 1889. In 1892 a third locomotive was ordered, again from Beyer Peacock, Works Number 3500 and was named Glyn. They were true examples of tramway design with totally enclosed motion accessed by three lifting covers on either side. The sides of the side tanks were extended forwards to the front of the smokebox with a hinged door access to the lubricators. The wheel arrangement was 0-4-2 but these tramway locomotives were designed to run cab first as a 2-4-0, thus complying with the Board of Trade requirement to have the driver at the front, although they did occasionally run chimney first. Further details of these intriguing locomotives and the history of the line are comprehensively covered in W J Milner's The Glyn Valley Tramway. Unfortunately the line closed in 1935 before the preservation era and the locomotives were lost to the scrap man.

From a modelling point of view the tram arrangement is ideal for a hidden geared drive along with the adoption of a simpler 0-4-0 wheel arrangement and was the method used by earlier manufacturers such as Robin Gosling and Finescale engineering. It is imperative that the models of these locomotives (and in fact all tramway locomotives) can run slowly and consistently, because they would look ridiculous at speed. Several models of the

18. Beyer Peacock works photograph of the Glyn Valley Tram Sir Theodore Works Number 2969 of 1888.
(CD1221 IMG0054 2-A-50 – MOSI, Manchester)

19. (Top left) This view of the GVT Sir Theodore shows the condenser pipes leading from the cylinder exhaust to the side tanks. The vertical pipes alongside would be for ventilation. It also illustrates how little room there is in the cab. In this small space has to be fitted the rear of the boiler with its turret, the water gauge with drain valve, pressure gauge, steam regulator and water level/blow-off valve (seen in the side entrance). In addition, the gas tank is concealed at the rear of the cab between the frames with the gas valve projecting into the side entrance. The gas tank is filled through the hole in the cab roof seen just behind the roof-mounted bell.
(WN139-2 – Geoff Lumsdon)

20. (Left) View of the underside showing how the SVS engine fits in neatly between the frames and the axles. The 2in wide by $2^3/8$in long 1in deep gas tank is also shown at the right hand end located between the frames and on the opposite end can be seen the control rod for the forward/reverse front lever. The gas tank has a ½in diameter column to provide a suitable filling point and gas valve location.
(WN139-3 – Geoff Lumsdon)

three GVT trams have been made with each successive model introducing more detailing. WN139 illustrates a model of Sir Theodore, complete with imitation condensing gear and a large number of real rivets. With the SVS engine located between the axles driving to the rear axle and the limited access of the tram body, the forward/reverse lever has been brought out to the front (chimney) end footplate. The Sentinel type gas tank sits to the rear between the frames well inside the cab and clear of the boiler. The turret, attached to the gas tank, mounts the gas valve at the side with the gas filler valve on top. Access to the filler valve is through the roof.

The works list shows that 'Glyn' is by far the most popular with WN's 153/4, 163, 179, 191. Number 179 is shown running at Robin Hoods Bay on Richard Calvert's 45mm track and, as with most tramway models, is dual gauge. This photograph illustrates the increased detailing with the speed indicator, sand domes, condensing gear, flat steam dome with

Ramsbottom safety valves and operating rods to the injector and steam whistle and a re-railing jack on the tank top. Even the rivets are starting to follow more accurately those of the prototype but remember these are real 3/64 and 1/32 in brass rivets. The displacement lubricator can be seen just in front of the cab with a slot in the skirt to access the drain valve lever. The photographs of WN163 show a different view of the GVT Glyn and again illustrate the greater attention to detail.

BRITISH BUILT TRAMWAY LOCOMOTIVES FOR OVERSEAS

One of the earliest tramway locomotive builders was Messrs' Merryweather who supplied 46 locomotives to the Southern Tramways of Paris from 1875 to 1877. They were the first steam trams in service in Europe and were soon followed by the adoption of Merryweather engines in Germany and Spain. There are no examples of the Merryweather locomotives in this book as they were considered far too small and too enclosed to be practical but there are two examples of British built tramway locomotives exported overseas, both of which were built by Beyer Peacock & Company.

BEYER PEACOCK & CO.
– SURABAYA STEAM TRAM

WN53 was based on the Surabaya trams supplied to Java and built by Beyer Peacock in 1900 and which were still in operation in 1973, probably the last steam trams to run anywhere in the world. Steam tram orders for overseas customers were important to Beyer Peacock who supplied many engines of different types to Java between the years 1882 to1910. The layout of the model is as the previous trams despite the fact that in reality the full size locomotives had horizontal boilers, the all-over cab tending to disguise this fact. The bodywork of these models is very pleasing to make but great care is required to ensure that the curves are consistent for any inaccuracy is instantly apparent. Another interesting point associated with fully enclosed tramway locomotives is that the body can be made as one complete unit held in place by screws into four outriggers. The full-length roof can be removed from the body separately. Removing these screws and possibly the buffing gear gives full access to the steam plant, the body being purely cosmetic. Several further Surabaya tram models have been built, (WN73, 79, 107and108). WN79 is illustrated in its original lined livery and then at a later date after having benefited from the attentions of Geoff Munday at Lightline.

BEYER PEACOCK & CO.
– SERAJOEDAL STEAM TRAM

Not all tramway locomotives were fitted with a full-length enclosed cab or with the ability to operate the engine from both ends. The tram locomotives built by Beyer Peacock in 1895 for the 3ft 6in (1067mm) Serajoedal Steam Tram Co in Java looked like a conventional side tank locomotive above the running boards but were fitted with skirts to enclose the wheels and motion gear. Fourteen of these 0-6-0 locomotives were spread over four orders with the last two being supplied as late as 1910. A works photograph supplied by MOSI, Manchester, illustrates the first locomotive of the initial fourteen, Works Number 3654 of 1895. An unusual feature of these locomotives was the addition of side curtains presumably to protect against rain or sun. Unlike the full size engine, the models WN48 & 49 were built with an 0-4-0 wheel arrangement and with a geared oscillating engine located between the frames.

22. (Top) The Glyn Valley Tram Glyn, WN163, was built to the same basic design by Mike Lax but with greater emphasis on detail. Note the dome detail with dummy safety valve and the whistle and injector operating rods. A toolbox has been added to the tank top along with re-railing jack and how about the speed indicator at the front left hand corner of the bodywork? The displacement lubricator and behind it the gas tank column are just visible in the doorway. There is also considerably more rivet detail on the bodywork. The small globe valve in the doorway is the water level/blow off valve.

(WN163-2 – Geoff Lumsdon)

24. (Above) Merryweather and Company tramway locomotive, wn110 of 1881, for the Rijnlandsche Stoomtramweg- Maatschappij standard gauge tramway – now preserved at the Nederlands Spoorweg Museum, (literally-Dutch Railway Museum), Maliebahn Station, Ultrecht, Netherlands.

(RSTM-2 – Kees Capel)

26. *(Top left) Surabaya Steam Tramway, one of several in the works list but here improved by the attentions of Lightline. Note the red outer and cream inner lining and the slight colour alteration to brown inside the lined panels. Unfortunately the photograph seems to have lost some colour contrast on the front panel.*

(WN079-2 – Geoff Munday)

27. *(Left) The Surabaya Steam Tram, WN79 Annie, but finished with a simpler lining. The full size locomotives were fitted with horizontal boilers, which are more difficult to fit into a tramway engine due to the length of the boiler. On the other hand the vertical boiler, the vertically mounted geared engine and rear gas tank fits very neatly into the 9in long frame and provides good access to these components. The full-length roof can easily be removed by loosening off one knurled nut to provide even better access. The body is removable as a single unit, being held in place by four 6ba screws, although with this model the buffers also have to be removed. This picture shows that the layout of the boiler, engine and gas tank is identical to that of the MBR&O tramway models.*

(WN102-4 – Roger Pattie)

28. *(Below) Beyer Peacock works photograph of the first of fourteen 0-6-0 locomotives supplied to the Serajoedal Tramway in Java. This locomotive was Works Number 3654, one of eight supplied in 1895 to be followed by two orders of two and then a final order for two as late as 1910. Note the unusual addition of side curtains presumably required to keep out the rain or sun.*

(CD1222 IMG0092 3-A-71 – MOSI, Manchester)

29. Serajoedal Steam Tram beautifully lined by Lightline. This is a conventional locomotive with side skirts below the footplate but built as an 0-4-0 rather than the correct six coupled arrangement of the full size locomotives. The brass wheel at the lower front of the side tank is the drain valve for the displacement lubricator. The forward/reverse lever can be seen in the cab opening.

(WN49-1 – Geoff Munday)

The gas tank was located in the left hand side tank and the boiler (complete with water gauge) was supplied by Finescale as used on their 'Dolgoch' model.

CONTINENTAL STEAM TRAMWAY LOCOMOTIVES

Whereas the steam tram had a short life in Britain and was rapidly replaced by electric traction, the conditions on the continent encouraged the use of steam traction well into the twentieth century. Continental tramways tended to be inter-urban where the costs of changing to electric traction were not justified by the intensity or type of traffic. Electric traction required a huge investment in fixed equipment such as rotary convertor substations along with extensive overhead conductors and their supports, whereas steam tramway locomotives carried their own fuel with them and needed only a minimum of fixed plant. The track was of course common to both these systems as well as the maintenance workshops. These tramways managed to survive into the 1920s and 1930s and some into the 1950s before they were replaced by the rapid development of the motorbus. Many early tramway locomotives were self-propelled cars with the engine and passenger accommodation mounted together on one common frame, but there were technical problems – not least the lack of space for the boiler and mechanical parts. Although the 'Rowan' car enjoyed some success in a number of European cities, self-propelled cars were only used extensively in Paris. The author has made no such models but a 'Rowan' type car may become a future project. Different countries interpreted the requirements for tramway locomotives to suit their own conditions and

views, with some tramway locomotives having minimal protective covers and this variation is illustrated by several of the models covered.

GRAFFENSTADEN, ALSACE LORRAINE-FABR. NR. 4805 OF 1897

An example of one such tram built in Alsace Lorraine by the works of Elsassische Maschinenbau Gesellschaft at Graffenstaden . It was number 46 of the former Mittelbadische Eisenbahn Gesellschaft, (Mid-Baden Railway Company), or MEG and is preserved at the Klienbahnmuseum Selfkantbahn. Typical of many continental trams, this example is basically a conventional locomotive above the footplate with the motion gear partly enclosed in similar fashion to the RTM tram discussed later. Whereas most tramway locomotives had well tanks this engine is fitted with wing tanks.

Several models of this prototype have been produced starting with WN62, then WN64 which was supplied to Germany, followed by WN66, 94, 121,125, 207, and 229. Numbers WN207 & 229 illustrate this very attractive and practical tram model, which is dealt with in detail in the chapter on the Graffenstaden. Incidentally, the first models were produced, using only the single photograph of MEG46 that appeared in the book The Continental Steam Tram by G E Baddeley, but further models had the benefit of drawings obtained at a later date. As with many continental tramway locomotives based on the metre gauge or above, the width of the model has been reduced to suit the average garden railway loading-gauge. In this case the full size engine was 2.5 metres wide or 132mm in 16mm scale. Another problem associated

31. (Top) Preserved Graffenstaden locomotive Works Number 4805 built for the metre gauge Mittelbadische Eisenbahn Gesellschaft in 1897 as their number 46 and now preserved at Klienbahnmuseum Selfkantbahn historic steam railway.

(MEG46-1 – Hans Franke)

32. (Above left) Smokebox end view of the preserved MEG 46 tramway locomotive built by Graffenstaden.

(MEG46-4 – Hans Franke)

33. (Above right) Cab end view of the preserved MEG 46 tramway locomotive built by Graffenstaden.

(MEG46-3 – Hans Franke)

with the larger gauge is the use of inside frames but in this case the locomotive was outside framed allowing the model to incorporate a dual gauge facility. In addition, the outside frames used inside cylinders which allowed the use of the SVS engine without the need to fit dummy cylinders. From the photographs of the preserved locomotive, the finish was in a rather miserable plain black without any lining but the models have been finished not only in black but also green and maroon with attractive lining.

HENSCHEL & SOHN, CASSEL, GERMANY-FABR. NR.6014 OF 1902

Germany was best known for its prodigious output of tramway locomotives, rather than the tramways that were located within its boundaries. Henschel and Sohn for instance started production of tramway locomotives in 1877 and eventually supplied some 500 of them. The second largest builder and exporter was Lokomotivfabrik Krauss of Sendling in the suburbs of Munich with a total of some 300 tramway locomotives. Hohenzollern came third with a total of about 200 trams, and two models

of their locomotives, one of which is a tramway type feature in this book.

Starting with the products of Henschel & Sohn. WN133 was based on their Works Number 6014 of 1902. Fabrieknummer 6014 was named Hummelo and was originally No 3 of the 750mm gauge Tramweg Maatschappi Zurphen-Emmerik(in the Netherlands This tramway was taken over by Geldersche Stoomtramweg Maatschappij (GSTM) in 1910 and then by Geldersche Tramweg Maatschappiy (GTM) in 1929, Hummelo then acquiring the number 603. Fortunately, the sister locomotive (Henschel Works Number 6848, named Vrijland, GTM number 607) is preserved at the National Smalspoor Museum, Valkenburgse Meer, Netherlands and is shown on the photographs provided by Kees Capel and Michael Porter.

34. Ready to go! Grafenstaden WN207 seen here on Maurice Snell's Windy Ridge Railway at Ulverston. The front and rear side lamps are working units with the wiring carried in the conduit between the tanks. The LED's are arranged in series with the body used as the return path.

(WN207-1 – Geoff Holme)

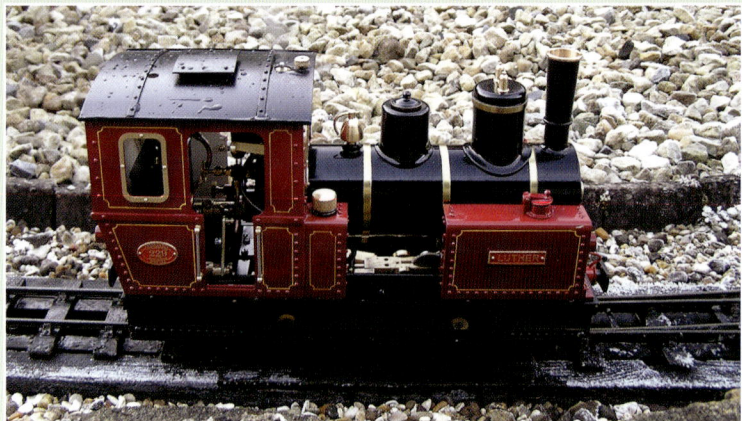

36. (Top left) This is one of the latest Graffenstaden locomotives, finished in red/maroon with yellow lining, rather than the plain unlined black of the original. The SVS engine can be seen between the side tanks under the boiler. This locomotive has a more commodious cab than usual which easily accommodates the gas tank along with the usual boiler fittings. As for the displacement lubricator, the small cab side tank was made just for it, if you will forgive the presence of the oil filler cap. An interesting point is the tapering of the cab rear sheet, which was in fact only fitted on MEG50 & 51, Works Number 5070 and Works Number 5071 of 1901.
(WN229-1 – Author)

37. (Left) Front view of the same model and looking splendid. The front headlights are working units using LED's with the rechargeable batteries in the right hand wing tank. The conduit running between the front lamp units carries the wiring for the LEDs, which are wired in series using the body as a return. The left hand wing tank contains the boiler check valve and Goodall water filler valve that is accessed by lifting the tank dummy water filler.
(WN229-2 – Author)

The layout of the model has the gas tank at the front on top of the frames followed by the horizontal boiler with the boiler fittings at the rear. The engine is again the SVS oscillating unit mounted horizontally between the axles with outside frames. The 9in long frames are symmetrical about the centre line with a 3¼in wheelbase and were spaced 2in apart for 32mm gauge only. This model along with WN110 (Backer & Rueb) was supplied to a customer in Holland, a definite case of 'Coals to Newcastle'.

The next Henschel & Sohn tramway locomotive, WN249, was based on the preserved locomotive Plettenberg Works Number 20822 of 1927, which operated on the metre gauge Plettenberger Strassenbahn AG located in Western Germany. Originally, this name belonged to No 9, which was Henschel & Sohn Works Number 20381 of 1924. The model was specifically required to use the SVS engine with geared drive suitable for operation on Mamod track. Apart from the small radius of 2ft 6in, this type of cast trackwork has the point lever connected to the point and when the lever is in the inside position can foul the buffer beam of the locomotive. Therefore the frame was made deep enough to lift the front and rear buffer beams clear of the Mamod

points. The full size locomotive had outside cylinders and inside frames, an arrangement not suited to the installation of a hidden geared engine. The photograph of the part built running chassis illustrates the difficulty in mounting the geared engine where inside frames have been used. The non-working outside cylinders were rejects, but it was still necessary to provide slide bars, crossheads and coupling rods. The boiler is the Lumpy Tom type with the gas tank located between the smokebox and the front of the tram.

ORENSTEIN & KOPPEL, GERMANY-FABR. NR.9134 OF 1920

Continuing with the German manufacturers, the next locomotive, again preserved, is No. 57 of the Rotterdamsche Tramweg-Maatschappij, built by Orenstein & Koppel, Works Number 9014 of 1920 and unlike the previous models, is of the 0-6-0 wheel-arrangement. Four photographs taken by Kees Capel show the preserved locomotive and were probably taken at the Dutch Railway Museum at Utrecht. This locomotive is thought to be preserved as a static display rather than in working condition and is listed as belonging to the RTM museum at

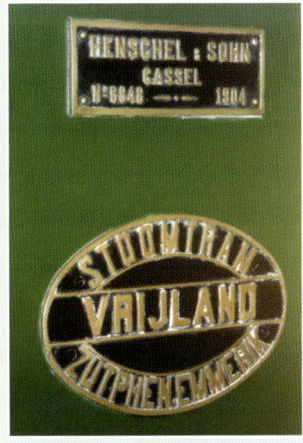

38. (Left) Photograph of Henschel & Sohn Works Number 6848 of 1904 preserved at the National Smalspoor Museum, Valkenburg Meer, Netherlands.
(GTM 607-1 – Vrijland Kees Capel)

40. (Above) The Henschel & Sohn works plate of preserved locomotive 607.
(GTM 607-3 – Vrijland Michael Porter)

41. (Inset) Model based on the tramway locomotive built by Henschel & Sohn, Works Number 6014 of 1902, for the Tramweg-Maatschappij Zutphen-Emmerik (ZE). These photographs were taken of the model supplied to Kees Capel in 2003 and operating in Holland during 2011. The black painted reinforcing strips on the body along with the minimal white lining effectively break up the flat box like overall cab to give a reasonably attractive tramway locomotive. The model is fitted with the correct Hummelo name and company plates and also the Henschel and Sohn works plates.
(WN133-3 – Kees Capel)

42. (Left) The tramway locomotive is shown with a suitable set of rolling stock. Notice the location of the gas tank between the cab front and the boiler smokebox.
(WN133-2 – Kees Capel)

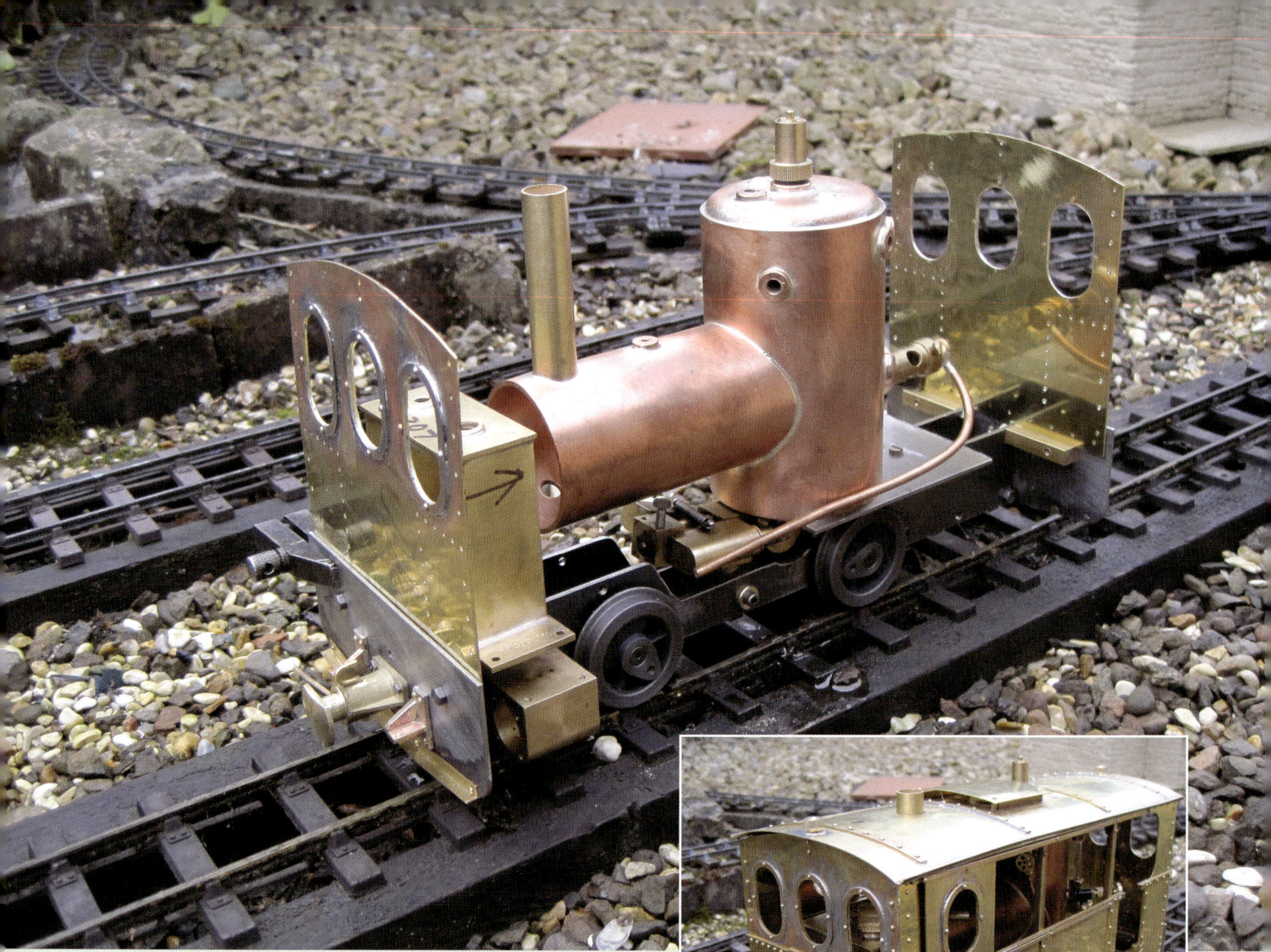

43. *(Above) Early construction of the Pletenburg tramway locomotive showing the difficulty of mounting the geared engine and drive on an inside framed locomotive.*

(WN249-3 – Author)

44. *(Right) The model of Henschel & Sohn Works Number 20822 of 1927 seen here in the brass before painting. One feature of the full size locomotive was the ability to slide the side window panels and this facility is retained on the model. Typical of Continental steam trams are the re-railing brackets on the buffer beams. The gas tank can be seen between the cab front panel and the boiler smokebox.*

(WN249-11 – Author)

45. *(Below right) Photograph of the model of Henschel & Sohn Works Number 20822 of 1927 now painted in green with the reinforcing strips highlighted in black and the lower valance in red. The buffer beams have the lower edges rounded as per the prototype and this along with raised buffer beams ensures that the model can operate on Mamod track without colliding with the point lever on the Mamod points.*

(WN249-15 – Author)

46. (Top left) Photograph of the front of the full size Rotterdamsche Tamweg-Maatschappij No 57 locomotive built by Orenstein & Koppel Works Number 9194 of 1920, photographed at the Dutch Railway Museum, Ultrecht.

(RTM57-1 – Kees Capel)

47. (Left) View of the same locomotive from the rear showing the angled rear of the cab rear sheet.

(RTM57-2 – Kees Capel)

48. (Above) Orenstein & Koppel Works plate for number 57.

(RTM57-3 – Kees Capel)

49. (Below) Rotterdamsche Tramweg-Maatschappij company plate for number 57. Compare this with the company plates on the model.

(RTM57-4 – Kees Capel)

Ouddorp, where it is now located. As with the Serajoedal Tram, the locomotive is conventional above the footplate with the tramway protection limited to an all round skirt, yet even this plating only partly covers the wheels. Typical of continental practice this 3ft 6in gauge locomotive has inside frames with the cylinders located inside the frames.

From a model point of view, the inside frames would be a problem in fitting the twin cylinder oscillating engine if it were not for the fact that the area between the boiler and the running boards is also enclosed which allows the geared SVS engine to be mounted above the wheels. Another point is that this locomotive is rather large and to remain within the gauge of most 16mm garden railways had to be built to the smaller scale of 14.25mm/ft. The end result is WN76 which is illustrated with several photographs showing the layout. The gas tank is located in the rear bunker and reversing of the engine is taken to a lever in the cab.

A further locomotive, No. 56 is also preserved and WN94 is based on this locomotive which was finished in a dark green unlined livery. Unlike No 57, this locomotive is preserved in working order and is shown operating at the

RTM museum at Ouddorp, Netherlands having been moved to this museum in 1966.

MACHINFABRIEK "BREDA" (FORMERLY BACKER & RUEB)

The earliest locomotives to run on Dutch tramways were constructed in London by Merryweather & Co. in 1878, a company who were more famous for their fire engines. There were 19 locomotives supplied to the Hague-Scheveningen tramway, with a further 5 for the Leiden-Katwijk standard gauge (1435mm) line of the Rijnlandsche Stoomtramweg-Maatschappij (RSTM) in 1881/82. As mentioned previously, a photograph of RSTM No.2 is shown, the locomotive now preserved at the Dutch Railway Museum at Ultrecht. Following on from this, development of tramways was very rapid so that by the turn of the century the country was covered with a dense network of light railways. Most Dutch tramways were inter urban and kept to the grass verge of country roads or followed the towpath of the extensive canal network. Crossing these canals was by way of lifting bridges and it was not unheard of for a tram to derail and fall into the canal. Tramway locomotives were supplied by several companies such as Henschel & Sohn and Hohenzollern

50. (Top left) Model based on No 57 of the Rotterdamsche Tramweg Maatschappij built by Orenstein & Koppel Works Number 9194 of 1920. Of particular interest are the side panels between the boiler and the footplate which allows the SVS engine to be fitted despite the locomotive having inside frames. As can be seen, part of one cylinder of the SVS engine is just visible through the hole in the cover. Note also the unequal spacing of the axles and exposed wheels indicating that this is an inside framed locomotive.
(WN76-1 – Michael Porter)

51. (Left) Excellent front ¾ view. Note the cylinder alongside the boiler, used as a water separator with the exhaust steam released through the uppermost pipe at the cab front. Notice how the side skirt terminates inside the buffer beam rather than being attached to it. The lack of side tanks means the Goodall filler system is rather exposed on the running board.
(WN76-2 – Michael Porter)

52. (Below left) A side view of the cab with the forward/reverse lever visible in the cab entrance.
(WN76-3 – Michael Porter)

53. (Below right) View inside the cab with the roof removed. The gas tank is located in the rear bunker with the Ronson type gas filler and the 90° elbow to the gas valve visible through the openings in the top plate. This photograph also illustrates the unusual angled rear to the cab.
(WN76-4 – Michael Porter)

but Holland had its own tram manufacturing company known as 'Machinefabriek "Breda" Voorheen Backer and Rueb'.

The next tramway model, WN 110, was based on a locomotive built by Machinfabriek "Breda" (formerly Backer & Rueb) on their Works Number 182 of 1900 and called Silvolde. It carried the number 13 of the 750mm gauge Geldersche Stoomtramweg-Maatschappij (GSTM) or Geldersche Steam Tramway Company. It is typical of the Breda products and in the book The Continental Steam Tram, the author G.E. Braddely describes them as 'pretty little things with large oval end windows'. Either way they were far more attractive than their British counterparts and lasted much longer. The sister locomotive, number 12, was withdrawn in 1935 but No.13 occasionally performed light goods and shunting services on the then Geldersche Tramwegan. In the summer of 1956, on the occasion of the 75th anniversary of the GSTM/GTM Company, it ran a special tourist service between Doetinchem & Doesburg. This event was repeated in 1957, after which the whole

tramway was wound up. The locomotive was then preserved by the GTW as a museum piece and is now at the National Smalspoor Museum, Valkenburgse Meer, Netherlands where it is regularly steamed. These tramway engines were classed as a light locomotive intended for small trains and requiring only single man operation. For Machinefabriek "Breda" the construction of tramway locomotives started in 1883 and ceased in 1910 after some 216 had been supplied to the Netherlands, 34 to Indonesia, 8 to Spain and one to South Africa.

Built to a scale of 16mm /ft, the tram model would have been rather small in length at 6½in, consequently the frame length was increased to 8½in to provide a boiler length of 5½in including the smokebox. The gas tank is located between the boiler and the cab front. The SVS oscillating engine is positioned between the 102mm wheelbase with the geared drive to the rear axle. Although this model was built for 32mm gauge, the inside frames and large wheels made the fitting of the SVS engine rather awkward.

54. (Above) The full size Rotterdamsche Tramweg-Maatschaapij locomotive No 56 built by Orenstein & Koppel Works Number 9193 of 1920 finished in dark green and unlined. This locomotive is preserved in working order at the RTM museum at Ouddorp, Netherlands.
(RTM56-1 – Kees Capel)

55. (Left) A second photograph of the preserved No. 56 in steam at the RTM museum.
(RTM56-2 – Kees Capel)

57. (Left) Model of Silvolde Machinefabriek "Breda" Works Number 182 of c1900. Despite increasing the length of the model it can be seen how tight it is to fit the horizontal boiler into these small Dutch trams. The gas tank is located at the front between the boiler smokebox and the cab front panel. The geared oscillating engine had to be sandwiched between the boiler and the large wheels with the further problem of inside frames.

(WN 110-1 – Peter Howarth)

58. (Above right) The same model photographed in 2011 now having moved appropriately across the North Sea to Holland and to the country where the original locomotive operated.

(WN110-3 – Kees Capel)

59. (Below left) Side view of the model of Groningen, in this case WN212. Unfortunately there is not a good side photograph of WN115 and therefore the opportunity has been taken to illustrate the neat appearance of the 'Breda' trams using a photograph of WN212, built by Mike Lax. The model is of the same design and fitted with the large company plates and the very special ribbon works plate with the correct works number and date.

(WN212 – Mike Lax)

Continuing with the products of Machinefabriek 'Breda, several models have been built based on Groningen, Works Number 236 of 1905 supplied to Dedemsvaartsche Stoomtramweg-Maatschaapij as their number 25. The model, WN115, followed by WN127, took the liberty of using a vertical boiler in the same way as the Wilkinson Patent Tram but still represents the looks of a typical 'Breda' tram. Despite the box like shape the typical 'Breda' tramway locomotive was fairly attractive with large oval end widows, hooded roof and the addition of several identification plates. Firstly, there was the locomotive nameplate, then the large owner plates complete with their number and finally the unique manufacturers scroll works plate. There was also the raised side skirts typical of Dutch trams along with the front mounted angled outriggers to act as jacking points when re-railing the locomotive. The gauge of the full size locomotive was 1067mm and as would be expected with this gauge was fitted with inside frames. The model on the other hand has outside frames with disc type cranks and a dual 32/45mm gauge facility. Again the body is made removable without affecting the mechanical side in any way and the geared drive ensures slow running which is absolutely necessary with this type of model.

SCHWEITZERISCHE LOCOMOTIV UND MACHINENFABRIK, WINTERTHUR

For the next continental steam tram a move to Switzerland is required. This was the single firm of Schweitzerische Locomotiv und Maschinenfabrik at Winerthur, near Zurich, or SLM for short. The firm was both successful and world famous for their rack railways and tramway engines, building about 300 tramway locomotives between 1877 and 1903 which were exported all over Europe and also to Russia and Brazil. Many of the earlier locomotives were fitted with the Brown Patent 'T' boilers with a vertical dome come-firebox behind a short horizontal part containing the firetubes leading to the smokebox. It was similar to that used on their rack locomotives and could be termed a 'T' boiler.

A feature common to most tramway locomotives and derived from the rack engines was the drive through a rocking shaft from cylinders placed above the footplate. This arrangement lifted the cylinders and motion parts clear of road debris but the rocking shafts tended to cause vibration which made many of them to shake themselves to pieces after only a short life. What the engine driver thought of having to negotiate his way around the locomotive with these exposed moving parts is not recoded. The photograph of an SLM tramway locomotive being rebuilt illustrates this unusual arrangement.

60. (Above) Showing what could be a typical Dutch scene as the Machinefabriek 'Breda' based Dutch tram locomotive WN115 crosses over a canal with a light three-coach load on Peter Howarth's railway at Blairegowrie.
(WN115-2 – Peter Howarth)

61. (Left) Looking down on the model with the roof removed to reveal the simple layout made possible by the non- prototypical vertical boiler.
(WN115-3 – Peter Howarth)

62. (Below left) A three-quarter view which illustrates the typical 'Breda' oval windows and the re-railing brackets. Some of these trams even had brushes in front of the wheels.
(WN115-4 – Peter Howarth)

63. *(Top left) An interesting photograph from Ron Smith showing an SLM steam tram being rebuilt at the Zytglogge depot, Bern in March 2001. The location of the cylinders above the running boards and the rocking lever that transmits the cylinder output down to the wheels can be seen. This locomotive has a horizontal boiler with a large central steam dome. Notice the bowed front typical of SLM tramway locomotives.*

(Steam tram under construction – Ron Smith)

64. *(Left) Preserved Strassenbahn Bern No12 built by Schweizerische Lokomotiv-und Machinenfabrik, Winterthur (SLM), Works Number 863 of 1894. Electric traction took over in 1902 and all but number 12 &18 were scrapped.*

(No 12 SLM Tram (7) – Ron Smith)

65. *(Below) This is another view of the preserved SLM locomotive (with an appropriate carriage). It is seen here outside the Burgenziel depot, Bern on the 22nd June 2003. The carriage or trailer dates from 1894 and carries the number 31. It is fitted with three braking systems so it can be used with the historic electric trams. This trailer was refurbished with the wrought iron end balconies reinstated.*

(No 12 SLM Tram (8) – Ron Smith)

66. (Top left) Schweizerische Lokomotiv-Machinenfabrik(SLM), Winterthur, tram locomotive Works Number 346 built for the Noord-Zuid-Hollandsche Tramweg-Maatschappij Haarlem-Leiden (NZHSTM-HL) 1435mm standard gauge railway. This model is fitted with the correct 'T' boiler of the 'Lumpy Tom' type. This type of boiler had a horizontal and vertical component and provided a good steam space without the use of a steam dome. In full size the boiler was built on the Brown's Patent with a vertical dome cum-firebox behind a short horizontal part. The curved pipe coming down the vertical part of the boiler is to the water level/blow off valve. The hexagonal head in front of this pipe is the Goodall valve fed from the check valve at the right hand side of the vertical part of the boiler (in the picture). The gas tank can be seen at the rear of the locomotive and note the extension to the steam regulator spindle to the end of the cab.
(WN111-1 – NZHSTM-HL No8 – Geoff Lumsdon)

67. (Below left) This shows the locomotive from the opposite side with the displacement lubricator alongside the boiler. Note the low side panels and the handrail so typical of SLM tramway locomotives. The reinforcing around the bottom of the body is clearly visible along with the rounded or bowed end sheets.
(WN111-2 – NZHSTM-HL No. 8 – Geoff Lumsdon)

As with many trams, the water tank was of the well type located between the frames and under the horizontal part of the boiler. Later, tramway locomotives were fitted with horizontal boilers with a large central dome. Two of these locomotives are preserved in Switzerland, namely No 12, built in 1894 as SLM Works Number 863 along with a suitable balcony coach No. 31 located at Burn, and locomotive No.18 and trailer No. 26 at Verkehrshaus in Luzern.

The model, WN111 illustrates a typical 4 wheel version of this type of tram based on SLM Works Numbers 346-347, supplied in 1883 as nos. 8 & 9 of Noord-Zuid-Hollandische Stoomtramweg Maatschappij Haarlem-Lieden standard gauge (1435mm) or NZHSTM-HL if you prefer it. The 'T' boiler of the original locomotives was faithfully retained in the model by using the 'Lumpy Tom' boiler with the gas tank located at the rear (firing) end of the tram. The bodywork is correct with bowed end panels, cut outs in the side skirts and a reinforced bottom edge to the skirts. Notice also the lowered side panels with guardrail, so typical of these engines. However, the SVS engine replaces the raised cylinder and motion gear along with outside frames to allow for a 32/45 dual gauge facility.

Several other models of this tram have been made as per the works list and have included dummy side rods to imitate the drive to the rocking shafts as with WN116, St. Etienne, based on number 21 of the metre gauge Compagnie des Chemins de Fer à Voie Etroite de Saint Etienne. The locomotive was built by SLM in 1882, Works Number 283. Although similar to the previous locomotive the layout of this tram uses a more conventional horizontal boiler in place of the 'T' boiler arrangement with a large central dome and the water gauge located alongside the centre of the boiler. The opening in the side skirts shows the connecting rod from the dummy vertical lever to the coupling rods. This model was built for 45mm gauge only with inside frames as per the prototype.

68. (Top left) Based on number 21 of Compagnie des Chemins de Fer à Voie Etroite de Saint Etienne built by SLM, Works Number 274 of 1882. This side view photograph shows the connecting rod between the dummy vertical lever and the coupling rod. The location of the gas tank and displacement lubricator is clearly shown. With this inside framed locomotive, the geared SVS engine is located above and between the axles and below the boiler. The boiler is horizontal with a large central dome. Notice that the wheel rims have been painted white. **(WN116-4 – Andrew Cottenham)**

69. (Below left) This end view shows the centrally mounted water gauge. The location of the water gauge and the large dome allowed for a more accurate reading on inclines as it was less affected by the inclination of the boiler. If the gauge were located at the firing end then it would give a misleading reading caused by the movement of the boiler water. **(WN116-4 – Andrew Cottenham)**

70. (Above) Another SLM Tram, WN143, fitted with the 'Lumpy Tom' boiler, shown hauling suitable platform end coaches on David Mercer's 45mm gauge Springfield & North London garden railway in July 2009.

(WN143-1 – Chris Webster)

71. (Left) In this photograph the tram is hauling a suitable end platform passenger coach built by Trevor Peat and looks particularly fine and prototypical. What is not apparent in the photograph are the deeper frames which allow the body to be raised 1/8in to clear the point levers on Mamod track.

(WN211-3 – Trevor Peat)

Finally WN143 and WN211 revert back to the 'T' boiler with the latter built with taller frames in order to raise the body by 1/8in for operation on Mamod track where clearance is required to the point lever. The locomotives are shown to good effect connected to suitable balcony ended coaches in the accompanying photographs.

WN167 HOHENZOLLERN FIRELESS TRAMWAY LOCOMOTIVE.

The German company of Hohenzollern A.G. fur Lokomotivbau, Dusseldorf, were responsible for the prototype on which WN167 was based. My attention was drawn to this locomotive by a works photograph on page 108 in the book A History of the British Steam Tram. Below this

photograph the caption described the engine, named Cleve as a twin cab narrow gauge tram locomotive for 750mm/30in gauge and weighing 6.3 tons empty and 8.3 tons when in use. Further information from Hans Franke in Germany revealed this locomotive to have operated in Germany close to the Dutch border. The railway was built to serve a mental hospital at Bedburg-Hau (Kries Kleve), transporting food, laundry and refuse. A locomotive turning facility was not incorporated at either termination of the railway and therefore a cab was fitted at both ends of the engine complete with dual controls. As with many such institutions of that time, there would be ample supplies of steam from the large hospital boilers, which made it practical to use a fireless locomotive that could

72. Side view of the model of the Hohenzollern double-ended tram locomotive used to transport goods to a provincial nursing home at Bedburg-Han near the Dutch border in the district of Cleve. The right hand side cab in the photograph houses the large gas tank. Between the cab and the boiler can be seen the end of the blanked off end of the centre flue which is constructed as a 'T' shape. Notice the chimney part is reduced as far as possible to give the impression of a fireless locomotive.

(WN167-1 – Author's collection)

73. Opposite side view of the Hohenzollern locomotive showing the other cab containing the boiler front end, the ceramic burner and the boiler fittings with the exception of the water level/blow-off valve, which can be seen on the footboard behind the cab. The second copper pipe is the water gauge blow down valve outlet.

(WN167-2 – Trevor Peat)

74. Nice view of the Hohenzollern locomotive with a short train of wagons. A photograph of the full size locomotive shows it pulling two large covered vans each with a raised centre portion at one end, (unfortunately this photograph is not suitable for publication).

(WN167-4 – Trevor Peat)

be charged from these boilers. Built in 1912, the photograph appeared in the Hohenzollern catalogue of 1922 and gave the gauge as 750mm. However, a further photograph provided by Hans shows the locomotive outside the hospital and the information states a gauge of 500mm. Unfortunately, the photograph is unsuitable for publication. There is no indication of the colour and therefore it was decided to finish the model in grey/black, probably the most suitable colour for such an ugly cnginc.

Considering the model, the obvious digression relates to the boiler. Whereas the original locomotive used a high-pressure reservoir that could be charged with superheated water/steam, the model uses a conventional centre flue boiler of 2¾in diameter, the 28mm flue having water tubes. By making the output of the flue as unobtrusive as possible, the general impression of a fireless locomotive is maintained. The SVS engine is located horizontally between the axles and the gas tank is located in one of the cabs. The boiler fittings, along with the ceramic burner, occupy the remaining cab with the exception of the water level valve, which was attached to the running plate. The combination of a short fat 'T' boiler, ceramic burner and water tubes in the flue, gives an excellent performance even in the coldest of weather. On the other hand it is doubtful if this locomotive would win a beauty contest.

REFERENCES:
• History of the Steam Tram by Dr H A Whitcombe.
• Beyer, Peacock Locomotive Builders to the World by R L Hills and D Patrick.
• A History of the British Steam Tram Volume 1 by David Gladwin.
• Article by Ron Smith: Steam Tram Runs Again in Bern, Continental Modeller October 2004.
• The Continental Steam Tram by G E Baddeley.
• De Stoomlocomotieven Der Nederlandse Tramwegen by S Overbosch.
• Typenskizzenbuch der Mittelbadische Eisenbahnen AG-Die Fahrzeuge nder MEG by Claude Jeanmaire, Hans-Dieter Menges. Archiv Nr. 13/14
• The Locomotives Built by 'Machinefabriek 'Breda' voorheen Backer & Rueb' by A D De Pater.

1. (Above) The preserved locomotive Works Number 4805 built for the metre gauge Mittelbadische Eisenbahn Gesellschaft number 46 in 1897 and now preserved at the Klienbahmuseum Selfkantbahn historic steam railway.

(MEG46-2 – Hans Franke)

2. (Below) A later model of the Grafenstaden shown here on Maurice Snell's Windy Ridge Railway at Ulverston, Cumbria.

(WN207-4 – Graffenstaden – Paul Timewell)

ANATOMY OF A LOCOMOTIVE – GRAFFENSTADEN 4805

This model is based on Graffenstaden Works Number 4805 of 1897/98, which operated as No. 46 on the metre gauge Strassburger Pferde – Eisenbahn Gesellschaft, located in Alsace Lorraine. Alsace Lorraine was a largely industrial area on the banks of the River Rhine, which was annexed to Germany from France during the early 1870s only to be returned to France under the Treaty of Versailles in 1919. This area has a complicated history but sufficient is to say that the main city was Strassburg (Strasbourg) that had an extensive standard and metre gauge tramway system. Under the Treaty of Versailles the network became split with part of the metre gauge system remaining in Germany and this included the section on which No. 46 ran. In 1923 the tramway was taken over by Mittelbadische Eisenbahn at Kehl. Gradually, the steam locomotives were replaced by diesel railcars but according to G E Baddely in his book The Continental Steam Tram some of the steam trams reappeared in the 1930s due to a power failure and during the 1939-1945 war. On the German side, two of these locomotives were seen in the back of a shed in the 1960s.

The area had its own locomotive manufacturing works the Elsassische Maschinenbau Gesellschaft at Graffenstaden, near Strassburg. The locomotives were 0-4-0's with outside frames and inside cylinders, so that the only moving parts visible were the coupling rods and this allowed them to be classed as locomotives with enclosed motion and thus tramway locomotives. They had commodious cabs at the rear and wing tanks alongside the smokebox. In later years some of the locomotives were fitted with a Westinghouse brake pump mounted behind the chimney and an electric lighting jumper cable in front of the chimney. The model featured in this chapter is one of these steam tram locomotives namely No 46 of the Mittelbadische Eisenbahn Gessellschaft, (MEG), built by Graffenstaden as wn4805 of 1897 which is now preserved in operating condition in Germany. Perhaps it is one of those that were seen in a shed as previously mentioned.

From the point of view of a model, there are several advantages to constructing this rather attractive engine. Firstly, the locomotive is outside framed and this makes it possible for

3. One of the earliest models of the Graffenstaden Tramway locomotive seen here on Brian Hicks East Lincolnshire Light Railway in 2001.

(WN094-1 Graffenstaden – Tony Corbett)

the wheels to provide a dual gauge facility. Secondly, the cylinders are located inside the frames, which would make it suitable for the installation of the geared oscillating engine, although in the full size locomotive this would have been direct drive. The long wheelbase means the geared SVS engine can be mounted between the axles, similar to several previous models and the large cab would easily provide

room for a rear mounted gas tank. On the model, the cab size has been increased by building the rear cab sheet angled in-over to the buffer beam, but strictly speaking this feature was only fitted on the sister locomotives No's 50 & 51.

For this chapter let us follow the model through the construction stages.

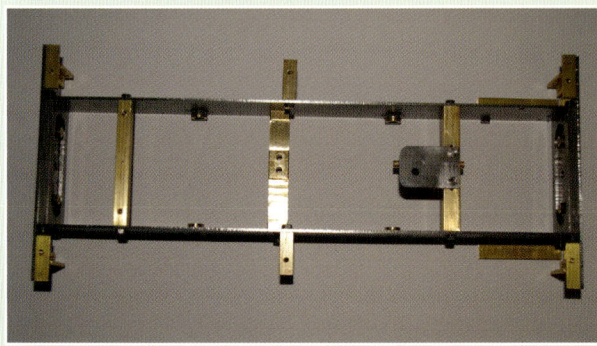

4. This is the start of the construction of WN221. The frames consist of 1/16in steel with 3/16in x 1in rectangular section brass or steel end stretchers. The 1/16in steel buffer beams are bolted to these stretchers. The intermediate stretchers are brass bar with the central one being the engine bearer. Notice also the central outriggers and end angles to support the footplates.

(Photographs 4–11 by the Author)

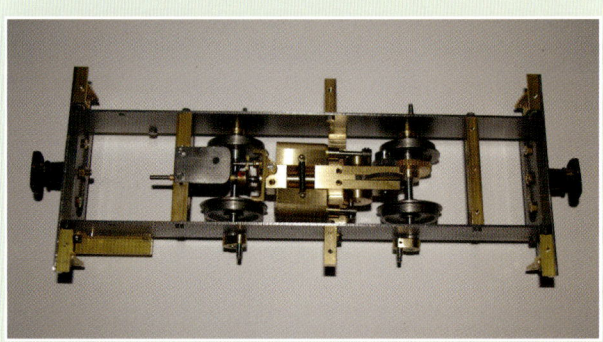

5. Now the engine has been fitted neatly between the axles along with the 2:1 spur gears to the front axle. At the opposite end of the engine, the lever and rod mechanism is partly assembled to operate the forward/reverse valve on the engine. The wheels are set for 32mm gauge but there is sufficient room to open the wheels to 45mm using the wheel boss screws and the indents in the axle. The two angle brackets fitted to the rear sides of the frames are to mount the gas tank.

6. The footplates and the smokebox support have been added and the reversing mechanism is complete. The conduit on the footplate is to interconnect the working headlights.

7. The wing tanks complete with front facia along with a connecting conduit and notice the wire in the conduit for the working headlights.

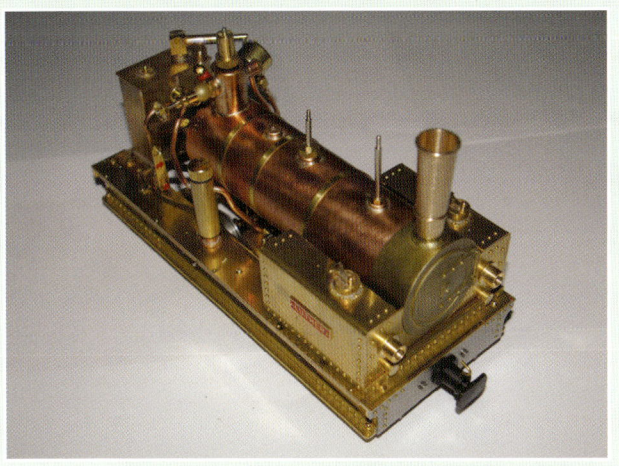

8. This photograph shows the wing tanks fitted and the cast smokebox supplied by John Prescott Engineering. This enables the boiler to be mounted and the model now starts to take shape. In addition, the side valance (brass angle) and the front and rear side panels have been attached to the buffer beams. These tramway locomotives were not fitted with full side panels.

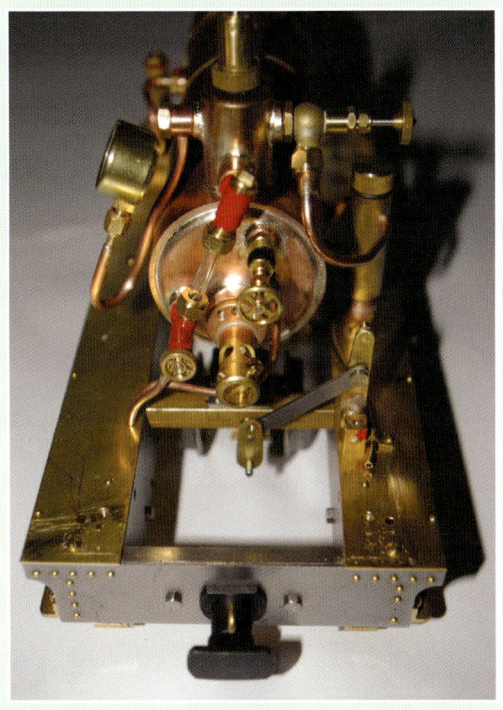

9. The rear of the locomotive with the gas tank removed. The boiler fittings are complete and include the gas burner, water level/blow-off valve, water gauge and pressure gauge. The pipes for the water level/blow-off valve are brought together to run down the side of the main frame. The short cab front tank will eventually cover the displacement lubricator. Just below the forward/reverse lever can be seen the conduit which will lead the wiring from the battery and switch to the rear cab headlights.

10. This is a photograph of the finished cab before fitting to the chassis. The type of construction is clearly shown with the cab being made up of 1/32in brass sheet, either ½ hard (CZ108), or where possible engraving brass (CZ120), connected by 3/64in rivets and accurate 6x6x1mm brass angle. Ordinary brass angle is not always at 90° but this brass is machined not drawn. The 1/4x1/4x1/16in brass angle at the base is however drawn and must be selected for accuracy. This 1/16in thick angle is required to attach the body and wing tanks to the footplates using 8ba screws.

11. The locomotive is complete and ready to be dismantled for cleaning, bead blasting and painting.

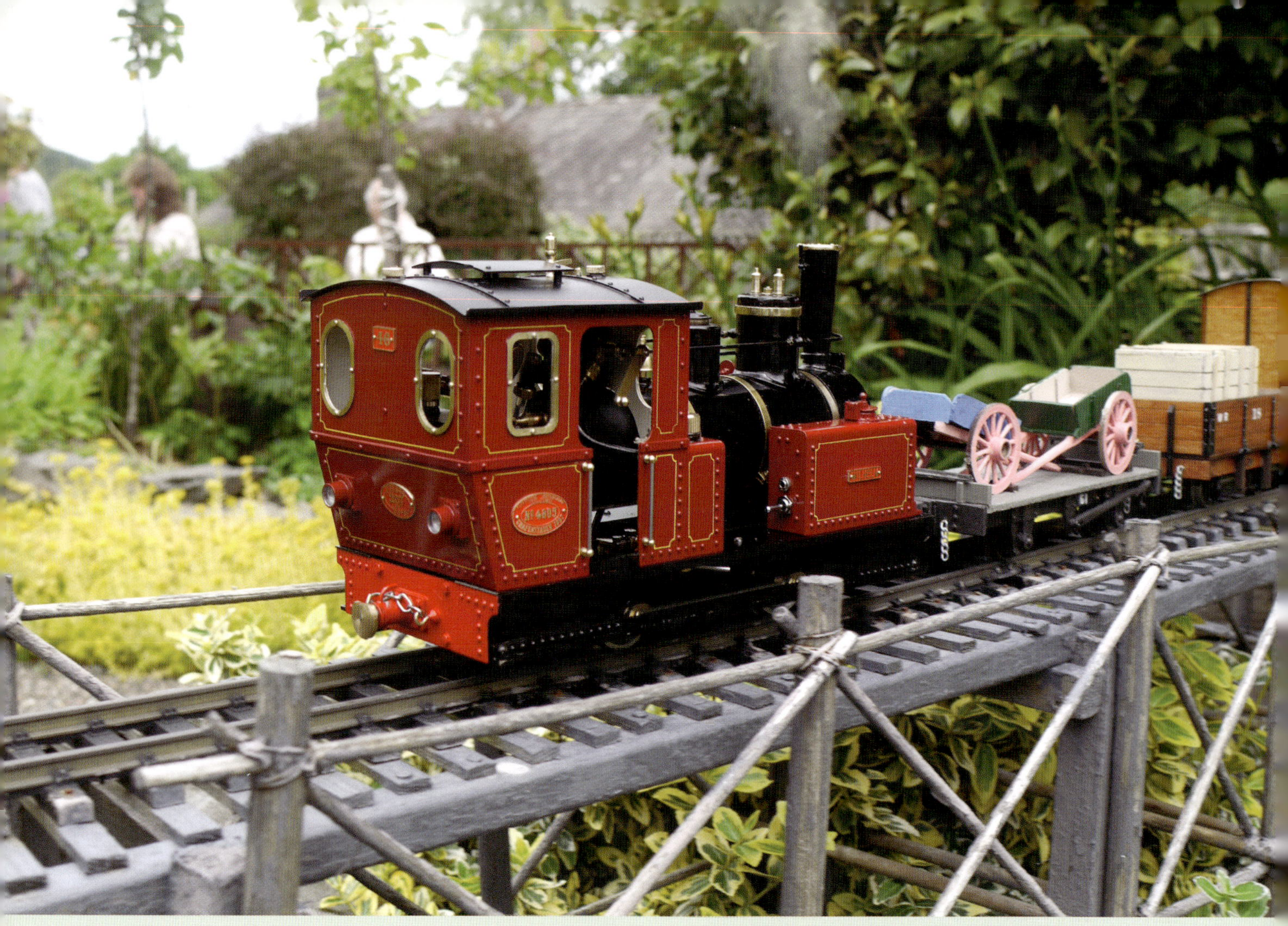

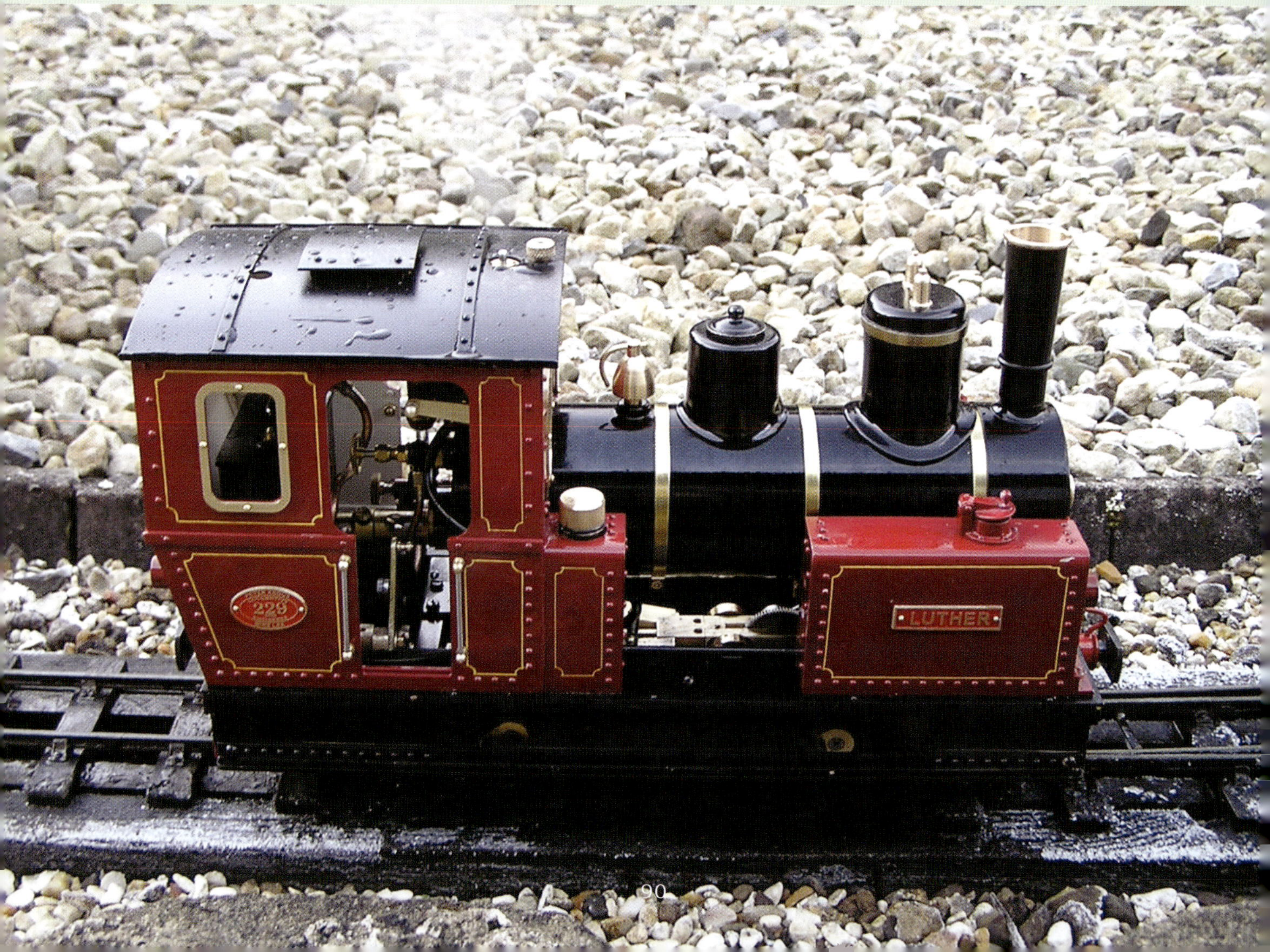
229
LUTHER

12. *(Opposite top) Graffenstaden tram with a rake of kit built wagons operating on the Windy Ridge Railway of Maurice Snell at Ulverston. Andell Models supplied the first flat wagon, while the handcarts are scratch built by Maurice's wife Jennifer.*

(WN207-3 Graffenstaden – Geoff Holme)

13. *(Opposite below) The finished WN221 beautifully painted and lined by Mike Lax. This really is a practical and neat locomotive capable of running on either 32 or 45mm track. Even the displacement lubricator fits neatly into the cab side tank.*

(WN229-1 – Author)

14. *(Above) Front view of this very attractive tramway locomotive based on No. 46 of the metre gauge Strassburger Pierde-Eisenbahn Gessellschaft.*

(WN229-2 – Author)

REFERENCES:

• The Continental Steam Tram- by G E Baddeley
• Typenskizzenbuch der Mittelbadische Eisenbahnen AG by Claude Jeanmaire, Hans-Dieter Menges.

CONSOLIDATION

By WN50 the development of the locomotive models had settled down to the use of a geared engine drive where possible, preferably in a model where the drive was hidden (such as a tram), or the gears were so placed as to be unobtrusive as in the case of a De Winton. A slow and consistent speed could thus be obtained without recourse to radio control, which in those days was still rather large to fit into a small 16mm locomotive. There was also the perennial problem of arriving at a garden railway meeting only to find the batteries flat or the system just not working. There were other changes, namely the replacement of the methylated spirits fired potboiler with the universally adopted gas fired plain centre flue type first introduced by Beck. The problem now was the supply of a suitable engine for gearing. The original Caton marine engine had been replaced by the CNC friendly Max II version, which unfortunately was considerably bigger and suitable only for the larger locomotives such as a Garratt. As with the original Caton engine, the Max II was made available as an inverted bedplate version but even then it was still too large. Several were adapted to mimic the Shay layout with the bedplate rotated through 90° and can be seen in the chapter on Shay locomotives.

The Cheddar Pintail V twin was not suitable even for a Heisler type locomotive due to the large forward/reverse valve located between and above the cylinders. The solution lay in another marine engine produced by Mike Legg under the SVS trade name. Unlike most marine engines, this unit was particularly small with twin double acting oscillating cylinders of 8mm bore and 12mm stroke and was available in a 4:1 geared version designed for paddle boats. The engine was so neat that with a single output shaft it could be fitted between the wheels of a 32mm locomotive sufficient to engage with a gear on the axle using 2:1 spur gears of 1in and ½in PCD. The first models to use the SVS

engine were two trams based on the Alford and Sutton Tramway, which appear in the chapter on tram locomotives. Soon the engine was developed into two other versions, the first variation fitted with an extra side bearing and extended output shaft for overtype locomotives and termed an overtype engine. The second variation had the output shaft brought back alongside the crankshaft to reduce the overall length and termed a boxer engine.

FOWLER GEARED PLANTATION LOCOMOTIVE **WN80**

The next locomotive not covered in the specialist chapters was WN80 based loosely on the Fowler Patent locomotives of Alfred Grieg and William Beadon, both of the Steam Plough Works, Leeds. The intention of the Fowler Patent was to build a small locomotive suitable for plantation type work but with the cylinders and valve-gear raised above the wheels and therefore clear of dust and dirt from the ground. Drive from the engine was via vertical connecting rods to the front axle with the engine located above the pony truck of the 2-4-0 wheel arrangement. The driven wheels were of very short wheelbase to negotiate very tight bends giving the locomotive a top-heavy appearance. For the model, it was quickly realised that the prototype was rather small, the wheelbase too short, there was nowhere to locate the gas tank and the linkage between the engine and front wheels impractical. However, the 0-4-2 wheel arrangement was retained and the location of the engine above the pony truck. Instead of connecting rods, the drive from the engine was replaced by 2:1 spur gears to the leading axle and the wheelbase was increased. This allowed a spare Lumpy Tom 'T' boiler to sit between the driven wheels with the horizontal part of the boiler above the engine. To balance the wheel arrangement, the rear frame was extended to accommodate the gas tank in a rear bunker. Now no longer representing the

1. (Top left) Originally based on the Fowler Patent plantation locomotives of Alfred Grieg and William Beadon, both of the Steam Plough Works, Leeds. The SVS engine can be seen between and above the front axle and the pony truck driving to the wheels using a spur gear arrangement. The displacement lubricator is in the right hand side tank with the water filling system in the opposite left hand tank.
(WN080-1 – Geoff Lumsdon)

2. (Left) Opposite side view showing the Lumpy Tom type boiler which at the time was spare. The gas tank is located in the rear bunker. Although the model was very practical with its straightforward layout of components, the locomotive lacks the spirit of having been based on a full size prototype. With the exception of two freelance tramway locomotives based on a photograph of a model, this was the only freelance model to be constructed.
(WN080-2 – Geoff Lumsdon)

original locomotive, the cab sprouted side tanks to cover the lubricator and water filler system. Although the incentive to build WN80 was based on the Fowler engines, the end result was virtually freelance and along with two freelance tram locomotives, were the only models to lack a prototype. At least in the case of the tram locomotives they were based on a photograph of an existing model. The experience of WN80 suggested that all future models had to be based on a full size locomotive.

WN89-HUNSLET ENGINE CO.
0-4-2 'EVA' CLASS

WN89 was based on the Hunslet Engine Works 'Eva' class of 1906. Built to the order of Martin & Co, contractors to the Howrah Amta 2ft gauge light railway, this class of locomotive were very successful, a total of 19 being built over a period of 49 years with changes only to the safety valves, the addition of electric lighting and a

change to welded steel side tanks. The last two engines, Hunslet Works Numbers 3866/3867 were supplied in 1955. For the purpose of building the model a works photograph and general arrangement plan was obtained from the Armley Mills Museum, Leeds, who at the time held the archives of some of the Hunslet designs. There are certain points to note with this locomotive. The front and rear buffer beams are curved along with the rear of the bunker, the fixed wheelbase is short and frames are split just behind the rear driven axle with the rear frames of greater width to accommodate a wide firebox. In the case of the full size locomotive, it was possible to take the weight of the front end and separate the front main frame along with the driving wheels, cylinders and valve gear. This allowed work to be carried out on the running gear with much improved access to the parts. Both front and rear drawbars are pivoted with the rear bar located on swinging links to allow for tight curvature of the track.

3. (Above) Works photograph of the Hunslet 'EVA' class of locomotive Works Number 904 of 1906. Notice the Martin & Co plates. This firm were the managing agents for several small narrow gauge railways, mostly in Bengal and Bihar including the Howrah Amta 2ft gauge railway.

(Hunslet 'EVA' class locomotive – Leeds Museums & Galleries (Armley Mills)

4. (Left) This photograph by Bruce Flaxman shows the rounded rear buffer beam, an unusual feature of this locomotive design and intended to assist with tight curvature of the track. Note how a slot with a pivoted draw bar has replaced the original centre buffer. The rectangular plates on the side of the cab in front of the entrance are the correct Martin & Co plates representing the managing agents for the Howrah Amta 2ft gauge railway.

(WN089-3 – Bruce Flaxman)

5. (Below left) In this ¾ front view photograph by Adrian Banks the unusual curved front buffer beam is also evident. There is also the boiler-mounted bell as seen on the works photograph.

(WN089-4 – Adrian Banks)

To build the model, WN89, the front frames used the Roundhouse Billy Chassis suitably cut down in length before being attached to a cross plate located behind the rear wheels and on to which was added the wider rear frames as was the case with the full size locomotive. The wheels of the full size locomotive were 2ft 6in in diameter and therefore the original Roundhouse 33mm wheels and axles were discarded and replaced with 40mm steel disc wheels on 3/16in dual gauge axles. On to this chassis a conventional 2in diameter plain centre flue boiler with poker type burner was mounted and the gas tank located in the area of the rear bunker. In the photographs, the rear centre buffer is seen attached to the buffer beam. This was quickly changed to a pivot arrangement to improve operation on the tight curves of a garden railway. The drawbar slides in a slot in the buffer beam and pivots from a point between the gas tank and the rear wheels. Despite being direct drive the locomotive was not radio controlled.

WN128-BOSNIA HERZEGOVINA 0-6-4 RACK/ADHESION LOCOMOTIVE.

In complete contrast, the next model was articulated on the Engerth principle. One of the principle objections to the tender locomotive is that the weight of the tender and its contents is a dead load unavailable for adhesion. As locomotives and railways developed, the need to reduce fuel and water stops resulted in larger tenders that in some cases could be a considerable proportion of the locomotive weight. It was therefore natural to attempt to utilize this weight of the tender for adhesion. It is generally thought that Engerth was the first to suggest this system, which was used on his geared locomotives where the rear four wheel truck which straddled the firebox was used for adhesion by being driven from gears off the fixed driven axles. A degree of flexibility

was provided in the frame adjacent to the third driven axle. They were not particularly successful due to poor flexibility and gave much trouble in practice. Eventually, the use of gears was abandoned and the design was limited to transferring part of the weight of the tender to the locomotive in order to improve adhesion. It is this later version known as a modified Engerth that is the subject of WN128.

The model is based on locomotive number 701 built by Wiener Locomotiv-Fabricks-Actien-Gesellschaft, Floridsdorf, for the 760mm Bosnia & Herzegovina State Railway in Yugoslavia. An engraving and information appeared in a supplement to Narrow Gauge Times, which was taken from an article in The Engineer first published in 1896. This engraving was so good that it could be used as a drawing to build a model. The prototype was in fact a rack/adhesion locomotive but this aspect of the design was not included in the model. However, the articulation of the tender was adhered to in the model and can be seen in the accompanying photographs. Despite the gauge of only 760mm these locomotives were quite large and therefore WN128 was built to a scale of 15mm/ft for operation on 45mm gauge

6. (Top left) Left side view of the model of the 760mm gauge Bosnia & Herzegovina 0-6-4 mountain locomotive number 701, built by Wiener Locomotiv-Fabriks-Actien-Gesellschaft, Floridsdorf. The full size locomotive was of the rack/adhesion type as indicated by the plates on the cab sides (SYSTEM ABT) with only the adhesion part included in the model. On a straight track there is little indication that this locomotive was semi articulated. The model is beautifully painted in two tone grey and black and lined by Mike Lax.
(WN128-1 – Geoff Lumsdon)

8. (Left) This is the locomotive as seen on a curved track to illustrate the articulated tender, which is pivoted to the main frame at a point under the cab. What cannot be seen is that the wheels of the leading axle of the four-wheel tender are mounted on a tube free to slide over a limited distance along the axle. Without this feature, the wheelbase would lock up on a double curve.
(WN128-4. Geoff Lumsdon)

9. (Left) This photograph, kindly supplied by Jim Hawkesworth, shows the American Locomotive Company Works Number 57092 of 1917. It was one of a 100 locomotives built at the Cooke Locomotive Works under WD Order No 10003 and carried the WDLR running number 1201.

(ALCO wn57092 of 1917 – Collection of Jim Hawkesworth)

11. (Above) Another excellent photograph taken with a suitable background that at first sight could be the real thing if was not for those oversize boiler fittings.

(WN182-2 – Richard Fort)

track only. The main chassis was based on the dimensions of the Roundhouse Argyle frames and used their cylinders and valve gear along with 36mm steel disc wheels on 3/16in axles. The 7in long x 2¼in plain centre flue boiler was carried on this rigid frame with the barrel extended to 9in to incorporate the smokebox. The front dome is used to pick up steam to the rear backhead mounted regulator as well as providing a location for the Roundhouse safety valve. The tender, which would have carried fuel and water for the full size locomotive, is carried on two free running axles. It was decided that the gas tank, though located within the area of the tender, should be supported by an extension to the main frame thereby removing the need to provide a flexible gas pipe to the poker type burner.

The outside frames of the tender project forward to a pivot located under the cab using a beam taken through the outside frames of the powered chassis. This pivot uses a double ball self-aligning bearing to give limited movement between the tender and the main chassis. With the full size locomotive, part of the tender weight

was transferred to the locomotive through this articulation. The problem with this type of single point articulation is that it cannot allow for the change from curve to straight or vice-versa as the rigid wheelbase will lock. How this was accommodated with the full size locomotive is not clear but with the model the inner tender wheels are located on a tube, which is free to slide along the axle to give sufficient side play. In all probability, the relatively less curvature of the full size railway could be accommodated with end float on the tender axles.

To test the articulation of the model, a special end-to-end track was laid using LGB R3 curves with straights to provide every configuration possible. The articulation was certainly impressive and capable of negotiating the 5ft radius curves with ease at full speed, but it must be admitted is a very complicated system with doubtful advantage in model form. To compliment the model, a full set of plates was added including the unique Abt rack plates and the locomotive was finished in various shades of grey with white/black lining, a very impressive model.

WN182-ALCO COOKE 2-6-2 WAR DEPARTMENT LOCOMOTIVE

This model is based on a War Department Light Railway 2-6-2 locomotive built by the American Locomotive Company, Cooke Works, in 1916 as wn57148 to the WD order LR1003. The model uses the Roundhouse S.R.R.L No24 sprung chassis with a 2in diameter by 6¾ in long plain centre flue boiler and poker type burner. At first glance, the two photographs of the model taken by Richard Fort appear almost full-size, only the displacement lubricator visible inside the cab on one of the pictures is letting the side down. WN182 is finished as the preserved locomotive at the C de F Cappy et Dompierre in Northern France. Radio control was not fitted.

WN188-AIRDMILLAN-FOWLER 0-6-2 WORKS NUMBER 20763 OF 1935

This 2ft gauge locomotive has the unfortunate distinction of being one of the last steam locomotives built by John Fowler and Company, Leeds, and was supplied to The Australian Estates Co. Ltd, Kalamia Mill, Queensland. The locomotive was named after a local district supplying cane to the Kalamia Mill. Although of 2ft gauge, the locomotive was fitted with buffers and draw gear to work 3ft 6in gauge stock over mixed gauge track. With an axle load

of just over 5tons, this 24in gauge locomotive could haul a load of 320 tons on a level track, a creditable figure for a 24in gauge engine. The locomotive was fitted with mechanical oil lubrication to the cylinders and valve gear and had steam breaking. Since tracks in Australia were usually unfenced, the locomotive was fitted with Pyle National electric lighting. It was replaced by diesel locomotives in 1962 and placed on display in the mill grounds. The Australian Narrow Gauge Railway Museum Society purchased the locomotive in 1975 and it was put into storage.

To build the model, a works photograph and general arrangement drawing were obtained from the Fowler archives at the Museum of English Rural Life, located within the University of Reading. WN188 was built with particular attention being paid to detail. There is little else to be said about this model, which follows a now standard practice of 2mm steel frames,

12. Works photograph of the John Fowler plantation locomotive Works Number 20763 built in 1935. John Fowler & Co. (Leeds) Ltd had a reputation for the quality of their locomotives, which is apparent in this excellent photograph. Notice the mechanical oil lubrication to the cylinders and valves, the Pyle National electric lighting and the double roof that would be specified for hot climates.

(35/25032 – Museum of English Rural Life, University of Reading-Fowler Archives)

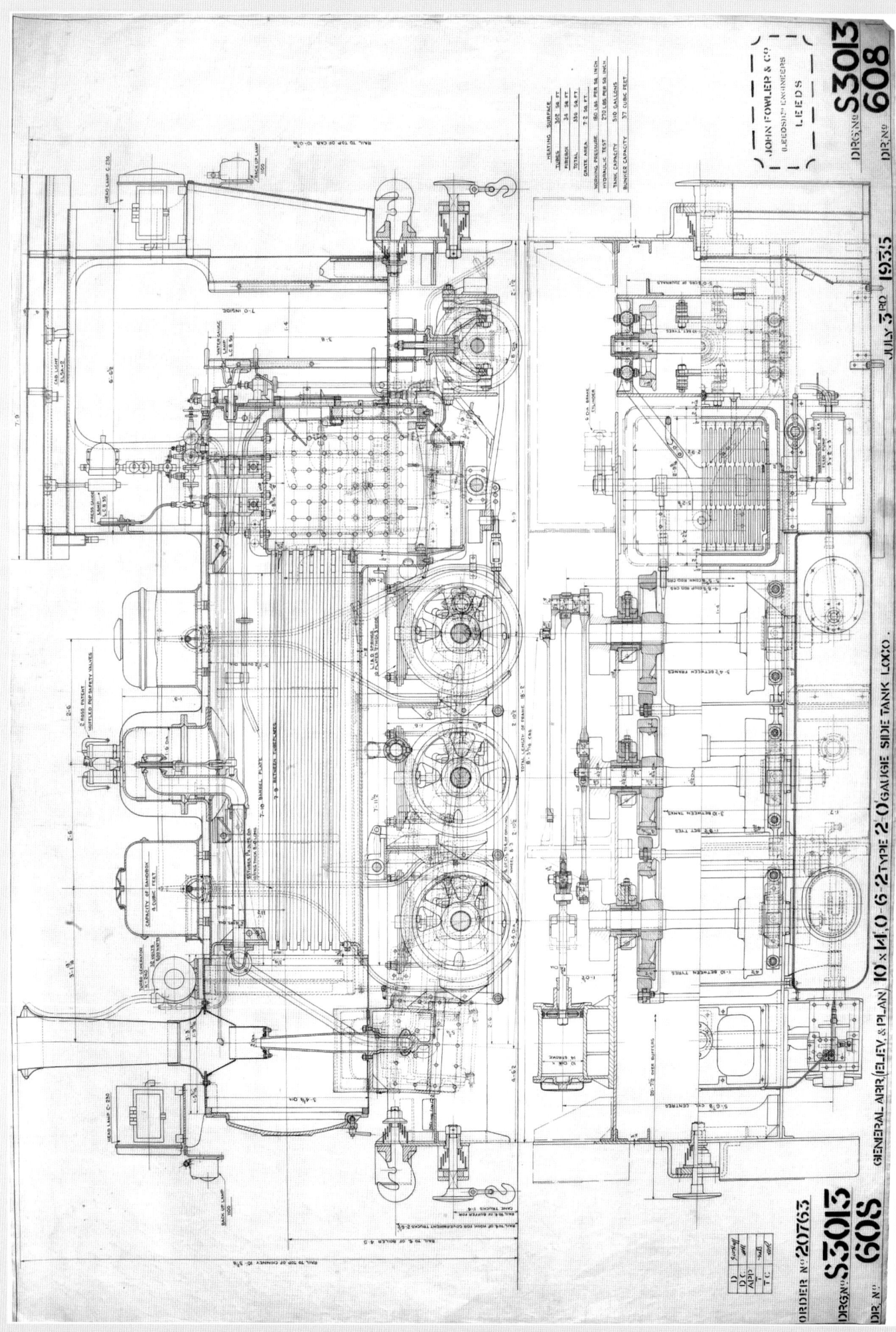

13. (Opposite page) General arrangement drawing of the John Fowler plantation locomotive wn20763 dated July 3rd 1935. The detail on these works drawings is quite outstanding and a tribute to the skills of the drawing office at a time when all such work was done by hand.

(S3013 608 – Museum of English Rural Life, University of Reading – Fowler Archives)

14. (Top left) John Fowler and Company plantation locomotive Airdmillan supplied to the Australian Estates Co. Ltd, Kalamia Mill, Queensland. The typical Fowler plantation locomotive with a very business-like no frills appearance included the addition of two sand domes either side of the steam dome on the top of the boiler barrel. The bright yellow colour finish is also typical of the Australian sugar plantation engines. The electric light on top of the smoke box and rear coalbunker are working units. The John Fowler works plates on the model are based on the full size plates taken from the works photograph and are unusual in not including the build date.

(WN188-1 – Mike Lax)

15. (Left) Rear view of the locomotive with the working rear headlight, the displacement lubricator in the cab and just visible is the radio control steam regulator.

(WN188-2 – Mike Lax)

16. (Below left) This is the gear side view of the later examples of overtype locomotives. The model now has running boards and sand boxes and the exhaust steam from the engine is neatly taken into the smokebox before blasting up the chimney. Early models simply laid the exhaust pipe up the rear of the chimney.

(WN209-1 – Author)(WN209-3 – Author)

17. (Below Middle The opposite side view showing the gas tank and lubricator. With such a small model and no cab or side tanks hiding these items is not possible. The lubricator is tucked in as close to the boiler and flywheel as was possible and is painted black, while a little lining on the gas tank and a small gas valve help to reduce the visual impact of this essential item.

(WN209-2 – Author)

18. (Below right) This is the open footplate end of the locomotive showing the clean functional arrangement of the boiler fittings. Note the oil cup on top of the gear cover and how easy it would be to remove the gas pipe assembly to get at the jet. The burner is from Finescale and originally was fitted with a ¼ x 40 union which has been replaced by soldering in a copper pipe (less joints the better).

(WN209-3 – Author)

¼in round and square frame spacers, plain brass axle bushes and cylinders and valvegear from Roundhouse Engineering. The boiler was 2in diameter x 6½in long plain centre flue with Roundhouse water gauge and safety valve. The gas tank was placed in the left hand side tank to allow radio control to be installed in the rear bunker. Due to the limited dimensions of the side tank, it was made with ¾in square 16g brass tube to give a tank size of 3.375in long by 13/16in deep by 1.562in high, allowing for a 1/32 overlap of the end plates. The rear trailing truck was lightly spring loaded in the vertical plane, only offering some support to the rear end along with a small degree of play introduced to the axle to ensure the wheels followed any undulation of the track.

STEPHEN LEWIN, POOLE FOUNDRY, SOUTH ROAD, POOLE

Stephen Lewin built a number of narrow gauge locomotives between 1868 and 1879 for industrial use and may have included one tramway locomotive. Although few in number, his locomotives have always held a fascination to locomotive historians and enthusiasts, especially the small Seaham Harbour engine which at one time was thought to be the oldest working industrial locomotive in the British Isles. This locomotive, the only surviving Lewin engine, is now being restored at the Beamish Museum in Durham. Within this small production from the Poole foundry there were several small locomotives with the engine located above the boiler as per traction engine practice. Two of these engines were built for Messrs A Guinness Son, & Co's Brewery, Dublin in 1877. The single cylinder engine, located above the boiler, drove through spur gears to the rear axle and thence through side rods to the front axle. A large flywheel was added to the other side of the engine. Despite their size and the gauge of 22in they were capable of hauling 40t on the level, which reduced to 16t on a 1 in 30 gradient. The engine ran at 280rpm for a speed of 6mph and the drive could be disconnected using a wrought iron clutch to allow the locomotive to be used as a stationary power plant. A bolted-on front water tank could be added to the front of the locomotive when it was used as a portable engine. They were appropriately named Hops and Malt and both locomotives survived into the 20th century, Hops being scrapped in 1917 and Malt in 1927.

Unlike the previous models of these locomotives, the next generation starting with WN56 used a special version of the SVS geared oscillating engine with the correct spur gear drive to the rear axle. The final drive spur gear doubled up as a crank for the side rod coupling to the front axle. The models were produced with outside frames for 32mm track and inside frames for 45mm track, the line of the gear drive remaining the same. Over the years the design has remained basically unaltered with attention being given more to cosmetic changes and the addition of running boards to WN209/230. The latest Overtype locomotives, this time built by Mike Lax, takes this further by introducing the rounded rear footplate as fitted to the full size locomotive but this does increase the overall length. Despite being oversize on 32mm track, there is no doubt that they are an interesting and very unusual addition to any garden railway and the provision of a flywheel gives incredibly slow and smooth running.

0-4-0+T HOHENZOLLERN MILITARY LOCOMOTIVE

Of all the locomotives in this book the Hohenzollern military locomotive must be one of the most unusual. It came about from a photograph in a German military book that was shown to me by Ian Jones. It was not just the over exaggerated tapered boiler but also the equally oversize steam dome, the conical chimney, the rather short wheelbase and the cute tender. The principal with the tapered boiler was to provide the maximum amount of water around the intense heat of the firebox for rapid steam raising, useful in an emergency. The large dome ensures a good clean steam take-off on gradients or rough track and increases the water space both of which are just as important with the model.

From the photograph, it can be seen that the engine lies under the tapered boiler, driving the front axle with the cylinders at the front just visible under the diminutive smokebox. The cylinders were located inside the frames and probably drove direct to the axle because there is no indication of a geared drive. A small four-wheeled water-carrying tender was supplied for normal duties, but could be detached for convenience when shunting. The caption, in German, indicated that this locomotive was the first Feldbahn locomotive built by Hohenzollern as their Works Number 473 in 1888. It was built for the Prussian Royal or Imperial Railway Regiment for a gauge of 600mm and had an axle load of 2500kg and a working weight of 6500kg and was a far cry from the later 0-8-0 Klien-Lindner radial axle Feldbahn locomotives. Even the German caption uses the word 'Grotesk', perhaps a fitting description, which can be judged from the photographs of the model.

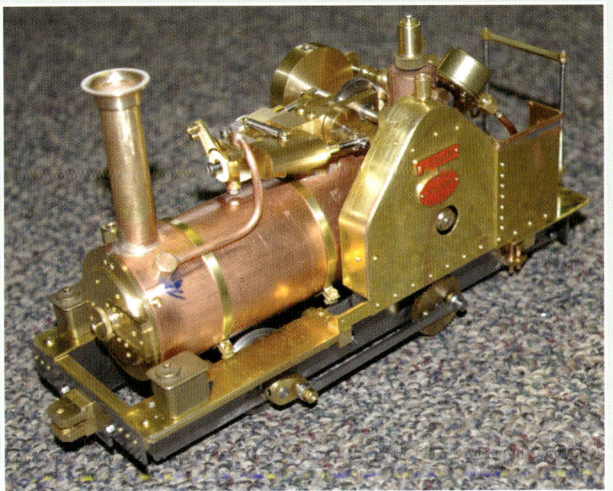

19. (Above) Photograph of the sister locomotive hauling a small train of goods trucks on Trevor's Mamod tracked line. These small 4 wheel geared locomotives, capable of running at a slow consistent speed, are well suited to the 2ft 6in radius Mamod cast track.

(WN230-3 – Trevor Peat)

20. (Left) The locomotive in the brass shows that the boiler shell is full length, which makes it unnecessary to provide a separate smokebox, a similar method being used on the Lumpy Tom boiler. One of the ball race bearings used on the SVS engine can be seen on the output shaft. Notice also final spur gear doubling as a crank for the side rod. Behind this there are two pipes cleated to the frame representing the blow down/water level valve and water gauge blow down valve drain pipes. The Goodall water filler valve is just visible past the chimney on the far side. Again where can you hide it on such a small locomotive without side tanks?

(WN209-4 – Author)

21. (Below left) Final development of the Stephen Lewin Overtype, this time built by Mike Lax, and fitted with the round-ended rear footplate. Since the gas tank is still fitted at the side, introducing the curved rear footplate results in a small increase in overall length. Just under the gear cover and in front of intermediate gear can be seen the adjusting slot for the motion plate. The intermediate gear of 2½in diameter is mounted on this plate, which swivels from the rear in order to adjust the gear settings. Once correct, the 6ba socket cap screw is tightened. If required, the gear setting for the engine to intermediate gear can be set using shims under the engine mounting.

(WN243-1 – Mike Lax)

From the model point of view, this was certainly an interesting project. Take for instance the tapered boiler. The top of the boiler is horizontal and the rear tube plate vertical, i.e. at right angles to the barrel. The front tube plate is however at right angles to the centre line of the taper along with the smokebox front. The rear bunker is available to accommodate a large modular gas tank located between the frames and the simple roof arrangement give excellent access to the boiler fittings. However, one of the main points was the location of the engine. By careful design the geared SVS engine was positioned below the tapered boiler to drive to the front axle yet be clear of the sprung pony truck. The extremely short wheelbase of the full size locomotive was increased to provide better tracking assisted by the vertically sprung pony truck. Despite the short wheelbase, this model runs very smoothly but is prone to slipping on greasy track especially at exhibitions later in the day when oil on the track causes problems. The four wheel auxiliary water tender has sprung wheels with the axles held up against the springs by an under-running tie bar and is fitted with a quick release draw bar connector to the locomotive.

22. *(Top left) This is the Hohenzollern Fieldbahn locomotive during construction, showing the general layout of the running chassis. The conical boiler is mounted at the front on the support brackets using four 8ba screws and at the rear on the paxolin pad. The gas tank is supported by angle brackets attached to the frames and will be covered by the rear bunker. The height of the rear bunker means that a large a 2¾ gas tank can be fitted providing extra endurance. The straggly pipe from the engine is the exhaust pipe, which feeds through the smokebox into the chimney, the twisted shape allowing the pipe to be fitted or removed with the locomotive complete. The pipe is deliberately offset through the smokebox to clear the centre flue, thereby reducing the overheating of the pipe, which can cause a cackling affect.*

(WN291-1 – Author)

23. *(Middle left) Close up of the SVS engine illustrating the difficulty of locating it in the frames. The engine must sit under the tapered boiler yet clear the vertically sprung pony truck and at the same time engage with the spur gear on the leading axle. Thick washers are fitted to the 6ba socket cap screws holding the engine frame stretcher in order to cover the slot in the frames used to align the engine. The brass screws holding the engine to this stretcher would be replaced by 6ba socket cap screws. The 32mm steel disc wheels are dual gauge to allow the locomotive only to be re-gauged to 45mm.*

(WN291-2 – Author)

24. *(Left) The front pony truck of the Hohenzollern locomotive shows the vertical springing and pivot. The wheels and axle unit can be removed and replaced with a 45mm set which consists of the same size wheels on a 45mm axle and two ¼ in spacers.*

(WN291-5 – Author)

25. *(Below) Hohenzollern on Brian Hicks' West Lincolnshire Light Railway.*

(WN187-2 – Andy Cooper)

26. The Hohenzollern 2-4-0T is operating on the garden railway of Mike Brown in December 2010. The top of the engine can be seen below the smokebox. Notice how the buffer beam has been cut away to allow the forward/reverse lever sufficient travel. The location of the engine did not lend itself to providing a remote forward/reverse lever. The pipe on the left hand side of the turret is for the water level valve, the disc wheel of which can be seen on the right hand edge of the side panel. From the valve, the pipe runs down the frame alongside the gauge glass blow down valve pipe.

(WN187-3 – Paul Howard)

27. An unusual photograph of the Hohenzollern locomotive is shown crossing the Zambesi Bridge on Brian Hicks' West Lincolnshire Light Railway.

(WN187-4 – Andy Cooper)

WN195-NORTH EASTON RAILWAY W WORSDELL CLASS M1 4-4-0 No1621

A diversion from all of the previous steam locomotives was a request to build a gauge one electric powered locomotive based on the North Eastern Railway class M1 4-4-0 locomotive designed by W Worsdell. William Worsdell's first design of a 4-4-0 locomotive appeared in late 1892 and was designated as Class M1 with the number1620. 18 further engines were built in 1893 and the twentieth in 1894. They were notable as the first British 4-4-0 engines to exceed 90 tons in working order. No.1621was a regular visitor to Alnwick, as it was based at Alnmouth shed and in the later years of its service ran between Alnwick, Alnmouth and Newcastle until withdrawn on the 28th of July 1945. Fortunately, this locomotive, number 1621, is preserved and in the National Collection at NRM York. The model was intended for extensive running on LGB type coarse scale track on the bookcase railway at Barter Books in Alnwick. It was not intended that this model would be an exact scale model, so the opportunity was taken to use the frames supplied for the Gauge 1 DEE

project (Southern Railway class D) but fitted with ball race bearings on all axles including the tender. For power, a Buhler 24 volt 13-21 electric motor was fitted to an ABC Gears 20:1 heavy duty gearbox with track electrical pick-up from the wheel rims using LGB sprung pick-up units. After completing the running chassis the mounting of the motor/gearbox, the bodywork, painting and lining was carried out by Mike Lax. Due to the considerable running expected of this model a spare gearbox was provided. Although the majority of the running is carried out by LGB locomotives, WN195 is still expected to run up to eight hours per day in winter and up to 10 hours per day in summer when required.

WN216-BURMA MINES No 9-NORTH BRITISH LOCOMOTIVE COMPANY.

Following on from the coal-fired model of the South African Railways class NGG11, WN215, it was decided to build a simpler rigid framed locomotive to gain experience in coal firing. Looking back it was probably not a good idea to have selected such a complicated articulated locomotive as an initial introduction to the world of coal firing. Consequently, the prototype chosen would have to be as simple as the Garratt was complicated, with particular emphasis on a large boiler and firebox, maximum unrestricted access to the backhead along with a chassis without leading or trailing wheels. The locomotive selected had all these advantages and in addition the outside frames widened after the rear axle to accommodate a boiler with a large grate area. Coal firing tends to favour locomotives with a tender and open rear to the cab, which improves the access to the boiler fittings located on the backhead and also to the firedoor for the loading of coal. In addition, the four-wheel tender was of low outline thereby improving access still further. The archive photograph of the original locomotive, supplied by the Mitchell Library, Glasgow City Archives, illustrates this interesting engine built by the North British Locomotive Company, wn18674 of 1908, at their Atlas Works. We are also fortunate in being able to reproduce the general arrangement drawing of the locomotive by courtesy of the University of Glasgow Archives Services, Andrew Barclay Sons and Company Ltd Collection, reference GBO248RHP58442/1

This locomotive was one of three supplied to the Burma Mines Railway under order L319 (Works Numbers 18672-4) with a further three supplied under order L637 of 1914 (Works Numbers 21105-07). The Burma mines Railway was located in the hilly far north east of Burma in the Shan States close to the border. Originally, the mines existed to extract silver long before the British discovered the mines in 1886. However, the huge slag heaps contained lead, zinc and copper that could be economically worked providing cheap transport to the smelter was developed. With the construction of the main line to Lashio in 1903 giving access to a smelter in Mandalay, the Burma Mines Railway and Smelting Co. was formed to lease the mines and smelt the ore. The mines themselves would be connected to the main line at Lashio by a 50 mile 2ft gauge line through difficult hilly country and was completed by 1908. It was for this line that the NBL locomotives were supplied.

The model, WN216, was developed using drawings supplied by the University of Glasgow Archive Services with the wheelbase slightly altered to coincide with the Roundhouse Engineering Argyle chassis. This made it possible to use their standard parts including the dual gauge axles. It was decided to reduce the 2ft 6in driving wheels from 40mm to 37mm using steel disc wheels supplied by Walsall Model Industries and outside cranks supplied by Finescale Engineering. The chassis

consisted of two side frames connected by suitable stretchers, which were bolted to a rear U shaped frame just behind the rear axle. This arrangement provided the increased rear frame width to accommodate the large firebox of the boiler.

A 3/16in diameter by 6mm stroke water pump was fitted over and in front of the leading axle driven by an eccentric on the trailing axle. The cylinders were the standard Roundhouse Engineering units with the exhaust connected to a blast pipe in the smokebox. The most interesting part of this model was the excellent Belpaire type locomotive boiler built by Brian Nicholls and provided with as large and deep a firebox as possible within the constraints of the frame. In addition, this locomotive has a long smokebox, which provided a bit more room for the internal fittings, although the fitting of the pipe unions on the boiler front tube plate requires a thin spanner and a degree of patience. Another point of interest with the full size and model locomotive is the action of the drawbar between the locomotive and the tender. This bar enters underneath the cab floor through a slot in the draw beam to a 'T' piece roughly halfway between the boiler and the rear of the locomotive. From each end of the 'T' piece a link connects back over to the end of the draw beam. The effect of entering a curve is to move the drawbar sideways as if it was pivoted further into the locomotive. Connection to the tender is to a pivot inside the tender front. The problem of tight curves were reduced by this arrangement and the tender could be closer coupled. For the model the disadvantage is that the location of the water pipes to the tender is restricted due to the sideways movement of the drawbar. The end result is shown in the photographs with the model finished in black with lining on the cab and tender sides. A further locomotive is proposed but this time it will be finished in grey/black with black lining similar to the Avonside and Hohenzollern engines.

WN274-DARJEELING HIMALAYAN RAILWAY CLASS A

There can be few people interested in railways that have not heard of the Darjeeling Himalayan Railway. This tiny 2ft gauge line starts at the southern terminus at New Jalpaiguri, a mere 480ft above sea level passing through the original terminus at Siliguri Town, across the plains to Sukna, a distance of over 7miles, and then begins its tortuous climb for 40miles to the summit at Ghum (7407ft) before descending down to Darjeeling (6812ft), a distance of 55miles. To keep to the contours of the hills required extensive use of short radius complete

29. Gauge 1 model based on North Eastern Railway W. Worsdell designed class M1 4-4-0 of 1893. This electric steam outline locomotive was designed for extended running on the raised bookcase railway at Barter Books in Alnwick using track pick-up from LGB style coarse scale track.
(WN195-1 – Mike Lax)

30. Close up of the gauge 1 class M1 4-4-0 locomotive on the bridge between two bookshelves on the raised track at Barter Books located in the old Alnwick station building in Alnwick. This railway is an important part of the bookshop display and is appreciated by the large number of visitors to what is one of the largest second-hand bookshops in Britain. Keeping the railway operating is not easy as the locomotives, made up of mainly LGB stock, are expected to run continuously up to eight hours per day in winter and 10 hours in summer.
(WN195-2 – Dave Champion)

31. (Right) This is the overall view of the part of the raised track. In the background is one of three murals commissioned by Barter Books and painted by Alnwick born artist Peter Dodd in 2001. This famous mural known as the Famous Writers Mural is 12m long and 5m at the apex and consists of over thirty life size portraits of famous writers in the English language.
(WN195-3 – Dave Champion)

32. (Below) By courtesy of the Mitchell Library, Glasgow City Archives, Photographic Collection. North British Locomotive Company works photograph of the Burma Mines No.9 locomotive, Works Number 18674, supplied in 1908 under order L319.
(Burma Mines No 9)

loops and Z-reversing stations. Over the years from the start of construction in 1879 the gradients have been eased and track formations changed, often due to monsoon damage, but the railway still includes gradients down to 1 in 25 and curves of 60ft radius.

To operate this extremely difficult line, the railway ordered four locomotives in 1879 from Sharp Stewart, (order no.E777) with a further four (order No E 778) in the same year. With a wheelbase of only 4ft 6in on a frame 15ft 3in long, these locomotives were fitted with full-length side tanks and inclined cylinders with Stephenson inside valve gear. These locomotives continued to work for several years but even after the first season of operation it was obvious that more powerful engines were required. Therefore a further order for two locomotives of an improved design was given to Sharp Stewart in 1881, extended to successive orders in 1881-82 to give a total of four orders

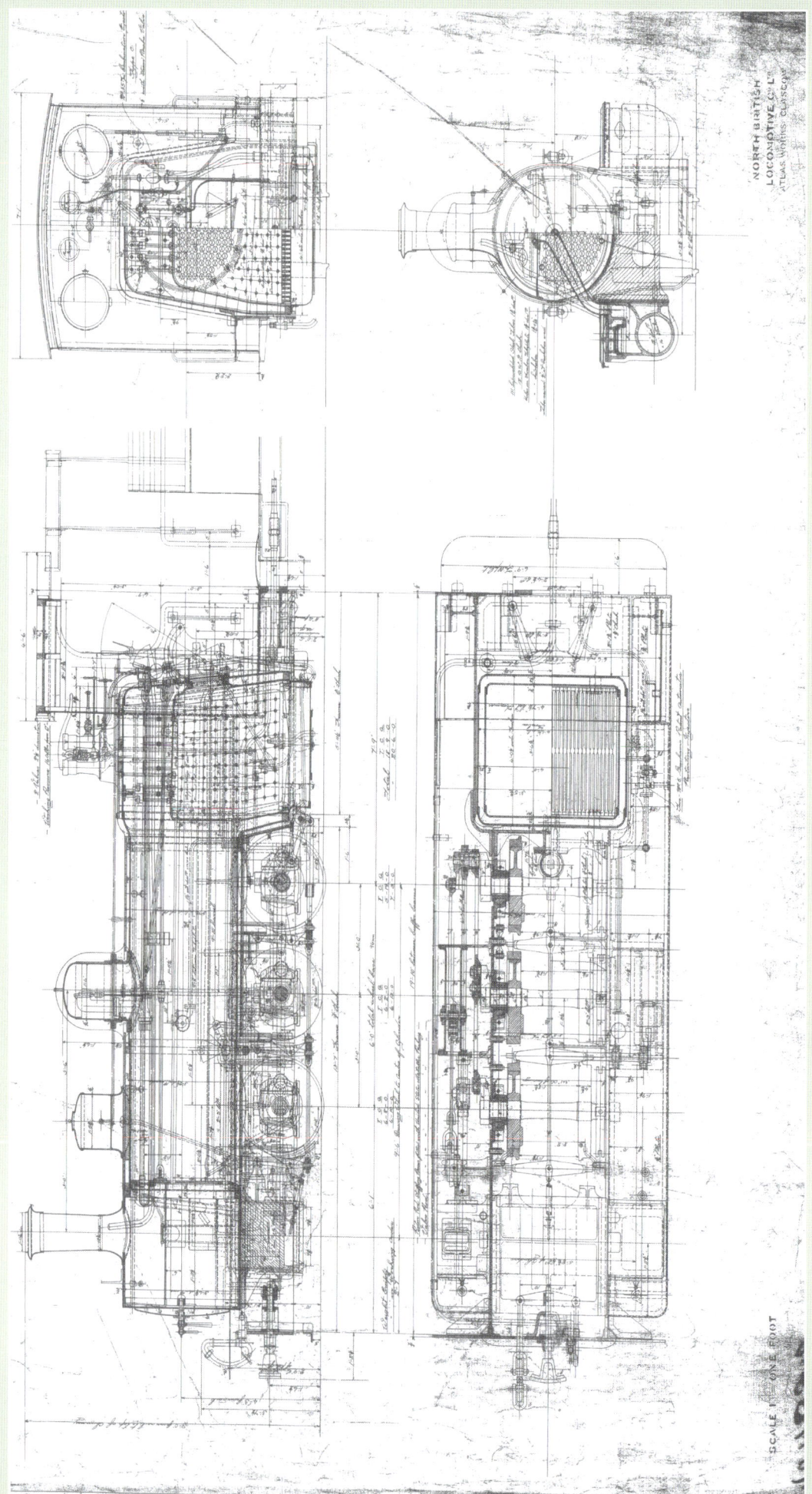

33. *(Above) General arrangement drawing of the North British Locomotive Company locomotive built for the Burma Mines in 1908 under order L319.*

(GBO248 RHP58442/1 Reproduced by kind permission of the University of Glasgow Archive Services, Andrew Barclay Sons and Company Ltd Collection)

34. (Right) This shows the model of the Burma Mines No9 shown in the brass before painting. The rear buffer beam of the locomotive can be seen to be split. This allows the trapezoidal mounted draw bar to move sideways as the locomotive enters a curve. The sideways movement acted as if the drawbar was pivoted much further into the area that would in reality be the firebox. The tender could therefore be close coupled despite the tight curvature of the track. Water can be added to the tender through the water filler, which is attached to a re-moveable plate. Notice the crane hook rings inside the tender that would have been used on the full size locomotive to lift off the tank. Also the axle boxes of the tender are fitted with a tie bar between them.
(WN216-3 – Author)

35. (Left) The coal fired boiler for the Burma Mines locomotive showing the wide firebox possible due to the increased width of the frames behind the rear axle. The bush on the side of the boiler barrel is for the check valve for the mechanical pump with a second bush on the other side for the Goodall valve. The centre boiler dome houses the steam inlet pipe with a blank plug required to close the top. The left hand bush on the boiler crown is for the 5/16 x 32 safety valve with the final bush nearest to the backhead used for the blower valve and pressure gauge turret. A blow down valve fits into the bush at the bottom of the firebox.
(Burma Mines locomotive boiler – Brian Nicholls)

36. (Right) Backhead detail of the coal fired boiler showing all of the fittings from left to right as follows:

• water gauge with blow down valve.

• left hand side hollow stay incorporating the blower pipe fed from the blower valve above.

• steam regulator in the centre of the boiler fitted with an internal steam pick-up from inside the boiler dome.

• right hand hollow stay incorporating the steam feed to the cylinders via the smokebox.

• (far right hand side) the water level and blow-off valve.

The steam regulator can be seen to feed to the displacement lubricator and then back to the right hand hollow stay. There is no superheating. A small turret screwed into a bush on top of the boiler mounts the blower valve with the steam pressure gauge attached above the steam blower valve.
(WN216-4 – Author)

of two locomotives. To reduce the centre of gravity, the water tanks were moved to a single well tank between the frames, which in turn required outside Walschaerts valve gear and the cylinders were set at an inclination of 1 in 8. The layout gave a low centre of gravity necessary for the tight curves and better access to the motion. Initially, this class of locomotive (numbered 9-16) was designated the No. 2 class but this was reclassified as the A class. As time went on nos. 9-16 were much altered with the addition of a collar tank to give greater water capacity and extended side wings to contain

more coal. On re-boiling further alterations were carried out such that by the time of their withdrawal they had adopted a similar outline to that of their successor, the B class.

The model WN274 was based on the first of the A class No. 9, as supplied to the railway in 1881. A general arrangement drawing was available from the University of Glasgow, Archives Services but an official photograph of No.9, which has appeared in several publications, could not be traced. The drawing reproduced within this book shows the frame as being widened behind

37. (Above) The finished coal fired Burma Mines No 9 locomotive on trials on the garden railway of Geoff Lumsdon. The cover over the safety valve has not been added.
(WN216-5 – Author)

38. (Left) The operators working area on the finished coal fired model showing the access afforded by the open rear of the cab, which is not compromised by the low outline of the tender. Notice the Roundhouse side-draining lubricator as there was insufficient room for a bottom drain valve. The disc handle in front of the lubricator operates the bi-pass valve for the axle driven pump. Water can also be injected into the boiler using the Goodall type valve next to the right hand check valve. Between the locomotive and the tender can just be seen one of the water feed pipes which are pushed to the side of the draw beam to allow the sideways movement of the trapezoidal mounted drawbar.
(WN216-7 – Author)

40. (Right) The chassis of the Darjeeling A class model showing the split frame as used on the original locomotive. This arrangement allowed for a wider firebox whilst retaining a narrow set of inside frames for the running gear. From the model point of view, the wider frames can be used to accommodate the gas tank. Changes had to be made to provide an increase in the length of the gas tank. Consequently the screws seen in the picture connecting the frames were replaced with countersunk ones and the cross stretchers behind the buffer beam were reduced and incorporated within the beam.
(WN274-2 – Author)

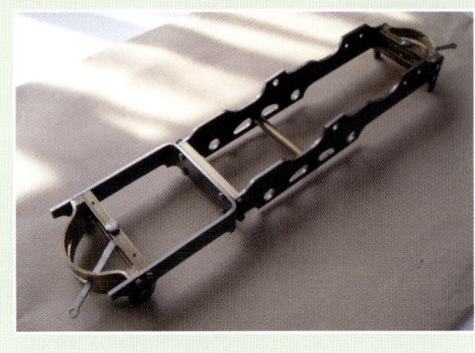

the rear axle to allow for a wider firebox on the boiler. This feature is retained for the model, which makes it possible to fit a reasonable size gas tank between the frames despite the frames adjacent to the driving wheels being only 1.875in apart. From the photograph of the complete frames it can be seen that they are quite complicated when compared to the frames of most other locomotives. In addition, the installation of the Roundhouse Engineering cylinders and valve gear at the correct inclination does produce certain problems. For instance, the use of a well tank between the frames on the full size locomotive means that the steam inlet and exhaust pipes are attached to the top of the valve chest/cylinders, whereas in the model the pipes are side entry. This requires careful removal of the underside of the smokebox to accommodate the two 'T' pieces. The inclination of the cylinders also lifts up the expansion link pivots and therefore the weight shaft, which has to be altered to clear the underside of the boiler.

As can be seen in the photographs, the boiler comes a long way into the cab area providing little room for the oversize model boiler fittings located between the backhead and the assortment of hand rails and roof pillars. To further complicate matters, the lack of side

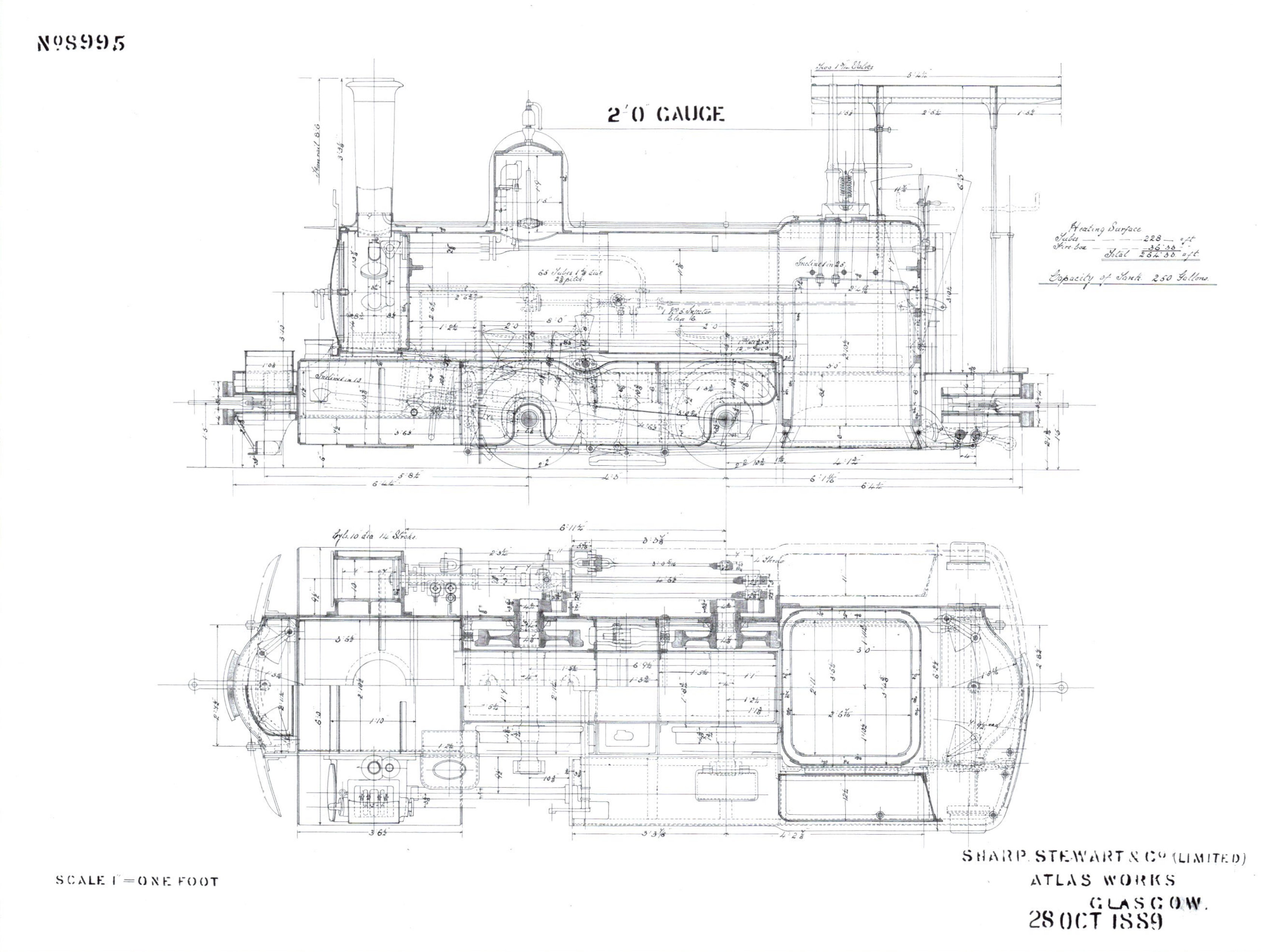

Nº 8995

SCALE 1 = ONE FOOT

2' 0" GAUGE

SHARP, STEWART & Cº (LIMITED)
ATLAS WORKS
GLASGOW.
28 OCT 1889

39. (left) General
arrangement drawing
of the Darjeeling
Himalayan class A
0-4-0WT locomotive
built in 1881 at the
Atlas works of Sharp
Stewart. The model
was based on this
drawing and the
photograph of the
Darjeeling Himalayan
No 9 (Works Number
3016). It was
delivered in 1882 and
was the first of two
locomotives supplied
under order E810.

**(GBO248 RHP57723-1
Reproduced by kind
permission of the
University of Glasgow
Archive Services,
Andrew Barclay Sons
and Company Ltd
Collection)**

tanks and the open cab provide little room for the Goodall type water filler, forward/reverse lever and gas tank filler. The end result is shown in the photographs of the locomotive in the brass and the finished in green/black based on the coloured drawings in the reference books. Lining will be added eventually. This model is the last one in this chapter but not hopefully the end of Darjeeling production. Proposed for the near future is construction of the Sharp Stewart No 1 class.

WN279 Darjeeling Himalayan Railway-Baby Sivok

There is a considerable amount of information on the A & B class locomotives, the solitary class D Garratt and the two C class pacific tender engines, but as would be expected, little information on the locomotives engaged in the construction of the railway. One of these locomotives was the small contractors engine named Baby Sivok, which fortunately still survives. The locomotive was obtained second hand and transferred to the DHR at an uncertain date, possibly being used on the Tessta valley extension in 1913-15 along with the other contractors engine Tiny. There is even some doubt as to its identity but it is generally thought to be Orenstien & Koppel Works Number 5130, recorded as a 20hp 0-4-0 tank engine and supplied in 1911 to

Gillanders Arbuthnot, the Agent for the DHR. The locomotive was described as a 'ballast engine named Sivoke weighing 8tons' in the DHR stock list of 1920 and may then have been used on the construction of the Raipur Forest Railway. It was then laid aside until rebuilt for the Indian Railway Centenary Exhibition in 1953, after which it was preserved at Siliguri Junction. During the rebuild, the locomotive acquired the small saddle tank and coalbunker along the pattern of the A & B class. There is a drawing and photograph of this engine in the book, The Iron Sherpa by Terry Martin.

From the model point of view there is an immediate problem hinted at by the name. Baby Sivok is very small with an overall length over the buffers of 15ft 6in or just over 12ft between the buffer beams. Since the engine was destined for one of the longest garden railways in the country a compromise was required. WN279 was therefore built to the wheelbase and valve gear dimensions of a Roundhouse Billy, giving a frame length of 241mm and an all important boiler diameter of 2in. Built to this size the locomotive would be too high, so care had to be taken to reduce the vertical dimensions and the overall result can be judged by the photographs. The cylinders and valve gear are as would be expected in Roundhouse Engineering products with the cast iron wheels and ¼ in diameter square-ended axles from Walsall Model

41. (Above left) The Darjeeling A class model in the brass before being sent off for painting with only the headlamp to add and the eccentric rods.
(WN274-8 – Author)

42. (Above right) There is not much room on the rear footplate of the locomotive for all the fittings. A lever will replace the disc handle on the steam regulator. Careful observation along the left hand side shows the angled turret that houses the gas filler valve and the banjo outlet

to the gas valve, while beyond that is the Goodall type water filler valve. The unused steam bush on the top of the boiler indicates that the pressure gauge and siphon have yet to be fitted. To the side and top of the boiler are the dummy operating rods, with the left hand one for the injector and the right hand one for the blower valve. Notice how the footplate has been split to make it easier to dismantle or assemble the back end of the model.
(WN274-9 – Author)

43. (Left) This photograph is looking down on the Darjeeling A class locomotive which is about to set off around the garden railway layout of Geoff Lumsdon during his open day on 4th September 2011. As previously mentioned there is not much room above the footplate for all the boiler fittings.

(WN274-12 – Tom Beattie)

44. (Below left) Left hand side view of the Darjeeling A class locomotive which has now been lined by Lightline. The pipe from the check valve runs through the dummy injector and thence to the Goodall valve located in the side bunker. The support brackets for the dummy injector and blower valve operating rods are mounted in blind bushes that have been silver soldered into the boiler, which is necessary where the boiler does not have an outer wrapper.

(WN274-15 – Geoff Munday)

45. Opposite side view of the painted and lined Darjeeling A class. Notice how neatly the gas tank has been shoe-horned between the frames in the area, which with a coal fired locomotive, would be the firebox. The original frame spacers at the rear of the frames have had to be incorporated in the rear buffer beam in order to provide extra length to the gas tank.

(WN274-16 – Geoff Munday)

Industries. A further problem was the location of a gas tank. The only suitable position was alongside the boiler in the coalbunker using two ¾in square tubes mounted one on top of the other, although part of the tank remains visible below the front section of the bunker. Mounting a vertical gas tank in the cab would be too prominent and there is little room behind the gas burner anyway. Next on the Darjeeling list should be the Sharp Stewart No 1 class.

WN263 VANCOUVER FIJI SUGAR COMPANY No4

Sugar cane was first planted on the Fiji Islands at Selia Levu on the windward side of Taveuni in 1873 and a sugar mill was imported from Sidney in 1874. Crushing began in 1875 with transport provided by bullock cart. The usual problems soon occurred with deterioration of

the road surface following heavy rainfall. The solution was to construct a tramway, 2.4km by 1876 with the cane hauled by horses along the tramway and bullocks hauling the cane from the bush. Further cane plantations soon followed along with deliveries of tramway equipment, for instance the delivery of 1225 sections of railway, 32 points and crossings and parts for 40 cane wagons in 1882. As part of this consignment there was included one steam locomotive built to a gauge of 2ft 6in by the Falcon Engine and Car Works of Loughborough.

The 1880s produced a rapid expansion of plantations, including three sugar plantations in the rich land located in the wide delta of the Navua River on the island of Viti Levu. It was one of these plantations, which in 1884, was to become the Fiji Sugar Company Limited and then, following negotiations with the

46. (Top left) Photograph of the full size locomotive, Orenstein & Koppel wn5130 of 1911 taken by Kieth Froom at the DHR Museum at Ghum in 2008.

(Baby Sivok – Keith Froom)

47. (Left) View of the left side of Sivok in the brass before being sent off for painting. The valve in the lower corner of the cab entrance controls the gas to the burner and in front is the forward/reverse lever. The pipe from the boiler check valve loops under the left hand side of the bunker to a Goodall valve just visible in the imitation coal, the valve being mounted inside the pillar attached to the rear footplate. The safety valve is located inside the dome cover mounted on the actual boiler dome, which also acts correctly as the steam outlet to the backhead mounted steam regulator. Notice how the dummy coal has a gap at either end to allow some circulation of air around the boiler and gas tank. The small hole at the base of the saddle tank was required during the construction of the tank and has since been filled in.

(WN279-16 – Author)

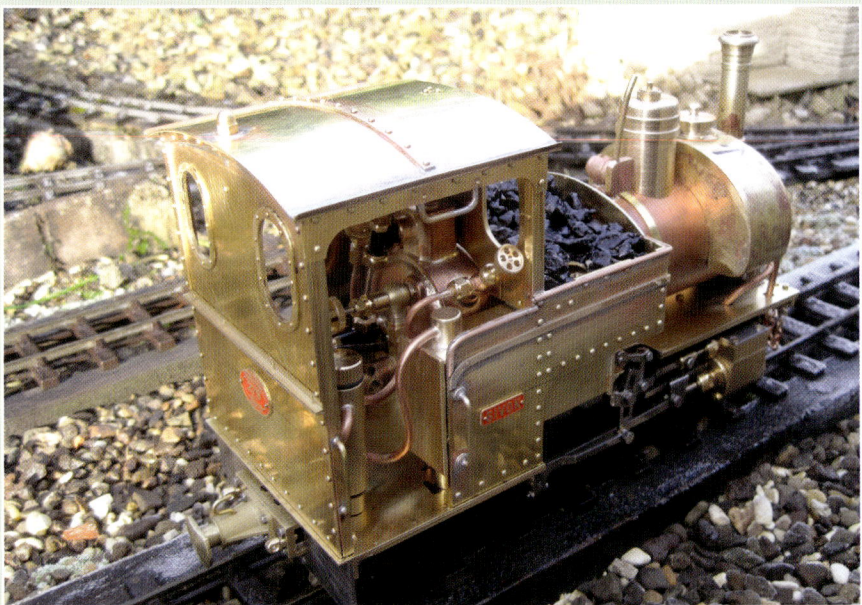

48. (Below left) This view, looking from the rear into the cab, illustrates the layout of the boiler fittings. Clearly visible is the displacement lubricator at the rear with the blow down valve through the cab floor. The backhead mounted steam regulator (disc handle to be replaced by a lever), the water level/blow off valve and water gauge are again clearly visible. As mentioned in the text the gas tank location was a problem with the only position possible limited to the inside of the cab side and bunker. Unfortunately, this means the tank is visible below the bunker side but there is no other suitable location on this small model. Locating the tank alongside the boiler is unusual and not ideal and requires adequate insulation from the heat of the boiler.

(WN279-18 – Author)

49. (Above right) The finished model of Baby Sivok painted in the same Brunswick Green as the Darjeeling class D Garratt previously supplied to Chris Moody. The Goodall water filler is hidden in amongst the imitation coal in the bunker. Although the locomotive is not lined, it has been possible to add the DHR lettering on the side bunker.

(WN279-1 – Author)

50. (Above left) Front ¾ view of the finished locomotive. The gas tank is just visible below the bunker side but is not particularly obtrusive. With such a small engine with limited side bunker and a plain rear cab sheet there is little room to hide the gas tank.

(WN279-6 – Author)

51. (Left) Vancouver Fiji Sugar Company No 4 in the brass before the fitting of the radio control receiver and battery. The rear bunker fitted on this locomotive provides a suitable location for the gas tank with room either side for the receiver and battery. The inside frames of this chassis limits the locomotive to operation on 32mm track only.

(WN263-4 – Author)

British Columbia Sugar Refining Company of Vancouver in 1905, became the Vancouver Fiji Sugar Company. The company at the change of ownership had three steam locomotives along with 6¾ miles of main line, four miles of branches and 7¾ miles of portable track. Up to this time the sugar was punted down to the mouth of the river for transfer to ships bound for Vancouver. Extending the plantations, upgrading the mill at Navua and building a 375ft bridge over the Navua River resulted in the provision of a single track down to a substantial wharf at Naitonitoni. Along with this expansion a fourth locomotive was delivered in 1907 from the makers W G Bagnall Ltd of Stafford, England. Locomotive No 4 was a large 0-6-0T of 14tons with inside frames and was the maker's Works Number 1825 of 1906. WN263 was based on this locomotive.

The model was built around a Cheddar Models 0-6-0 inside framed chassis fitted with a type of Joy valve gear. This chassis had been in stock for several years and was believed to have been used on their 0-6-0 tender locomotive. As with all Cheddar Models steam plant, it was of exceptional quality with sprung axles, substantial valve gear, bushed coupling and connecting rods and clever reversing mechanism. Two servos were fitted integral with the frame and the steam regulator was located inside the frames behind the cylinder connections. The chassis was very close to the required dimensions and very few alterations were required to accommodate the proposed boiler and bodywork. This locomotive outline included a reasonably sized rear bunker into which was fitted the gas tank, radio control receiver and batteries. A displacement lubricator was fitted rather than the hydrostatic oil lubricator used by Cheddar Models on their locomotive. As with all inside framed locomotives a dual gauge facility was not possible, the model being set for 32mm gauge only.

52. The finished locomotive named Navua No 4 after the mill on the Vancouver Fiji Sugar Company plantation. The radio control switch can be seen in the recess in the side tank. This location away from the receiver and the batteries absorbs the long leads, which are always a problem in the confines of a small 16mm scale locomotive. The receiver and battery are located in the rear bunker either side of the gas tank. The model is finished in Victorian maroon with white lining and the correct Bagnall works plates.

(WN263-14 – Paul Howard)

WN273 KALIGHAT-FALTA No3

The Kalighat-Falta Railway was one of four lines built to open up undeveloped parts of India in and around the Calcutta area. They were built and managed by McLeod & Co on behalf of the Indian government with the Kalighat-Falta Railway being completed in 1917. To operate each line, four orders were placed by McLeod and Company with the firm of W. G. Bagnall but the advent of war in 1914 resulted in two cancelled orders, including the locomotives for the Kalighat-Falta Railway. However, Bagnalls had on hand twelve 750mm 2-6-2 locomotives destined for the Egyptian Delta Railway. Again, due to the war, only six were sent to Egypt, the remaining six being re-gauged to 2ft 6in and sent to various railways in India including the Kalighat-Falta which received works numbers 2028-2030. They were a very successful design with a further five ordered by McLeod, two in 1930 and the remaining three as late as 1953. For obvious reasons, they were referred to as the Delta class.

Works number 273 was based on Bagnall works number 2028 of 1916 which became Kalighat-Falta No3. To assist in building this model, a copy of the works photograph of number 2028 was obtained from the Staffordshire Records Office who hold the records for W. G. Bagnall Ltd. Weighing in at just under 29 tons, this was a large locomotive with a frame length of 24ft and a width of 7ft 6in. With this in mind, the scale of the model was reduced to 15.5mm/ft. The main frames of 2mm steel were designed to use the wheelbase and cylinder/valvegear dimensions of the larger Roundhouse locomotives, namely the Argyll chassis. This gives a driven wheelbase of 52+52mm, whereas the full size locomotive had

a wheelbase of 7ft equivalent to 108.5mm. The frames work out at 379mm long. In view of the size of the model, the frames included the side springing as was adopted on the leading and trailing wheels of the full size locomotive. Despite its size, the model will operate on a minimum radius of 4ft 6in, whereas the Kalighat-Falta railway had a minimum radius of 573ft or 30ft in 16mm scale. A point of interest is that the model is fitted with Roundhouse simplified Walschaerts valve gear, whereas the Delta class locomotives, being a product of W. G. Bagnall, used Bagnall-valve gear.

REFERENCES:

• Fowler Locomotives in the Kingdom of Hawaii by Jesse C Conde-Narrow Gauge Railway Society.

• Indian Locomotives Part 3-Narrow Gauges 1863-1940 by Hugh Hughes.

• Model Engineer Vol. 120/No3007 – 8th January 1959.

• Stephen Lewin and the Poole Foundry by Russell Wear and Eric Lees.

• The 4-4-0 Classes of the North Eastern Railway by K Hoole.

• North British Locomotive (1912) A reproduction of NBL company catalogue of Narrow Gauge Locomotives 1912 introduced by John Thomas.

• Loco Profile 23-Darjeeling Tanks by Brian Reed.

• British North Steam Locomotives Built 1857-1956 for Railways Overseas. John H Court.

• Article in The Narrow Gauge No119.

• McLeod Light Railways and their The Bagnall Locomotives by Allan C. Baker.

• Bagnalls of Stafford by Allan C. Baker & T. D. Allen Civil.

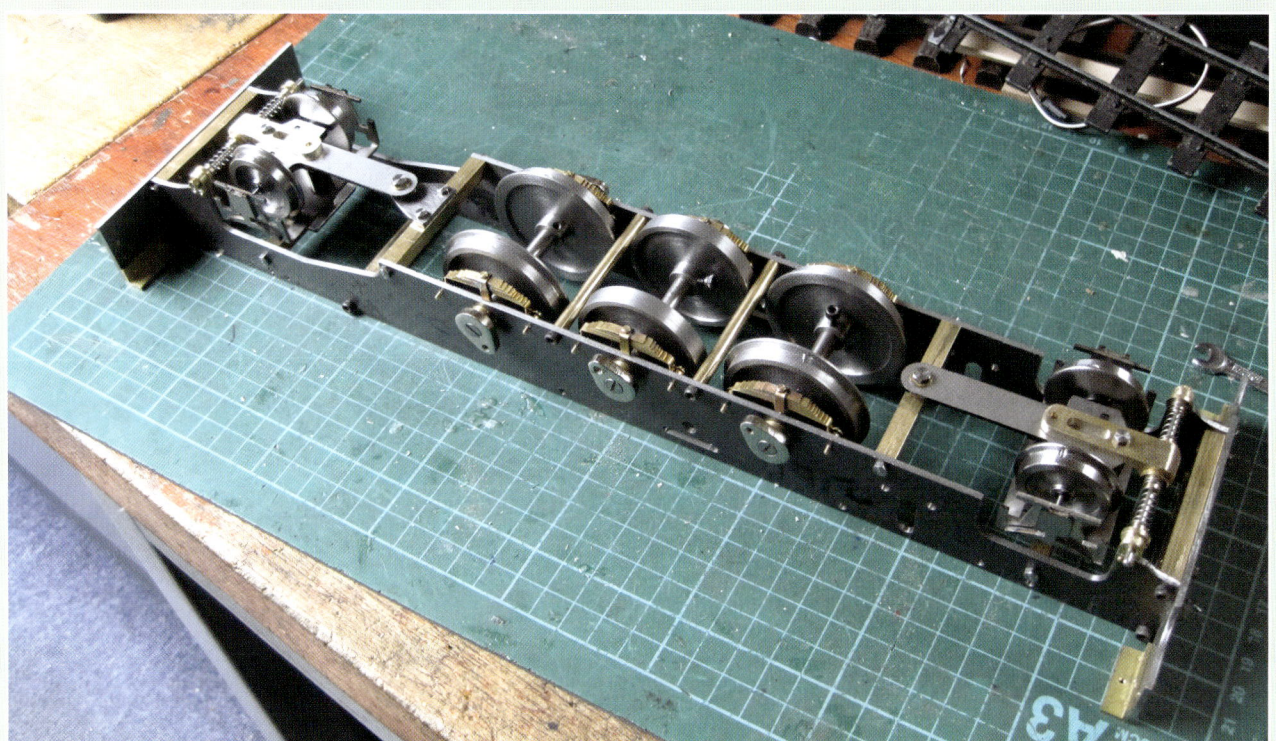

53. (Above) The layout of the frame showing the leading and trailing wheel side springing. Notice that the frame is 32mm only and includes the underslung springs of the full size locomotive.

(WN273-3 – Author)

54. (Right) There is nothing subtle about Indian locomotive colour schemes as shown in the two photographs of the finished model. This right hand side view illustrates the size of the locomotive and the long overhang behind the rear driven axle. Notice the Indian lettering for ER (Eastern Railway) on this side with the English lettering on the left hand side.

(WN273-25 – Author)

55. (Below right) The opposite side front view of this large locomotive. Notice the front cowcatcher which for a model must be set higher than would be the case with the full size locomotive. On garden railways the model is subject to greater fluctuations of track level that could lead to a costly 'failure to proceed' should the cowcatcher catch a raised rail joint.

(WN273-28 – Author)

THE 7/8TH SCALE LOCOMOTIVES

One of the problems associated with the scale of 16mm/ft (1:19) occurs because the particularly diminutive narrow gauge locomotives, such as the Stephen Lewin Overtype, are difficult to reproduce in such a comparatively small scale. One method of tackling these models is to increase the scale slightly and this method has been used on several projects. The smaller locomotives then become a practical size that will still look acceptable alongside the larger engines. The chain driven Sentinel Industrial locomotives are a good example and these, with careful interpretation of scale, are not out of place alongside other 'correct to scale' models.

There is however an alternative approach to small locomotive construction by adopting a larger scale of 7/8in/ft (1:13.7), but this in turn can introduce further problems. For instance, one could use 7/8th scale for locomotives based on 2ft gauge, giving a correct track gauge in model form of 45mm (1¾in), but this produces a model some 40% larger than an equivalent 1:19 scale locomotive – and would definitely be out of place on a 16mm layout. There is however, the alternative of building a model to the larger scale but based on 18in or 20in gauge for operation on 32mm track, though the scale is not quite correct, (18in on 32mm gauge is 21.3mm/ft).

Now this opens up the possibility of building some of the most attractive and unique little engines with huge amounts of character. Just consider the Hunslet locomotive Jack at Armley Mills. Thinking of the unusual, how about the Samuel Geoghegan 'Guinness' locomotives or perhaps one could consider the Hartley, Arnaux and Fanning No 74.

So, here we go with examples of 7/8th scale models starting with the Guinness locomotive.

WN208. THE SAMUEL GEHOGHEGAN GUINNESS LOCOMOTIVE

The Guinness locomotive WN208 must stand out as perhaps the most unusual model produced in a long line of distinguished oddities. The reason the full size locomotive design came about was due to the failure of conventional designs to cope with the special conditions of this particular industrial site.

PERMANENT WAY

The brewery of Arthur Guinness, Son & Co. Ltd at Dublin, had its own branch line from the Irish 5ft 3in standard gauge, but for internal use, installed an extensive 22in narrow gauge railway with a maximum gradient of 1 in 40 on a site which, due to the slope of the ground occupied three different levels, all within a limited area. The total length of this narrow gauge line was about seven miles and it connected all parts of the works. The intention was to operate the line using steam locomotives and the problem of connecting two of the different levels was solved in a most unique way, by the construction of a spiral tunnel, which replaced an earlier slow and costly method using a hydraulic lift. This spiral tunnel lifted the track 35ft in 2.65 turns at a radius of 61ft 3in without exceeding the set gradient of 1 in 40. A further 15ft of rise, from the Quay to the bottom of the spiral, was affected by a zigzag incline railway arranged with a curve to alter the direction of travel on the incline. This meant that points were not required thereby simplifying operation and saving time. In fact a train could travel the entire length, including the inclines, without shunting or changing the engine to the other end of the train.

THE LOCOMOTIVES

The brewery experimented with various types of locomotive for operation on their 22in gauge works railway, nonc of which fully satisfied their requirements. The first locomotive weighed only two tons, making it suitable for light work only. It was difficult to keep this engine in working order, because the running gear was too close to the ground, where it was easily damaged and prone to excessive wear. The next two locomotives, supplied in 1877 by Stephen Lewin, were heavier and more powerful and had the cylinders mounted on top of the boiler with a gear drive to the axle. Unfortunately, the axles lacked springing, making them particularly hard on the road. They were rather slow and the single cylinder engine could be difficult to start. Models of these locomotives are discussed in another chapter. The next class, weighing 6tons, were built by Sharp Stewart and had conventional outside cylinders and valve gear (with direct drive), side tanks and circular ends for footplates. They proved better adapted to the conditions of the site and whilst the outside motion was easily accessible for maintenance, the close proximity to the ground resulted in excessive wear and constant adjustment, due to dirt and rubbish. They were Sharp Stewart's Works Number 2764 and Works Number 2765, delivered in 1878 as No 4 and No 5, and managed to last until 1925.

Faced with the difficulty of finding a locomotive suitable for the duties required, the Engineer to the Brewery, Mr Samuel Geoghegan, decided to design a unique class of engine that would overcome the objectionable features of the three previous classes, yet combine the best points of each. The locomotive design retained the four-coupled wheels of wrought iron disc pattern with outside bearings and counterbalanced cranks. Extra vertical coupling rods were then provided to link the rear wheels to the crankshaft of the engine, which was located above the boiler, again using overhung cranks. The four-coupled wheels were part of a separate and removable sprung bogie formed of eight steel leaves in four pairs, two on each side. One pair was on top of each pair of axle boxes, and the other pair under the bottom.

The ends of the springs were attached to front and back plates with a central pin so that, by removing both of these pins and the vertical coupling rods, the complete sprung bogie with wheels, axle and brake gear could be run out for maintenance. The weight of the engine and boiler was transferred to the spring frame through normal locomotive leaf springs attached above the axle boxes. The engine was

1. (Top) This side view of No 23 at Amberley Chalk Pits Museum, Sussex, illustrates the main points of these unusual locomotives. What cannot be seen is the tie bar between the axle bearings, which is obscured by the coupling rod. The spring frame however, is evident as are the main springs supporting the weight of the engine and boiler. The horizontal bars, above and below the axle boxes, are twin leaf springs tied to the locomotive main frames at vertical plates at each end. The crankshaft bearing can be seen in the hornblocks with the engine crosshead visible through the window in the frames. The stubby chimney is just visible at the top right hand end of the frames.

(Guinness 23 – Dave Pinniger)

2. (Above) This is a photograph of the preserved locomotive, No 20, in the Belfast Transport Museum at Cultra. This front view shows the high side frames required to support the engine; unlike the Stephen Lewin locomotives with the engine mounted on the boiler as per traction engine practice. The cylinder covers can be seen behind the squat chimney. Notice the drag hook held up by a chain to the handrail. They were attached as close to the centre of the locomotive and as low as possible to allow for the tight curves of the railway.

(Guinness 20 – Dave Pinniger)

located above the boiler with the cylinder block attached to the main frames. The crankshaft axle boxes were provided with horn-plates to allow vertical movement with a link to the spring frame, thereby maintaining the distance between the crankshaft and the rear axle. This link also allowed for a slight oscillation of the axle.

The boiler was of the Ramsbottom type with a working pressure of 180psi, a cylindrical firebox and 64 1½in diameter fire-tubes. The coupled wheels were 1ft 10in dia. with a wheelbase of 3ft and a loading of 3.6tons on the front axle and 3.8tons on the rear. The locomotive was capable of hauling 120tons on the level and 25tons on a gradient of 1 in 40. A special transporter wagon was arranged so that the small locomotive could be lifted and fitted inside the truck, allowing it to be used on the 5ft 3in gauge line for shunting. The locomotive wheels drove through friction to discs on countershafts, which in turn were geared 2:1 to each axle of the four-wheel haulage truck.

Initially, the system worked well and avoided having to use 5ft 3in gauge shunting locomotives but, as the loads increased, the cumbersome process of lifting the little locomotives in and out of the haulage trucks together with their limited power, eventually resulted in the purchase of steam locomotives for the larger gauge. Eventually, nineteen of these small locomotives were built, the first by the Avonside Engine Company of Bristol in 1882 and the remainder by W Spence & Son, Cork Street Foundry and Engineering Works, Dublin. The Avonside Engine Company locomotive was

Works Number 1337 of 1882 and entered service as No 6 on the brewery railway. It was withdrawn in 1936 and was scrapped in 1947. The remaining Spence locomotives were numbered 7 to 24. Fortunately, several of the locomotives have been preserved, including one at Amberley Chalk Pits Museum, complete with a haulage truck.

THE MODEL-WN208

As with the Stephen Lewin overtype locomotives, these engines were very small with a total length of only 12ft (or 192mm in 16mm scale). Even allowing for lifting the gauge from 22in to 24in, the scale would be just less than 18mm/ft. It was decided therefore to build the model to a scale of 22mm or just under 7/8ths scale. This would allow a decent size boiler of 2in diameter with sufficient width between the frames to accommodate the geared SVS engine. To provide an overall gearing of 8:1 from the 4:1 of the engine, the layout would require a separate countershaft to act as the output shaft to the top cranks. This area was covered anyway. It was never the intention to provide any springing and so the frames were arranged to include the axle bearings. All two-axle bearings and the upper crankshaft bearing could therefore be accurately drilled into the frames. All of the dummy spring frame parts would then be added to the frame to give the right effect. The side tanks, which also have to house the vertical coupling rods, were used to house the gas tank, gas regulator valve and the displacement lubricator. As with the full size locomotive, the drag hooks were kept as low as possible and are attached to the main frame towards the centre of the locomotive.

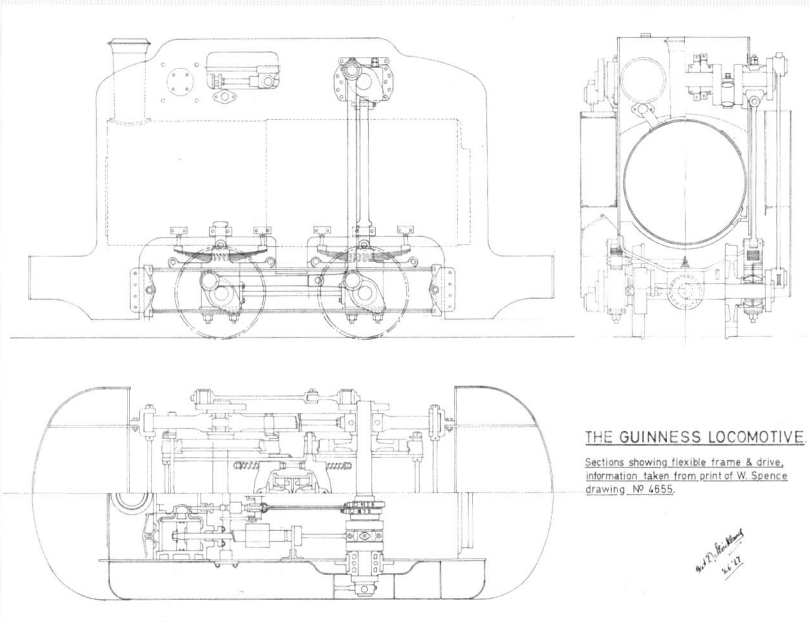

THE GUINNESS LOCOMOTIVE.
Sections showing flexible frame & drive, information taken from print of W. Spence drawing № 4655.

3. Guinness Locomotive drawn by Bill Strickland

This is an excellent drawing of the Guinness locomotive by the late Bill Strickland, which illustrates the arrangement of the independent spring frame. The frame is formed of eight steel leaves in four pairs, two on each side, one pair on top and another below the axle boxes. These spring pairs are located in this way, so that the spring frame complete with wheels, axles and brake gear can be run out for maintenance or repair by removing the pins and connecting rods and lifting the main body. The locomotive components most affected by dirt and rubbish are therefore easily accessible, whilst the engine and motion, located on top of the locomotive, are well clear of the ground.

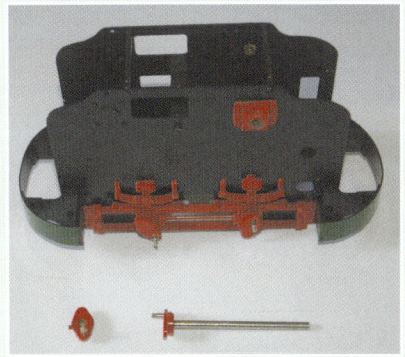

4. *(Left) The most important part of the locomotive model was the side frames, which have been drilled to take the axle boxes and the top output shaft bearings. This method ensures that the coupling rods and the axle/shaft centres correspond exactly to each other. The dummy sprung bogie detail was then added, purely for cosmetic reasons. At either end of the sprung frame can be seen the 6ba socket cap screws that hold the lower frame spacers. The rounded front was then attached to the end of the frames with suitable brackets and brought round to the plate outriggers at the end of the curve. Notice too, the unusually shaped balanced cranks on the axles and the top output shaft. The frames can be seen to include the axle bearings, whereas on the full size locomotive, the axle bearings were attached to the sprung bogie and the frames would be clear of them. Note the dummy tie bar between the axle boxes, which again in full size practice, was to maintain the distance between them.*

(WN208-01 – Mike Lax)

5. *(Above left) The small backhead of the model is even more cluttered than the full size locomotive, but even so all the required valves and gauges are there. The small valve, coinciding with the handrail in the photograph, is the water level and blow off control used to set the starting water level and also to blow off the steam pressure at the end of a run to prevent the possibility of producing a vacuum in the boiler. The side tanks for the Guinness model have to include a 'cut-out' to allow for the vertical coupling rods. On the model, the left hand tank covers the gas tank, whereas the right tank houses the displacement lubricator.*

(WN208-06 – Mike Lax)

6. *(Above right) This left hand side view of the finished locomotive shows the location of the gas tank and the gas regulator valve, with the vertical coupling rod running between them. The complicated and unique springing arrangement (albeit non-working) on the model, is easily seen in this photograph. For the full size motive power, the object was to provide a separate sprung frame that could be removed easily from the main body of the locomotive. A tie bar maintained the distance between the driven axle and the crankshaft of the engine.*

(WN208-07 – Mike Lax)

7. *The finished locomotive is here viewed in the steaming bay of its new home on Dave Pinniger's Ambledown Valley Railway. The driver figure is a 7/8th scale engine driver from Rob Bennett. Notice the unusual boiler front detail and the 'W. Spence' works plate on the front of the boiler. Dave has obviously decided to dispense with the engine covers.*

(WN208-09 – Dave Pinniger)

8. *The locomotive is seen at rest in the station area of Bishops Amble and being fussed over by two 7/8th scale Rob Bennett figures. The detail of the sprung bogie is well illustrated in this photograph, including the tie bar between the axle boxes. The gas tank filler and regulator valve can be seen above the left hand tank. Notice how the figure stands on a footplate inside the frames, although several photographs of the full size locomotives in operation show this area of the footplate planked over.*

(WN208-10 – Dave Pinniger)

REFERENCES:

• The Locomotive Magazine No 72 Vol VII April 1902 page 62. Article titled Narrow Gauge Locomotives for Shunting at a Brewery.

• Narrow Gauge and Industrial Railway Modelling Review No's 60 & 61. The first magazine has a very detailed article using archive material courtesy of Engineering Magazine. The second magazine includes an article by Peter Foley titled Guinness Brewery Portfolio.

• Industrial Railway Record No 22, December 1968. Article by Paul Ellison titled Guinness Brewery Tramways.

• The John Knowles & Co. (Wooden Box) Ltd 18in Gauge System

WN250 Jack and WN260 Gwen

The company of John Knowles & Co. (Wooden Box) Ltd. operated an 18in gauge tramway as part of their Mount Pleasant Works clay processing plant near Woodville in Leicestershire. John Knowles was a railway engineer and in the course of his work came across deposits of aluminous fireclay. He decided in 1849 to form a company to exploit these deposits for the manufacture of firebricks. Further expansion of the site uncovered seams of surface clays that were particularly suited to the production of high-grade stoneware pipes, in demand due the advancement of sanitary engineering. By 1870 there were two mills known as the brick mill and the pipe mill and by 1880 twenty kilns and a boiler house had been added. The company continued to expand, so that by the centenary of the works, the site covered seventeen acres and included thirty-three round kilns and three rectangular ones along with two tunnel kilns. With new materials replacing clay pipes, the company closed down this side of the business in 1965, followed by the closure of the railways and eventually, the firm was taken over in 1969. Incidentally, the inclusion of Wooden Box in the company name, referred to the location of the premises, which were a short distance from Woodville Crossroads, where there was a wooden sentry box from the time when road tolls were levied.

The most interesting part of the workings, as far as this chapter is concerned, revolves around the installation of an 18in narrow gauge railway for use around the Mount Pleasant Works. During the year 1897, a decision was taken to order a steam locomotive. The order was given to the Hunslet Engine Company and the locomotive was delivered on 22nd November 1898 as Hunslet Works Number 684 and it bore the name Jack. A works photograph of Jack is reproduced courtesy of the Hunslet Engine Company. The basic design used an 0-4-0 wheel arrangement with outside cylinders and frames having a wheelbase of 3ft and wheel dia. 1ft 6in. Outside Walschaerts valve gear was fitted and in order to keep the centre of gravity of the engine low, the feed water was stored in a well tank located between the frames at the front of the locomotive. This arrangement prevented the cylinders from having the inlet and exhaust pipes inside the frames. Instead, these pipes were fed into the top of the valve chest and cylinder, which required the smokebox to be wider at the base to cover the pipes – an arrangement that resulted in the exaggerated shape of the smokebox.

Several modifications were made to Jack during its long working life, including the addition of an extra sand dome on top of the boiler, as in the 'Waril' class. The firebox mounted Salter safety valves were changed to a pair of dome mounted Ross pop units. The whistle type and location were changed to the dome. In later years, the cab gained a rear backsheet and the smokebox-mounted displacement lubricators were removed and replaced by a mechanical

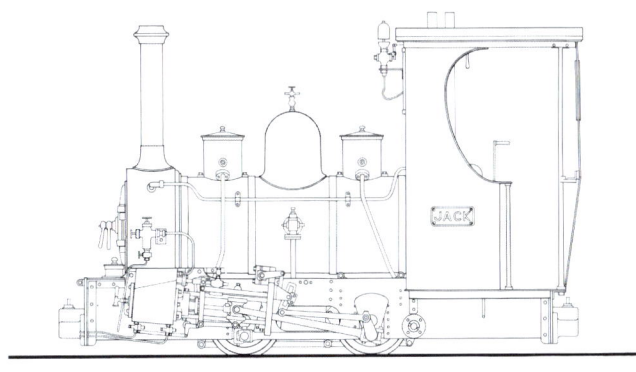

JACK

Hunslet Engine Co Ltd 684 of 1898

feet 0 1 2 3 4 5

drawing by Roger West

9. (Above) Works photograph of the Hunslet Engine Company locomotive Jack, wn684 of 1898.

(HE684 – Hunslet Engine Company)

12. (Left) A side elevation of Jack, Hunslet Engine Co. Ltd. wn684 of 1898 reproduced by kind permission of Roger West and The Industrial Railway Society.

(Drawing by Roger West)

13. (Below left) Front and rear end elevation of Jack reproduced by kind permission of Roger West and The Industrial Railway Society.

(Drawing by Roger West)

14. (Below right) A view of the 7/8ths scale Jack, WN250, taken when the model was still in the brass.

(WN250-1 – Author)

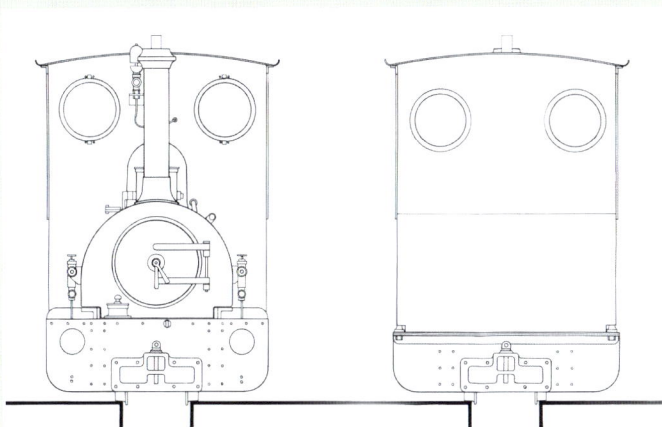

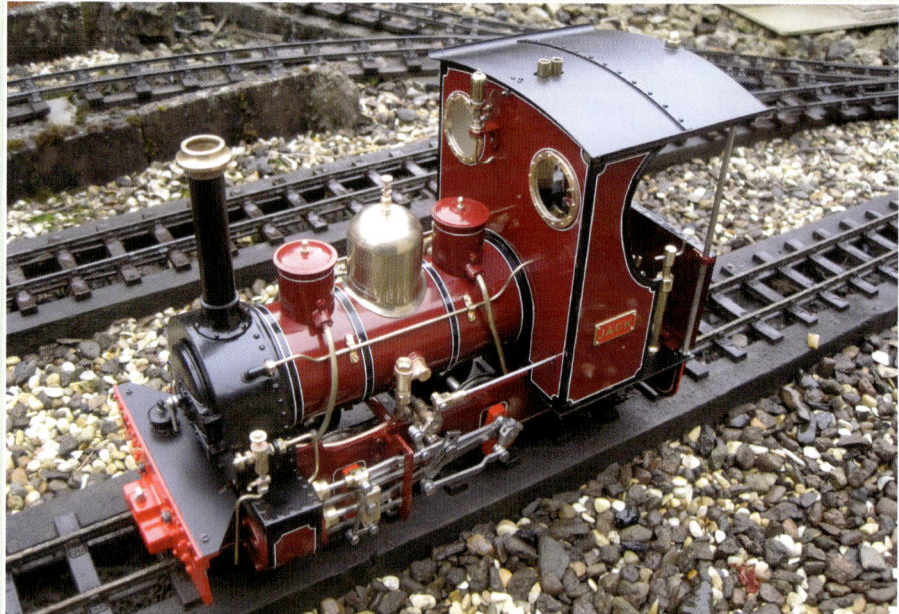

15. *(Top left) The finished model based on the Hunslet Engine Co. Ltd. locomotive Works Number 684 of 1898 and supplied to John Knowles (Wooden Box) Ltd. Since the locomotive is preserved at the Leeds City Industrial Museum at Armley Mills, the opportunity was taken to base the model in its present condition with the exception of the cab rear panel. To improve access to the boiler fittings, the original style of bottom half cab rear sheet was installed. This arrangement was changed to a full rear cab sheet on the prototype Jack sometime between 1946 and 1951. The excellent finish and lining on the model are a tribute to the work of Mike Lax and really make this one of the most attractive model locomotives in this book.*
(WN250-3 – Author)

16. *(Left) Notice the correct pin coupling block and the water filler cap in front of the smokebox, which actually covers the Goodall type water filler. The check valve on the left hand side of the boiler has had to be offset to clear the expansion link pivot, a point to be noted for any future model of the same engine.*
(WN250-4 – Author)

17. *(Below left) The Roundhouse Engineering Walschaerts valve gear and cylinders. The axles and wheels are also from Roundhouse, but the outside cranks were specially made for this model and are based on the cranks shown on the works drawing of the 'Eva' class. The second of the John Knowles narrow gauge locomotives left the Hunslet Engine Company works on the 12th July 1920, and was destined to perform the bulk of the work on the narrow gauge railway for the next thirty eight years, with Jack relegated to the position of spare locomotive. Gwen was built as a coal fired version of the Hunslet 'Waril' class, twelve of which had been supplied previously between 1915 and 1917 to the Deptford Special Reserve Depot. Details of the 'Waril' class are discussed in the next section.*
(WN250-6 – Author)

lubricator. Jack remained at the works until 1958 to be then given to the City of Leeds Museum from where it was eventually moved to the Leeds Industrial Museum at Armley Mills in March 1980. Jack was restored to full working order in 1984 and is occasionally steamed on special steam days.

Before starting this model, a copy of the excellent book Tramways and Railways of John Knowles (Wooden Box) Ltd, co authored by Roy Etherington and Roger West, was obtained from Andrew Neale. This allowed the locomotive to be built based on the drawing of Jack by Roger West but adapted to use the Roundhouse 'Billy' Walschaerts valve gear. It was built to a scale of 7/8th/ft for operation on 32mm or 45mm gauge track. The side elevation and front and rear end-elevations drawing is reproduced by kind permission of Roger West and The Industrial Railway Society. Roundhouse cylinders, wheels and axles were fitted to the purpose built 246mm long by 39mm deep 2mm steel frames with specially made outside cranks and crossheads. The boiler was a fairly standard 2in diameter by 6in long plain centre flue type with the steam pickup in the centre dome and blind bushes to locate the dummy sand domes. Without side tanks or a full cab the gas tank had to be the Sentinel type located between the frames. With

the locomotive preserved at Armley Mills, a visit was arranged and photographs taken, a rare addition to the process of building the model. These photographs allowed the model to be built to the existing appearance of the full size locomotive, including the painting and lining, which was carried out by Mike Lax. The end result is shown and must be one of the prettiest models in the book and one, which despite being 7/8th scale, does not appear to be oversize on a 16mm garden railway.

Gwen is represented by WN260, built after WN258 Esme, and was virtually identical but has had the addition of a full cab rear sheet as fitted to the full size locomotive. The top half of the rear cab sheet was made removable for ease of access and the loco is normally run in this condition. It was assumed that Gwen was fitted with the riveted smokebox as fitted to the 'Waril' class, although all of the photographs of Gwen show the simpler welded type. Both Jack and Gwen were fitted with a welded front smokebox after 1946. Gwen was finished in Victorian maroon, edged in black and fully lined.

18. Works photograph of Deptford Special Reserve Depot 0-4-0 WT No 3, Hunslet Engine Company No 1198 of 1915 as built.

(HE 1198a – Hunslet Engine Company)

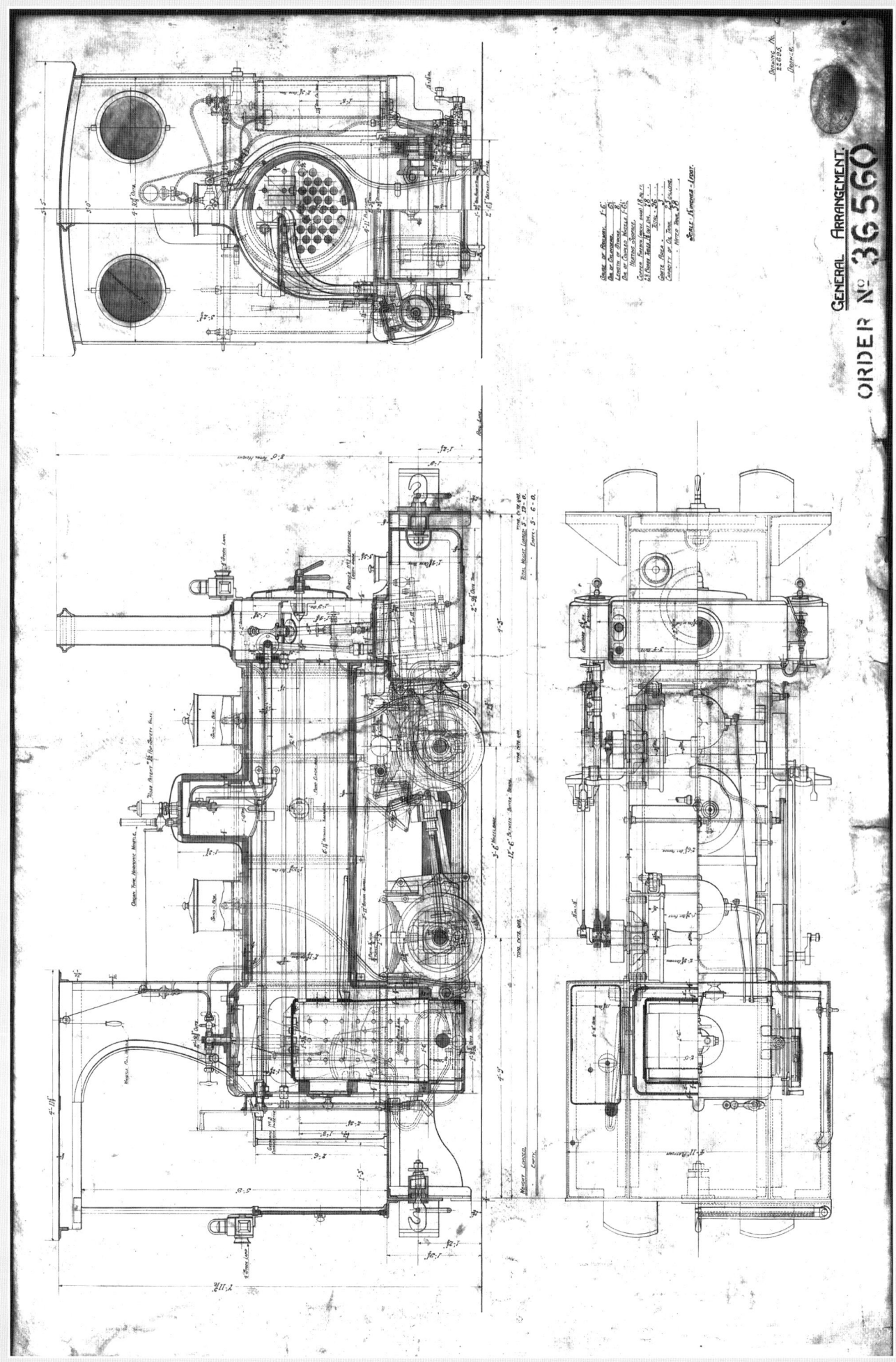

GENERAL ARRANGEMENT

ORDER N° 36560

19. (Opposite) The manufacturer's general arrangement drawing of the Hunslet 'Waril' class 0-4-0WT design supplied for use in the Deptford Special Reserve Depot. Acknowledge: Hunslet Engine Company.

(HE22695 General arrangement drawing – Hunslet Engine Company)

20. (Above left) A left hand side view of Gwen, based on the John Knowles coal fired Hunslet 'Waril' class Works Number 1404 of 1920. The model was built to the works drawing, which showed the sand pipes running to the front and rear of the driving wheels. All of the photographs of Gwen show these pipes were run to the insides of the driving wheels. The pipe leading from the check valve runs to the Goodall valve, located under the dummy water filler on the front footplate. The two pipes just visible below the cab floor are the drainpipes from

the boiler gauge glass and the blow-off/water.

(WN260-2 – Author)

21. (Above right) Of interest is the forward/reverse rod on the right hand side. This is the same as in the full size locomotive rather than the more usual Roundhouse left hand side location. The spectacle plate windows can be opened and, as with the sand boxes and hand brake lower mechanisms, these were supplied by Brian Wilson from Australia who is author of the book Steam Trains in Your Garden. These castings are of very fine quality and were used on both Gwen and Esme. An interesting point is that the smokebox of Gwen, seen in the photographs in both the reference books, show it as having a welded front rather than the riveted type fitted to the Deptford locomotives and Jack (later replaced with a welded front).

(WN260-8 – Author)

THE DEPTFORD SYSTEM AND THE SAND HUTTON 18IN GAUGE RAILWAYS WN258 ESME

Following on from the 7/8th scale Jack, WN258 was based on the 'Waril' class locomotives built by the Hunslet Engine Company for the 18in gauge Royal Army Corps Depot at Deptford. Twelve locomotives were supplied in three batches, starting with No's1 to 3, Hunslet Nos 1196 to 1198 in 1915, No's 4 to 8 Hunslet No's 1207-1211 of 1916 and the final batch No's 912 Hunslet No's1288 to 1291 of 1917. The design of these locomotives was basically an enlargement of the earlier Hunslet engine Jack described previously (No 684 of 1898). The design continued with the 0-4-0 wheel-arrangement on a wheelbase of 3ft 6in, a forward slung 56 gallon well tank and outside Walschaerts valve gear. The outside fly-cranks were counterbalanced and complimented by inside wheels of 1ft 6in diameter. The boiler was set at a relatively high centre of 3ft 5 ¼ in and was oil fired. A works photograph of No 3, Hunslet 1198 of 1915 and the General Arrangement drawing of the 'Waril' class is shown.

With the cessation of hostilities in November 1918, the depot was slowly run down and in 1926 the site was leased out to Convoys Ltd who continued to use the railway for several years, before change of use and road transport made the little railway obsolete. Previous to this, three of the locomotives No's 10 to 12 and 75 wagons had been sold to the Sand Hutton Light Railway in 1921, later to be joined in 1927 by No 4, another of the Deptford engines. Unlike the other locomotives, No 10 was given the distinction of the name Esme, after the second wife of Sir Robert J M Walker, the fourth Baronet of Sand Hutton in Yorkshire. The four locomotives were converted to coal firing for the remainder of their lives on the Sand Hutton Railway. The railway made a small profit up until 1929 but closure of the local brickworks, road transport and the death of Sir Robert in 1930 resulted in the inevitable closure of the line in 1932.

WN 258 is based on Esme, Hunslet 1289 of 1917 and is very similar to the previous models of Jack and Gwen. It is however not quite as attractive, due to the absence of any lining as was the case with Sand Hutton Railway locomotives. As pointed out previously, Esme was not fitted with a full rear cab sheet, which in any case is a far more practical arrangement in model form.

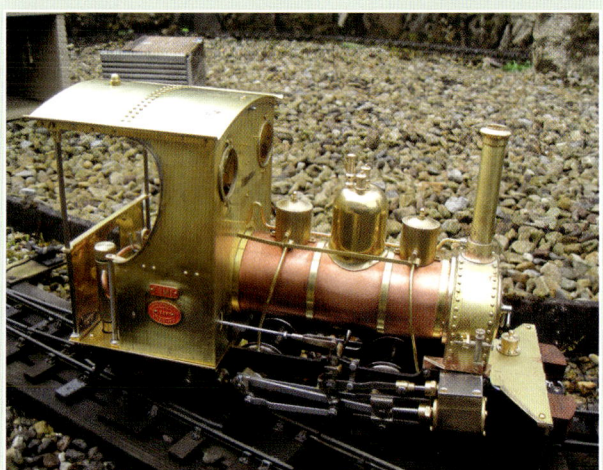

22. (Top left) This is an interesting photograph of the footplate of the 'Waril' class model Esme during construction. Note how the gas tank is located between the frames under the cab with the gas filler column angled back-over to coincide with the sliding door opening in the rear cab sheet. Despite the size of the 7/8th scale cab, the pipework behind the boiler back head is still congested. **WN258-5. Author)**

23. (Middle left) In the brass before stripping down for painting. The works plate is inside the cab and accounts for the two rivets sticking out of the cab front sheet. They will be cut and peened over after painting and then touched up. Similarly the dummy displacement lubricators will have the pipes to the valve chest added, which means they need only be bent once. As with Jack the dummy water filler on the front footplate gives access to the Goodall water filler. **(WN258-7 – Author)**

24. (Inset) This is the model of the 'Waril' class locomotive Esme, Hunslet Engine Company wn1289 of 1917, finished in the colours of the Sand Hutton Light Railway. **(WN258-10 – Mike Lax)**

25. (Below left) With a full head of steam and on its first outing, Esme is seen operating on Chris Haley's 45mm gauge garden railway of at Coupland in North Northumberland. For a 7/8th scale 18in gauge locomotive it should be on 32mm track but where possible it is always a good idea to provide the dual gauge facility. **(WN258-12 – Chris Haley)**

REFERENCES:

• Tramways and Railways of John Knowles (Wooden Box) Ltd. by Roy Etherington and Roger West.
• 18 inch Gauge Steam Railways by Mark Smithers.

A DE WINTON IN 7/8TH SCALE WN221

Following the issue of the book De Winton of Caernarfon by Alfred and David Fisher and Dr Gwnfor Pierce Jones, it was decided to build a De Winton model but this time in 7/8th scale. This wonderful book supplied all the information that anyone could require on the De Winton products, with suitable illustrations of the method of construction and a drawing of Chaloner. From this information, it was possible to build a model that would more accurately follow the method used on the full size locomotives as built by De Winton.

The tried and tested arrangement of a geared SVS engine, along with the now more to scale ceramic burner SD1 boiler and gas tank in the rear bunker, was retained. However, the simpler full plate frame with inserted axle bushes of previous locomotives was replaced by a thicker 1/8in by 5/8in bar frame with the axle boxes located under the frame. The full size locomotive used semi-circular brass bearings which were housed in line shafting type pillow blocks of cast iron, bolted to angle iron on the bottom edge of the frame. With the

model, a fabricated bearing, resembling this arrangement, was bolted to the inside of the substantial frame. This allowed for a more accurate method of setting and aligning the bearing centres, which in practice proved to be the case. Dummy bolts were then added to the bearing block to simulate the full size item. A particular feature of the De Winton frame is the curved 'J' shaped angle attaching the frame sides to the buffer beam and this has been represented on the model. However, in reality, a heavy brass spacer behind the slate catcher front/rear plates aligns the frames. The 'J' angle irons are silver soldered to this plate.

The arrangement of the boiler, SVS engine and gas tank basically adopted previous practice with the boiler now dropped through the side frames, the depth limited by the firetube of the burner clearing the rear axle. With the frame spacing set at the diameter of the boiler, there was adequate room to provide a dual gauge facility for 32/45mm. Building WN221 in keeping with full size practice, was certainly more difficult but the extra time and complication is more than justified by the end result.

26. (Left) This photograph illustrates a different approach to the construction of a De Winton locomotive. The original design used a simple plate frame with brass axle bushes inserted, whereas this model uses a 1/8in by 5/8in bar frame with the axle boxes mounted underneath as per the prototype. However, these fabricated axle boxes are attached behind the frame, instead of bolted to an angle plate attached to the bottom of the frame. Notice the dummy bolt heads on the axle boxes. The boiler is lowered through the frame as far as possible before the ceramic burner comes in contact with the rear axle. The 'J' angle irons, at each end of the frames, are a particular feature of the De Winton chassis but apart from reinforcing the lower end of the slate catcher, they are for decoration only, the rigidity of the frame coming from a heavy inside spacer.
(WN221-2 – Author)

27. (Right) Notice how the 7/8th scale figure is looking over the top of the boiler, as would be the case with the full size locomotive. Dummy wooden buffers are still to add along with the works and nameplates.
(WN221-10 – Author)

29. (Above left) The attraction of the small 18in gauge locomotives is captured here with this photograph of Serapis in steam on Mike Lax's garden railway. Note the unusual feature of the valance connecting the wing tanks to the smokebox. The brass pipe at the front of the roof is the imitation safety valve cover, whereas the real safety valve is in the polished brass boiler dome. The side tanks have removable top covers with the left hand tank dummy filler cap providing access to the Goodall water valve. The access to the right hand side tank was provided as a second option for the location of the radio control battery.
(WN275-8-1 – Serapis-PA)

30. (Above right) This opposite rear side view shows the large cab area and the rear bunker housing the gas tank and receiver batteries. The small disc handle valve is for the water level and blow off facility. More of the dummy safety valve cover can be seen along with the insulating washer between the smokebox and the front valance.
(WN275-9 – Serapis-PA)

28. This is the engraving of Serapis probably originated from The Engineer in 1885 and appeared in the Bagnall catalogue Number 13 of 1895. It has since appeared in several publications and is the only representation of these interesting locomotives.

WN275 THE BAGNALL LOCOMOTIVE SERAPIS

In the early days of model locomotive construction, it was quite normal for there to be little information available, but gradually the situation has changed with many models now built using archive drawings. Serapis has however remained elusive, no photographs or drawings, just an engraving – probably taken from The Engineer for the 6th March 1885 and reproduced in later publications. Even Mark Smither's book gives little information, other than the cylinder size and of course the usual engraving. There was also the problem of a suitable commercial chassis, due the inside valve gear. With the advent of the Roundhouse Karen chassis this situation changed. Here was an outside-framed 0-4-2 chassis with inside valve gear, albeit with slightly inclined cylinders and inside valve chest. Serapis had outside valve chests on top of the cylinders, driven by a rocking arm shaft from the inside

Stephenson link motion. The engraving showed a very neat 18in gauge locomotive with wing side tanks and a large footplate area, which included a rear bunker. This area was covered from the elements by a simple roof mounted on eight pillars. The five locomotives were built by W G Bagnall, Works Numbers 710 to 714 in 1885 with all locomotives being named from Egyptian mythology. Originally ordered in 1885 for the ill-fated Saukin-Berber Railway, they were delivered to the Royal Arsenal at Woolwich where they found useful work, lasting until the end of the First World War – that is with the exception of Serapis, which was scrapped in 1912.

From a modelling point of view the prototype offered space for the gas tank in the rear bunker, a useful area between the frames for the radio control and with outside frames the facility for dual gauge. An unusual feature is the front valance connecting the side tanks to the smokebox. To prevent excessive transfer of heat to the wing tanks, the smokebox is actually separate with an insulating disc inserted between. Several locomotives operating at the Woolwich Arsenal had their original open footplates fitted with cabs and therefore the liberty was taken to add a cab front sheet to the model. The end result is shown in the photographs and illustrates how attractive these 18in gauge locomotives can be in 7/8th scale.

REFERENCES:
- Bagnalls of Stafford – by Alan C Baker and T D Allen Civil.
- 18 inch Gauge Steam Railways by Mark Smithers.
- Narrow Gauge by the Sudanese Red Sea Coast by Henry Gunston.

WN233-EATON RAILWAY
LOCOMOTIVE URSULA

And finally a model based on the 15in gauge locomotive Ursula built to the slightly larger scale of 1in/ft.

The Eaton Railway was one of a small number of 15in gauge railways and was built for the 1st Duke of Westminster by Sir Arthur Percival Heywood. Previously Sir Arthur had demonstrated his 15in gauge railway at Duffield Bank to the Dukes nephew, the Hon. Cecil Parker and could see that a railway at Eaton Park was a perfect opportunity for a practical experiment

with the 15in gauge. Eaton Hall, built 1870 to 1890, was the last of the great ducal palaces with over 190 rooms and required up to 2000 tons of fuel and 3000 tons of stores all brought in by horse and cart from Great Western Railway goods yard at Balderton station some three miles away. The new railway proved to be an immediate success by providing an efficient haulage service from Balderton station to the estate for coal and supplies using one 0-4-0 locomotive called Katie.

In addition the railway gave a pleasant ride for visiting dignitaries including the Royal Family and for local schoolchildren with parties of 50 to 80 passengers not uncommon, the record number being 375 persons on 3rd April 1906. The engine driver, Harry Wilde recorded the names of notable passengers on the railway, which included Sir Winston Churchill, King Edward VII and HRH Albert Edward, Prince of Wales. On a trial run to test the maximum capacity of the engine a gross load of just over 22 tons was hauled at an average speed of 10mph. Unfortunately Katie did have a problem with adhesion on slippery track and therefore a further steam locomotive called Shelagh was supplied in 1904 and then a third locomotive Ursula in 1916. These two engines were of 0-6-0 wheel arrangement and despite the small gauge, Shelagh on trials proved capable of hauling 33 ½ tons from Balderton to Eaton in 22 minutes. In 1922 a 20hp Motor Rail Simplex petrol locomotive joined the railway by

31. This is a photograph of the replica of Ursula taken by Ian Lenthall on the open day at the Eaton Railway, Chester, on the 4th August 2007. This locomotive is part of the Heywood collection at the Perrygrove Railway in the Forest of Dean. To compliment the holly green livery and superb lining, and the black and gold capitals for the Eaton Railway, the locomotives carried a copious amount of polished brass including edging to the side tanks and spectacle plate.

(Ian Lenthall)

32. (Left) This second photograph shows the side view of Ursula hauling passengers on the same day. Notice the complicated Heywood valve gear designed to do without the expansion link and die block of conventional valve gear. The restored railway at Eaton Hall is 1½ miles long and consists of a large loop with a spur leading to the engine shed.

(Ian Lenthall)

33. (Right) The model based on the Eaton Railway locomotive Ursula built by Sir Arthur Percival Heywood at his Duffield Bank workshops and supplied to the railway in 1916. Notice how the rear of the boiler is finished with an outside ring with rivets. This ring imitates the flanged rear boilerplate of the full size locomotive. Three rivets have been replaced by 8ba screws, used to retain the polished brass ring (part ring on the model), in front of the spectacle plate. The rear handrails are of stainless steel and the rear plate has a convenient cut-out for access to the gas jet. The gas valve can be seen on the far side with the gas tank located in the left hand side tank. On the right hand side can be seen the displacement lubricator and a Goodall type water filler is located under the dummy water tank filler. The steam regulator is fitted to the backhead and a banjo union alongside feeds to a water level/blow off valve fixed to the right hand side footplate, the lever of the valve just visible behind the sideplate. Notice how the ½in steam pressure gauge is flange mounted on the spectacle plate.

(WN233-2 – Author)

34. (Below right) These locomotives carried a large amount of polished brass that has been reproduced on the model. Whereas many narrow gauge locomotives had a polished dome these engines included polished edging to the side tanks and spectacle plate. This feature is reproduced on the model by slitting 3/32in brass tube using a 1/32in slitting saw mounted in the milling machine with the brass tube fed through a special jig. The spectacle plate is held in place by the polished brass ring around the boiler, which is bolted through to the rear boiler ring. This view also illustrates the complicated nature of the Heywood valve gear reproduced in dummy format on the model.

(WN233-3 – Author)

which time Katie had been sold on to another railway. In 1942 the remaining steam engines were scrapped and by 1946 the Eaton Estate had been taken over on a twelve-year lease by the War Department who had no use for this quaint little railway and in 1947 it was taken up and sold.

However this was not the end of the story for in 1996 the opportunity arose to purchase a very accurate replica of the 15in gauge locomotive Katie built for the original railway in 1896. The present Duke acquired one of the four replicas and arranged for the construction of a track for Katie within the Eaton Park Estate which partly followed the original track and gave a track length of 1.5 miles consisting of a large loop and spur to the engine shed. The Estate workshops were given the task of restoring the original wagons and carriages. The track was completed in 2000 and the first open day followed in 2004.

WN233 was based on the third locomotive

35. *(Left) Underside view showing the location of the hidden SVS oscillating engine. The cramped nature of the frames meant that the boxer style of engine had to be used and was mounted to close to the front axle to permit a dual gauge facility. Usually this engine is mounted above the axle and the spur gear can be turned to permit the dual gauge facility.*

(WN233-6 – Author)

36. *(Above) Finally Ursula hauling a correct set of Eaton Railway passenger stock supplied by Ian Lenthall on the 45mm track of Malcolm Foreman at Longhoughton.*

(WN233-6 – Author)

Ursula. This model was built to a scale of 1in to 1ft for operation on 45mm gauge track. It was originally intended for a track that was built on a slope which required continual attention using radio control. Operation of geared locomotives however gave a much more relaxed run. Ursula was therefore fitted with a hidden geared engine and dummy outside cylinders and valve gear. Another advantage of the hidden geared engine drive was that the valve gear had only to look like the working version on the full size locomotive. Unfortunately this valve gear was of a unique design adopted by Sir Arthur Heywood using a linear linkage rather than the slide and die block assembly to operate the valve gear. The model was finished in holly green lined out in red and white with polished brass dome and brass edging. The underside was painted in the best imitation of the full size replica along with the red front to the buffer beams.

REFERENCE:
- The Eaton Railway for The Duke of Westminster, Eaton Estate Office, Chester.

37. (Above) Kathleen is seen here working at the quarry.

(IRS008778 Photograph kindly supplied by the Industrial Railway Society)

38. (Right) The completed model painted in Victorian Maroon and beautifully lined by Matt Acton of Berry Hill Works. Notice in this photograph how the running board and valance effectively hide the outside valve chest. The displacement lubricator can be seen at the rear of the cab and is easily accessible.

(WN283-3 Kathleen – Matt Acton)

39. (Below right) This photograph illustrates the arrangement of the boiler fittings in the open cab. There is easy access to the manually operated steam regulator located on the boiler back plate and the water gauge glass is readily visible. The frame mounted gas tank can be seen attached to the far side frame on the enclosed side. The firebox end of the boiler shows the external flange which in the model is a silver soldered brass ring with rivets.

(WN283-6 Kathleen – Matt Acton)

WN283 The Vulcan Foundry Locomotive Kathleen

When looking through the book, De Winton of Caernarfon, there was a photograph on page 185 of the 2ft gauge Spooner designed locomotive Kelso built by the Vulcan Foundry of Newton le Willows, works number 832 of 1878. A further photograph appears on page 255 reproduced from the works photograph but this may be works number 810 of 1887 with the name Kelso added, thereby saving the cost of another works photograph. The third member of the trio was Kathleen, works number 805 of 1876, supplied to the Alexandra Slate Quarry. All three locomotives had inside frames with inside valve gear and an open cab with a front spectacle plate only. Enquiries to Andrew Neale produced a simple side elevation of Kelso and a photograph of Kathleen.

It was decided to build the locomotive using a Roundhouse Millie chassis, which by definition, is a compromise between accuracy to the prototype against the convenience and cost of a complete ready to run chassis. Looking at the photographs, the locomotive Kathleen had several advantages over Kelso, in that it was fitted with attractive running boards curved at the front in a similar manner to that of the Spooner designed Single and Double Fairlie. The valance, attached to the running boards of Kathleen, effectively hides the valve chest of the Roundhouse cylinders and the running boards themselves hide the slip eccentric valve rod. In addition, access on one side only of the footplate rather than the rear access of Kelso provides a suitable location for the gas tank which can be mounted to the frames on the enclosed side. One of the features of these locomotives was the marine type boiler with an external bolted flange for the rear tube plate. This is represented on the model by adding a brass ring to the end of the barrel with suitable rivets. The model was built for manual operation only and this is particularly suitable to the smooth running characteristics of the Roundhouse basic chassis.

REFERENCE:
- De Winton of Caernarfon by Alfred Fisher, David Fisher and Dr Gwynfor Pierce Jones.

WN285 Manning Wardle locomotive ARQUEBUS in 7/8 scale.

The Royal Arsenal at Woolwich, located adjacent to the river Thames, possessed one of the most complete systems of internal railways in the country. It existed to provide an efficient means of transport between workshops, storehouses, magazines and depots as well as providing a passenger service for employees. Originally a primitive horse operated tramway, it was in 1866 that orders were given to construct an 18in gauge railway, the small gauge being necessary to provide access to severely restricted areas and buildings. By 1898 the Royal Arsenal Railway was said to consist of 30 miles of 18in gauge and 25 miles of mixed standard and narrow gauge permanent way. At the end of the First World War the site extended to 1300 acres with over 60 18in gauge locomotives but at the end of hostilities it was realised that there was little need of the narrow gauge. At the end of 1922 only ten locomotives had been retained.

1. Works photograph of Arquebus Manning Wardle works number 1030 of 1889, the last 18in gauge locomotive supplied to the Woolwich Arsenal by this manufacturer.

(Andrew Neale collection)

The first narrow gauge steam locomotive for the railway was built and supplied by Manning Wardle in 1871 with the official opening of the railway in 1873. It was makers number 353 Lord Raglan and remained in use at Woolwich until shortly after the outbreak of World War One. It proved to be so successful that a further twelve locomotives using the same leading dimensions were supplied by Manning Wardle along with six engines for the Chatham Dockyard. Although they used the same leading dimensions, the design was developed over the years. Gone was the ungainly double buffer beams of Lord Raglan to be replaced by single iron clad curvaceous oak beams and the simple columnar handbrake was replaced by bevel gearing to provide a horizontal hand wheel drive. There was even a difference in frame design between the two military sites. The Woolwich locomotives were provided with the lower edges of the main frames tapered upwards towards the ends, whereas the Chatham locomotives maintained parallel frames. However, it is the last of the Woolwich locomotives that is the subject of WN285.

WN285 was based on Arquebus , the last of the Manning Wardle Woolwich locomotives supplied for the 18in gauge railway. It was works number 1130 of 1889 and differed in several minor ways from previous locomotives. The most notable feature is the simpler canopy that dispensed with the decorative edges of previous locomotives and the addition of front and rear spectacle plates and cab side panels. The front spectacle plate has reinforcing strips bent over on to the saddle tank and the sand boxes were cylindrical. The cab footplate has been dropped, providing easier access without the need for a cab step.

As with Serapis, the model was built on the Roundhouse Engineering Karen chassis but in this case the frames were cut off behind the rear axle and then extended to the buffer beam to give the correct 0-4-0 wheel arrangement. Attaching this frame has to be accomplished without interfering with the dual gauge facility, the reason being that when the wheels are set for 45mm there is very little clearance between the wheels and the frame. Another very important point with this type of locomotive is the small diameter of the boiler at 1ft 9in and the raised round top firebox. Fortunately,

2. Front ¾ view of the model of Arquebus showing the reinforcing bars on the front spectacle plate. The cab side plates conveniently hide the two radio control servos located on either side with the steam regulator servo rod connected to the steam valve just visible. Notice the unusual side hinged smoke box door held by two handles and the lowered centre to the buffer beam providing access to the smoke box. Even more noticeable is the excellent lining by Matt Acton.

(WN285-14 Matt Acton)

3. (Top left) Rear side view of Arquebus showing the cab detail. The gas tank can be seen between the frames with the hole in the cab rear sheet for access to the gas filler valve. The handrail on the rear cab sheet should be inside the cab. The wooden buffer beam is spring loaded along with the handmade swivelling hook. Sticking out precariously above the roof is the dummy Becks patent whistle.

(WN285-15 Matt Acton)

4. (Left) Three 7/8 scale 18in gauge locomotives standing on the rebuilt frames of the full size Avonside Engine Company Woolwich (1748 of 1916) at Crossness Pumping Station on 21-12-2014. They are WN250 Jack, WN285 Arquebus (unlined) and WN267 Woolwich.

(Ian Bull)

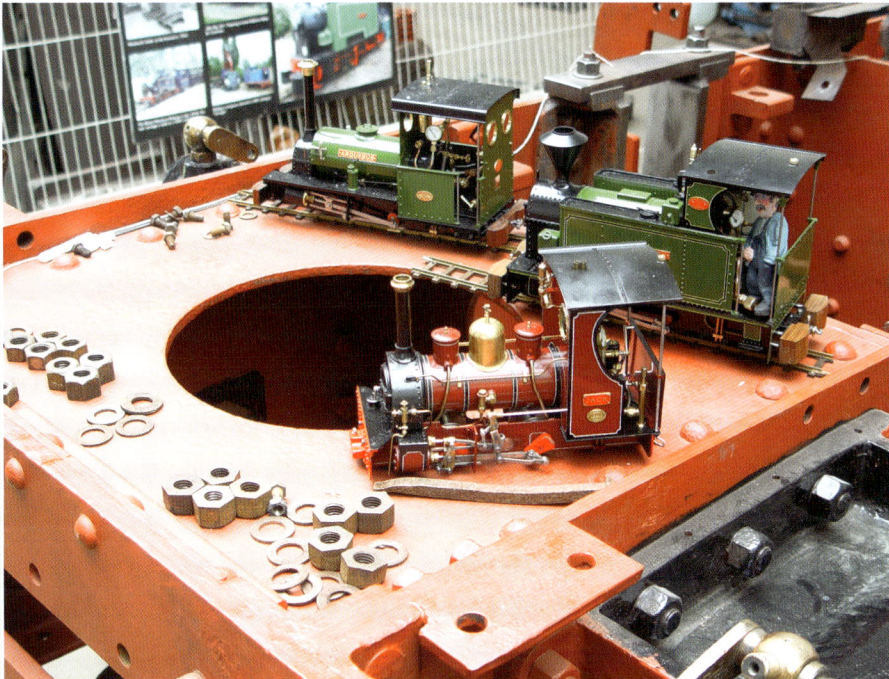

a standard 2in diameter boiler can be fitted by lifting the boiler up into the saddle tank. This boiler extends beyond the saddle tank to give a suitable representation of the raised firebox. On the other hand, none of these locomotives were fitted with a rear bunker which along with the saddle tank, leaves virtually no room in which to locate the radio control. The area between the rear frames is largely taken up by the gas tank leaving a small gap between the gas tank and the rear axle/wheels. The servos are located on the cab floor either side of the boiler.

All of these 18in gauge locomotives would make excellent models but Arquebus, with its simpler canopy and front and rear spectacle plates, has to be the most attractive as illustrated by the photographs.

REFERENCES:
- 18 Inch Gauge Steam Railways by Mark Smithers.
- Narrow Gauge Railways-Two Feet and Under by Leslie S. Roberts.
- Royal Arsenal Railway at Woolwich by B.R. Clarke & C.C. Vietch

INDUSTRIAL LOCOMOTIVES

It is difficult to specify any narrow gauge locomotive as purely industrial, since many of these engines would eventually do some passenger carrying, whilst those that lasted into the preservation era would become 100% passenger hauling locomotives. A good example of this progression is the Ffestiniog Railway, originally built to transport slate from the mines down to Porthmadog. The railway eventually developed to include passenger carrying and now, as a premier preservation line, is operated solely for the purpose of carrying tourists. So here are examples of those locomotives that served the quarries, mines and major civil engineering projects and, with the exception of workman trains, never carried fee-paying passengers and were therefore destined to disappear long before the preservation era. As usual there are a few exceptions, and this includes the products of the firm of De Winton, which despite the industrial nature of the locomotives, still have a few survivors in the preservation railway scene.

SENTINEL WAGON WORKS LTD, SHREWSBURY

In the first chapter on the early models, mention was made of the Sentinel locomotive, WN8. The Sentinel Wagon Works at Shrewsbury was well known for its production of steam wagons,

1. Sentinel 80hp Industrial, S6895
(By kind permission of the Industrial Locomotive Society – Frank Jones collection)

standard gauge geared shunting locomotives and steam railcars. They were characterised by having a vertical multi-tube boiler of very compact design, supplying a totally enclosed steam engine. The boiler consisted of an inner and outer shell, flanged top and bottom, inwards and outwards respectively; the inner shell being slightly tapered so that its top flange could pass through the lower flange of the outer shell. The inner or firebox shell contained the fire space followed by all the boiler water tubes and included at the top a superheater coil. When so inserted, the flanges met top and bottom and were secured by studs and sealed by suitable jointing material. It was therefore possible to split the boiler to carry out repairs or cleaning, by simply removing the nuts on the flange studs and lowering the inner shell completely, giving access to all the water surfaces. The internal layout could be varied to allow for the use of different fuels. The boilers were made in 100hp and 200hp versions for an operating pressure of 275psi or 300psi and the steam could be superheated to 650°C.

The engine was totally enclosed with two 6¾ x 9in single acting cylinders using separate inlet and exhaust enclosed camshaft operated poppet valves. At 500rpm the engine could develop 100hp and two engines could be used side by side to give 200hp. A six-cylinder version was also used for steam railcars. Each inlet and exhaust camshaft had five settings to cover 80% and 30% in forward /reverse and a central position with all valves open to warm the engine before starting. The engine was very much a steam version of an internal combustion engine. Apart from some modifications, the engine and boiler remained the basic design for road wagons, locomotives and railcars for over 40 years.

The first railcars came out in 1923 with the object of providing a more flexible and efficient alternative to the branch line train. These were exported to many countries, supplied in gauges from 2ft 6in to 5ft 6in with single or double engine and single or double bodies. The first locomotives followed in the same year and were made in 80hp, 100hp and double engine versions of 200hp for gauges from 2ft to 5ft 6in. WN152 is an example of the smaller 80hp 'Railway' type and was based on a photograph of one of these locomotives which was supplied to the McMillan estates in Kenya. The full size arrangement of the locomotive specified the boiler located at one end, the water tank in the middle and the engine at the other end. An attempt was made to replicate this layout in WN152 but the long thin vertical boiler produced a terrible howl that proved impossible to silence. Consequently, the conventional layout of a central 2½in vertical

boiler, front mounted engine and rear gas tank was adopted which can be recognised as the standard vertical boiler tram system. In full size practice, the centrally mounted engine drove both axles by separate chains but with the model this was replaced by a gear drive to the front axle and chain drive between the axles.

Due to the efficiency and free steaming of the 'Railway' type locomotives, their introduction met with considerable success and efforts were made to capitalise on this opportunity by extending the range. This resulted in the industrial or convertible 80hp locomotive. The purpose was to produce a sturdy but cheaper narrow gauge locomotive, suitable for small industrial sites and civil engineering contracts. They also had to compete with the rapidly developing internal combustion engine locomotives, both petrol and diesel. One very important feature was the ability to convert between 24, 30 and 36in, with all necessary holes drilled in the framing. This allowed a contractor or industrial user to transfer the locomotive to another site of a different gauge and would make it easier to resell if it was no longer required. The basic construction consisted of a built up steel frame with a standard Sentinel boiler mounted in the rear cab and the enclosed engine in the front. A chain drive was taken from a sprocket fitted to the crankshaft on the right hand side of the engine to a sprocket on the front axle. Sprockets fitted to the left hand ends of the two axles transmitted the power to the rear axle. For heavy-duty work, it was possible to provide two different gear ratios utilising a countershaft fitted under the crankcase and running in oil. Different gear ratios were fitted to each end of the crankshaft, either of which could be brought into use as required so that the locomotive could be used on a low ratio for shunting or on a high ratio for faster fast running. The final drive to the wheels was then from sprockets on the ends of the countershaft individually to each axle. Water was carried in a cylindrical water tank mounted horizontally between the cab and the engine. Normal shoe type brakes operated on each wheel and a large sand box was provided on the water tank.

From the model point of view, there are three problems, namely the small size of the full size locomotive, the chain drive and finally the size of the vertical boiler. The overall dimension of the locomotive was 11ft 9in long over the buffer beams and 5ft wide. This is indeed a small size for a 16mm scale model and therefore the models have all been built somewhat oversize. As more and more models were produced there has been a gradual reduction in size. The full size boiler was just over 3ft 6in in diameter with an overall

2. (Above left) B/W photograph of the Sentinel 'Railway' type locomotive number S5990 at the Barrasford Quarry, Northumberland, working for Northumberland Whinstone. Notice how the cladding has been added to enclose the upper part of the cab to give some protection for the engineman.

(Industrial Locomotive Society – Frank Jones collection)

3. (Above right) A model of the Sentinel 'Railway' type of locomotive with full cab and of very similar appearance to a tramway engine. For practical reasons the boiler has been placed at the centre of the frames with the geared engine visible at the front end. The engine drives to the leading axle using 2:1 spur gears and as can be seen on the photographs, connects the axles using the 4mm pitch stainless steel chain. With the full size locomotive the engine was located at the centre of the frames and drove with separate chains to each axle.

(WN152-1 – Geoff Lumsdon)

4. (Left) This photograph clearly shows the chain drive along with the chain adjusters on each axle. Whereas the front axle is fixed on the model due to the gear drive to the engine, the rear axle can be unlocked and adjusted using the turnbuckles. These turnbuckles were obtained from a model boat supplier and feature the correct left and right hand threads. The gas tank is visible at the opposite end to the engine in a layout typical of models of the vertical boiler trams and the De Winton locomotives. However, unlike most other models the axle boxes are slung below the bar type mainframe. Gusset plates reinforce the buffer beams from the main frame.

(WN152-2 – Geoff Lumsdon)

5. (Above) Sentinel 80hp 'Industrial' locomotive, S6900, at the Darwell Hole Reservoir construction, Hastings Water Works on 29-09-1948. This is a superb view of the Sentinel Industrial 80hp locomotive on which several models have been based. What is very clear from this view is the compact nature of the vertical boiler, which would be impractical in a model at 16mm scale. In fact the locomotive itself was rather small being 11ft 9in long over the buffer beams and only 5ft wide. The engine is covered with a protective box but some locomotives had just a rain canopy on four pillars. What cannot be reproduced in model form are the intricate Super-Sentinel works plates, which referred to numerous patents. The photograph shows a typical industrial location, almost certainly a quarry and a load consisting of tipper trucks.

(Sentinel S6900 – George Alliez courtesy of Andrew Neale collection)

6. This is the opposite side view to the photograph in the Early Days chapter of the first model of the Sentinel 80hp Industrial locomotive, including a particularly industrial background. Note the oil cup on the running board for lubricating the engine to front axle chain. The excellent Caton engine is seen at the front and was particularly suited to this model.

(WN008-2 – Author's collection)

height of approximately 5ft, corresponding to 2¼in dia. and just over 3in in height. Whilst it would be possible to build a 16mm scale model using a boiler of this small size, it would require an equally tiny engine and would be of doubtful practical value. The solution adopted on all the models was to discard the idea of a vertical boiler and use instead a horizontal boiler in the place of the water tank. Initially, the horizontal boiler was a pot type using methylated spirit firing with a Roundhouse firebox, as in the case of WN008, which was mentioned in the Early Days chapter. A photograph is still included in this chapter since it has a distinctly industrial flavour to it. The photograph of WN24 illustrates the arrangement using a simple potboiler and curved fireguard surround for methylated spirit firing along with the Caton Marine engine. The LHS chain drive can just be seen under the chain guard.

Whereas this model used a chain drive, the next Sentinel, WN30, has opted for a rod drive in an arrangement often used on diesel shunting locomotives. These early Sentinel models had the advantage of using the excellent Caton engine which had a geared reduction of 2:1 to a counter shaft under the engine similar to that used by Sentinel on their heavier locomotives. Despite these variations from the full size locomotive the models still capture the essence of these utility engines.

Several years were to pass before a further model of the Sentinel 80hp Industrial locomotive was attempted, by which time the Caton engine was no longer available and gas firing had taken over from methylated spirits. For WN114, the SVS oscillating engine with integral 4:1 gear reduction was the unit of choice but this still required a further 2:1 reduction to provide an

overall ratio of 8:1. This could not be obtained on the chain drive due to the size limitations of the locomotive. Even with the smallest available sprocket mounted on the engine, the axle-mounted sprocket, required for 2:1 reduction, was equal to the diameter of the locomotive wheels. The solution was to use an under-slung countershaft to give this reduction, with a chain drive from the RHS to the front axle using two 12 tooth sprockets.

The axles were then connected using a chain and 12 tooth sprockets on the left hand side of the locomotive. It can also be noted that the chain was of a much smaller size with a pitch of only 4mm, rather than the original chain of 6mm pitch and it was supplied pre-stretched. Based on the photograph of Sentinel S6742, the model carries the name of the Woodside Brickworks of E Handley but the box over the engine was replaced with a rain cover, as fitted to S6751 (Northumberland Whinstone). With the correct sandbox over the water tank (boiler), this model really looks the part. Incidentally, the short stub chimney is hardly noticeable and occupies the position of the water tank filler on the full size engine. Overall, the model is smaller than the previous examples, due to the smaller size of the SVS engine and building the model for operation on 32mm gauge only.

Although the chain drive on both sides of the locomotive was correct to the full size engine, it was awkward to fit in the drive to the front axle with the under-slung countershaft and the short distance between the sprockets. WN281 was therefore built with a straight spur gear drive between the engine and the front axle. This required two lay-shafts and the final spur gear to be mounted on the front axle. With both models, the rear axle bearings were mounted

8. (Left) The same locomotive still operating in 2012 but at some stage in its life has been painted in blue. The works nameplate date has been changed to when Ron Cushion owned it. Ron was the first owner of this model, who before and after this model gave valuable assistance in the construction of several models during our Thursday evening sessions in the workshop.

(WN024-3 Sentinel Samson – Graham White)

9. (Below left) A very similar model to the previous one but using a side rod drive more associated with modern diesel locomotives. The required gear reduction of 2:1 from the Caton marine piston valve engine was obtained using a layshaft located under the engine bedplate.

(WN030 Hannibal Sentinel – N D Kirkbride)

10. (Below right) WN114 was based on this locomotive, which was photographed in the yard of E. Handley, Woodside Brickworks (Croydon) Ltd. Notice the open awning type cab rather than the enclosed cab of other examples.

(Industrial Locomotive Society – Frank Jones collection)

11. The model based on the Sentinel Industrial locomotive S6742 but now using the SVS engine and arranged for 32mm gauge only. Not only has the model become a more accurate representation of the full size engine, but has now been reduced in size. Despite the fact that the model has a horizontal boiler in the place of the vertical boiler and water tank on the full size locomotive, the model really does capture the spirit of these unique industrial locomotives. Note the chain drive from the countershaft under the engine. The sprockets are the same size and thus the countershaft is required to give the 2:1 reduction with an overall engine to front axle gear reduction of 8:1. The 12 tooth sprockets used are the largest practical ones with the smallest being 10 tooth for this pitch of chain (4mm). Note how the rear axle is clear of the frame with the bearing attached to a separate sliding plate located by the socket cap screws either side.

(WN114-1. Sentinel – Geoff Lumsdon)

14. (Above right) View of WN281 in the brass, showing the different arrangement of drive from the engine using multiple spur gears. The two inner gears are mounted on idler shafts extended to support the gear drive cover. This method removes the need for a countershaft under the engine but is of course not as the full size locomotive. Notice the gas tank located between the rear frames with a vertical turret to accommodate the gas valve and filler. The gas valve has been turned to come up inside the rear cab plate and the displacement lubricator drain valve lever is just visible below the cab floor.

(WN281-1 – Author)

13. (Above left) Unusual top view photograph of a derelict Sentinel 80hp Industrial locomotive in the mid 1950s at the Cliffe Hill Granite Co.

(Jim Hawkesworth collection)

15. (Below) The finished Sentinel locomotive at rest in the siding with a George England saddle tank and a further part completed locomotive in the background.

(WN281-3 – Author)

on a sliding plate to adjust the chain tension, although once set, it has not been found necessary to carry out further adjustment. Again, these models are not strictly correct to the full size engine but they still capture the spirit of these unique locomotives and are a very practical garden railway engine.

THE SENTINEL 200HP STANDARD GAUGE LOCOMOTIVES

The final Sentinel locomotive was based on the standard gauge 200hp 0-6-0 locomotives built for Dorman Long in 1954. The post war production of Sentinel had been a continuation of the 100hp &200hp chain driven locomotives, updated from their pre-war designs. Then in 1953, Sentinel (Shrewsbury) Ltd began work on a new concept of steam locomotive using a Carden shaft drive with 0-6-0 rod driven wheel

arrangement and a new design of boiler fired by oil. This concept would incorporate the latest ideas in industrial locomotives but applied to the Sentinel system. They were large locomotives with a modern diesel style outline, including a totally enclosed cab with full height sliding doors. The first of these locomotives, built at Shrewsbury, was completed by mid 1954 and was given the number X49. The new design incorporated a Sentinel vertical boiler to the rear of the cab, which was balanced by two standard Sentinel engines mounted side by side at the front. The engines drove to a common gearbox mounted in front of the leading axle. From there the gearbox was coupled to the middle axle by a carden shaft. The water tank and oil fuel tanks were located between the engine and the cab. Eight locomotives supplied to Dorman Long in 1956 followed the prototype engine but unfortunately they were not a success, suffering

16. Prototype Sentinel 0-6-0 oil fired carden shaft drive side rod locomotive X49 in the works yard of Sentinel at Shrewsbury

(Sentinel X49 – (20) Andrew Neale collection)

17. Is it a steam locomotive? The model is based on the Dorman Long rod driven Sentinel locomotives. In the model the boiler is under the main front cover with the gas tank at the very front. The engine is located at the rear with a Carden shaft drive to the front axle. The casings on the full size locomotive were rather high in relation to the cab, which spoilt the overall appearance. With the model, the casing is lower and gives a much neater and more pleasing appearance.

(WN158-1 – Geoff Lumsdon)

18. Right hand side view of Sentinel S9602 (number 8) of 1956 at the Dorman Long Lackenby Steel Works, Cleveland.

(Sentinel-Dorman Long No8. Photo: late Frank Jones – Andrew Neale collection (18))

19. The location of the boiler is clearly shown in this side view.

(WN158-2 – Geoff Lumsdon)

20. Sentinel S9590 (number 4) of 1956 at the Dorman Long Lackenby Works, Cleveland.

(Sentinel-Dorman Long No4 – Photo: late Frank Jones – Andrew Neale collection (19))

21. A top view showing the small hole in the front sloping top plate to facilitate filling of the front located gas tank. The larger hole in the top casing is the boiler flue exhaust with the safety valve visible behind. Notice the dummy toolbox with the hole in the lid to provide access to the Goodall water filler valve.

(WN158-3 – Geoff Lumsdon)

from excessive heat in the cab, problems with starting and running the oil burners plus poor weight distribution. Three others were supplied to Guest Keen Iron & Steel Co of East Moors, Cardiff, who at one point refused to accept them on the grounds of reliability. Sentinel carried out several modifications, but with the decision by Dorman Long in 1959-60 to dieselise its fleet, the rod driven Sentinels rapidly went out of service with three locomotives being converted to diesel hydraulics in 1961/2. Had the design been developed much earlier, these locomotives may have been more successful but it was already too late, the time of the industrial steam locomotive was long past.

Despite the fact that a narrow gauge version was never developed, it was decided to build a smaller version with the scale being reduced to 12.5mm/ft, whilst still retaining a suitable cab height. WN158 was the end result and shows what might have been developed if this design had appeared 20 years earlier. The model is arranged with the engine located in the rear compartment behind the cab, with the boiler under the main bonnet and the gas tank right at the front. The boiler flue exhausts at the front of the main casing before it slopes down and is kept to a minimum to retain the correct appearance of the full size locomotive. On the other hand the SVS engine exhaust is released in the correct position behind the cab. As with the prototype, the engine drives via a carden shaft but in the model, it is from the rear mounted engine to the front axle using 20T:15T crossed helical gears. The gas tank is filled through a hole in the front inclined casing. WN158 is certainly an unusual looking steam locomotive.

CLAYTON WAGONS LTD, ABBEY WORKS, LINCOLN

The firm of Clayton Wagons Ltd was registered in 1920 and built a small number of vertical boiler locomotives, including steam railmotors, but unfortunately the company went into liquidation in 1929. Their type 'A' railmotor had inside frames and consisted of a vertical boiler at one end of the frame, a horizontal two cylinder engine beneath the floor of the cab, with the water tank and coal bunker at the other end. The engine drove through reduction gears to one of the axles and side rods transmitted the drive to the other. The vertical boiler had an inner and outer shell sealed by machined flanges, cross water tubes and superheater coils, similar to the Sentinel Waggon Works design of boiler and was constructed to operate at a pressure of 275psi. It is thought that only two or three of the 'A' type were built. In addition, a further design, known as a type 'C', was proposed for the narrow gauge and this was to form the basis for the two models WN43 and WN77. The layout of the 'C' type had outside frames with the vertical boiler at the front and a water tank and bunker at the rear.

The exact location of the 100hp two cylinder totally enclosed engine is unknown. However the drive to the rear axle was via rods from a jackshaft rather on the lines of a modern diesel locomotive. The outline of the bodywork was closely followed in the models but the steam layout, as with the Sentinel, required a different approach. For both models, the vertical boiler was mounted in tram fashion in the centre, the gas tank in the rear water tank/bunker

22. Clayton 'C' geared vertical boiler locomotive. The 2¾in diameter boiler is rather prominent with this model and do note the Caton marine engine lying along the centre line at the front of the cab. The vertical lever inside the doorway is the engine forward/reverse valve. The engine drives via a Carden shaft to the other end of the locomotive to pick up the countershaft using crossed helical gears.

(WN043-1 – Peter Duckering)

23. Other side of the locomotive with the rear mounted gas tank just visible behind the coal rails in the bunker.

(WN043-2 – Peter Duckering)

24. *(Above) A superb photograph of Anaticular after lining by Lightline. Notice the inverted squares on the corners of the lining panels. Incidentally, the brass headlights are working and can be selected for either end.*

(WN043-3 – Geoff Munday)

25. *(Right) Second Clayton 'C' vertical boiler locomotive with the rather grandiose name of Sir George Newnes.*

(WN077 – Author's collection)

area and the engine at the front. For WN43 the Caton marine engine was laid along the frame with a Carden shaft drive to the correctly located jackshaft, the gearing being 2:1 crossed helical. However in the later model, with the rather grand name of Sir George Newnes, it was necessary to use an SVS engine, which was geared directly to the jackshaft, thus reversing the location of the shaft. Either way, the use of a jackshaft and side rods is a very practical way of transferring power from the engine to the axle, when the distance between them is too much for direct gearing. Returning to the full size locomotive, it is unlikely that any type 'C' were actually made. Railmotors on the other hand were more successful and were built up to the demise of the company.

ROBEY & CO, LINCOLN

The Lincolnshire firm of Robey & Co. was founded in 1854 by Robert Robey and was just one of many concerns making steam engines in the 19th and early 20th century. The major products were steam wagons, steamrollers, portable steam engines and all types of horizontal and vertical stationary steam engines. In more recent times, Robey & Co. also produced winding engines and other mining products. Amongst all this activity, there was also the construction of a small number of steam locomotives. Information on Robey locomotives is very limited with the most comprehensive source being an article by Frank Jux in the magazine The Industrial Locomotive volumes

50 and 51, entitled 'Notes on Robey Steam Locomotives'. The article included a simple side elevation of wn15776 Perla and wn15903 along with a photograph of the former engine. Another example of the Robey product is illustrated in a copy of an engraving titled 'Improved Saddle Tank Geared Locomotive'. The peculiarity of these locomotives was the long extension of the front frames required to house the engine with the crankshaft appearing through the RHS frame. The drive was then through 2:1 gears to the front axle; the larger gear on the axle also providing a location for the crank pin. Access to the engine was obtained by lifting a plate over the front extension of the frame.

The photograph of Perla, Robey Works Number 15776, was the inspiration to produce WN72 but unfortunately the side elevation information became available only after construction had started. This side elevation drawing appeared in an article by Frank Jux in The Industrial Locomotive number 51, published by The Industrial Locomotive Society and was the work of his colleague Pete Roberts. The drawing is reproduced here by kind permission of his widow Mrs I Roberts. The model used the SVS oscillating engine located between the frames at the front end with the F-R lever appearing above the footplate. Spur gears of 2:1 reduction take the drive to the front axle with the larger gear on the axle providing the crankpin just as the prototype. Steam is provided by a 2in diameter plain centre-flue boiler having a poker type burner and in the absence of side tanks, the gas tank is located between the frames behind the rear axle. As with the full size locomotive, an access cover to the engine is located in front of the smokebox. It is interesting to note that Perla used refined petroleum as fuel, which was

IMPROVED SADDLE-TANK GEARED LOCOMOTIVE.

26. (Above) Engraving of a typical Robey geared saddle tank locomotive with the rather long nose hiding the two-cylinder engine. Notice the end of the engine crankshaft just visible ahead of the front wheel. The Robey geared saddle tank locomotive, wn15776 of 1895, on which the second and subsequent models are based, would have been very similar to this example.

(Robey-cat76 Engraving – Courtesy of the Robey Trust)

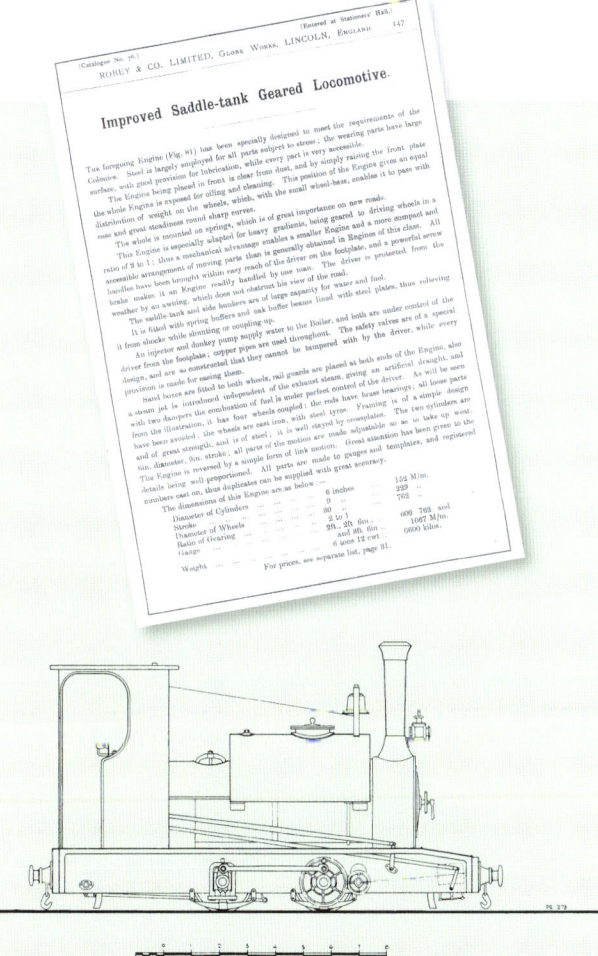

Robey 0-4-0 geared saddletank locomotive works number 15776 of 1895 (Machinery Order 8901) named PERLA. Gauge 50cm. Cylinders 5¼"x 8". Fuel petroleum oil.

27. (Top) Detail specification of the locomotive in the engraving.

(Robey-cat76-detail _ Courtesy of the Robey Trust)

29. (Above) Side elevation drawing of Robey wn15776 of 1895 drawn by the late Peter Roberts and reproduced by kind permission of Mrs I Roberts.

(PR273 Robey 15776)

28. (Above) This is a digitally enhanced photograph that was originally supplied by Paul Teather.

(Robey Perla Archive photograph – collection of Paul Teather)

30. The model based on the 500mm gauge geared saddle tank locomotive Perla built by Robey & Co. wn15776 of 1895, machinery order 8901, for Rose Innes & Co. The saddle tank on the full size locomotive had two compartments within the main tank, one for water and a smaller section for petroleum, which was used to fire the burner.

(WN072-3 – Fergus Morgan)

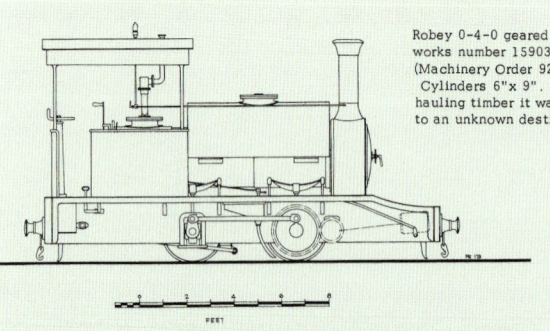

Robey 0-4-0 geared saddletank locomotive works number 15903 of 1895 (or 1896) (Machinery Order 9267). Gauge 2'6". Cylinders 6"x 9". Originally ordered for hauling timber it was eventually delivered to an unknown destination in January 1899.

32. Side elevation drawing of Robey 15903 of 1895/6 drawn by the late Peter Roberts and reproduced by kind permission of Mrs I Roberts.

(PR173 – Robey 15903)

31. Front side view showing the gear drive from the engine crankshaft to the gear on the front axle, just as full size. In front of the gear drive can be seen the 6ba socket cap screw locating the engine mounting frame stretcher. The toolbox on the front is a later addition by the owner probably to hide the forward/reverse lever.

(WN072-4 – Fergus Morgan)

34. Robey geared saddle tank. Second model of 15903. The only disadvantage of these models is the long steam pipe running from the steam regulator in the cab to the engine at the front and this pipe can be seen in this photograph. Typical of models of this era the steam pipe has been left unpainted but the practice now is to paint most of the steam pipework including the displacement lubricator.

(WN103-1 – Geoff Lumsdon)

35. (Left) View of the model in the brass clearly showing the cover over the engine. Note how a hole in the rear cab sheet makes for easy removal of the gas jet. The socket cap screw and washer in front of the leading wheels attaches the engine cross frame bearer to the side frames. These high tensile steel screws ensure that the engine bearer does not move once the drive is set up.
(WN103-3 – Geoff Lumsdon)

36. (Above right) Another model based on Robey 15903, but this time fitted with a front cab sheet.
(WN231-6 – Geoff Lumsdon)

37. (Left) The classic Balmforth Locomotive with a large vertical boiler mounted on a four-wheel chassis with outside cylinders. At one end is the water tank and at the other the coal bunker. It may not win a beauty contest but it is certainly not lacking in character.
(Balmforth Locomotive – Andrew Neale collection (11))

contained in a tank at the rear of the saddletank and the gauge was 500mm.

Sometime during the construction of WN72 the article by Frank Jux 'came my way', with the side elevation of Works Number 15903 of 1895/6, a 2ft 6in gauge locomotive originally built for British Goldfields, South Africa. The intended customer for this locomotive could not however pay for it and consequently the locomotive remained at the works until a buyer was found in 1899. This was the very last Robey geared saddletank locomotive and typical of the majority of Robey locomotives, does not appear to have been photographed. It would however be very similar to the illustrated engraving from the Robey catalogue 76, reproduced by kind permission of the Robey Trust. WN87 follows the same layout as the previous model with the exception of the drive from the engine to the front axle. The gears outside of the RHS frame always seemed rather exposed to trackside debris and so this model was built with the gears retained within the frames. This model was then followed by a close copy (WN103 illustrated in the photographs). WN231 is again of the same locomotive but the cab has gained a front spectacle plate and looks the better for it.

THE BALMFORTH 'COFFEEPOTS'

William Barmforth set up his own works at the Peelings Foundry, Rodley Lane, Rodley, just west of Leeds in April1861. He specialised in quarry cranes and in1864, together with Francis Robson patented 'Apparatus for Hoisting Stone' which combined a steam engine and crane with a degree of portability. Over the next few years Balmforth started to build small contractors locomotives using the same technology as their steam cranes. The first locomotive with 'William Barmforth' cast on the valve chest covers dates from around 1876 and was built for 3ft gauge. Only a few locomotives were constructed with the last one being built about 1900 and the firm failed in 1916 only to be taken over by Samuel Butler & Co Ltd. All of the locomotives had vertical cross tube boilers when new, outside inclined cylinders at the driving end and four coupled wheels with outside cranks. The inside Stephenson link motion was operated through rocking shafts.

From the model point of view the Balmforth locomotives have the advantage of a reasonable sized boiler which works out in 16mm at 2½in diameter and able to take a boiler 4in high. This is the standard SD1 boiler fitted with a centre

flue and water tubes as used on all the vertical boiler models. As with the full size locomotive, the boiler is dropped down between the frames and arranged to give the correct height above the frames of just over 3in. The pan type ceramic burner has the firetube above the rear axle and connects to the gas tank located in the dummy coalbunker. With any industrial locomotive model it is essential to provide slow running characteristics since many full size engines would be operating at below 5mph. Unfortunately, this would be difficult to achieve with the direct drive cylinders of the Balmforth and with such a small locomotive it

38. (Right) The latest Balmforth locomotive shown during construction to illustrate the basic design. The side frames are riveted to the buffer beams using brass angle but the main strength comes from the two frame stretchers located under and bolted to the boiler mounting plate. Sandwiched between the side frames and the stretchers the axle bearing 'W' irons are accurately located by the 6ba socket cap screws and the boiler mounting plate before being riveted to the side frames. The dummy cylinders are attached to the side frames but await the piston rod, crosshead and connecting rod before the hole is drilled locating the lower trunk guide. The 'hidden' oscillating engine is attached by its mounting bracket to the frame stretcher/boiler mounting plate.

(WN236-1 – Author)

39. (Left) Right hand side view of the Balmforth locomotive in the brass before dispatch to Mike Lax for painting. The dummy cylinders and valve gear are rather effective with the valve rods operating from an eccentric on the front axle. To the front right side of the water tank top there is the hole for access to the Goodall type water filler valve. As with all of these open type locomotives it is difficult to hide the oversize non-prototypical items, in this case the large displacement lubricator.

(WN236-5 – Author)

40. (Below left) Opposite side view of the Balmforth coffee pot locomotive showing the reduced forward/reverse Roundhouse operating lever and drive rod to the hidden SVS engine. The 'corrugated iron' roof is made up of corrugated aluminium sheets glued to a tinplate under roof which in turn has been soldered to the roof support frame. For good measure the roof sandwich was riveted to the roof frame. The entire roof assembly can be removed as one by removing the four 7BA mounting-screws.

(WN236-6 – Author)

41. (Above) The model painted and suitably lined and has the boiler lagged with mahogany strips held by brass boiler bands.
(WN236-8 – Ted Burge)

42. Cab end three-quarter view of the first Balmforth model showing the gas tank in the coalbunker. The copper drum under the water tank is an exhaust steam water separator designed to reduce condensate before it is released at the chimney. The forward/reverse lever in this early model is attached to the engine and accessible by the curved slot just visible in front of the water tank filler.
(WN065-2 – Andrew Cottenham)

would be very difficult to fit radio control. This is another situation for the geared SVS engine neatly located inside the dummy water tank and driving via 2:1 spur gears to the adjacent axle. Looking at the photograph of WN65 the F-R lever is visible through the slot in the tank. The dummy cylinders are driven from the same axle. An eccentric is fitted to give movement to a rocking arm and thence movement to the valve rods but the motion of the valve gear is not in correct timing with the cylinders. WN 65 was based on the Balmforth Brothers 8in. locomotive of c1897 and used on the Sheffield Waterworks Langsett Reservoir site.

A second model followed as WN92 and later a third model as WN236. With the later model the engine is better concealed by operating the

forward/reverse lever from under the dummy water tank through to a reduced Roundhouse lever in the open cab. The cylinders are fitted with trunk guides and the valve rods have tail guides; a noticeable feature of the full size locomotive.

DE WINTON & CO. UNION WORKS, THE SLATE QUAY, CAERNARVON

For anyone interested in the narrow gauge and in particular the 2ft gauge, the firm of De Winton is synonymous with the small vertical boiler locomotive with a 'launch type' engine direct coupled to the front axle. The original company was that of Owen Thomas at the Slate Quay, Caernarvon, but the firm was joined in the 1860s by Jeffreys Parry De Winton, an accomplished engineer, and soon became well known as builders of marine engines, horizontal and vertical stationary engines, boilers, stone crushing machines and locomotives. Approximately 60 locomotives were built at the Union Works between the years 1869 to 1897, the majority of them for the 2ft gauge with only a few for 3ft gauge and above. For most of these locomotives the standard arrangement consisted of outside plate frames with the boiler mounted low between them and central to the two axles. On locomotives built for 2ft gauge, the frames were formed with a bulge to accommodate the boiler. The vertical launch type engine was located in front of the boiler with the crankshaft integral with the front axle and drive to the rear axle by side coupling rods. At the front of the frames there was a small water tank and a coalbunker at the rear. There were variations to this standard layout with straight frames (as Victoria of 1897), inside frames (as Watkin of 1893) and a reversal of engine and water tank (as Arthur of 1895) and many other minor changes. In fact it is doubtful if any two locomotives were the same.

From the model point of view these delightful locomotives present a major problem. With a typical boiler size of 2ft 7½in diameter by 4ft 10½in high, a frame length of 8ft 6in and overall width of 3ft 6in they are very small. Built to these dimensions it is doubtful if these models would be practical for garden railways. The answer was to build the locomotive slightly oversize and take advantage of a 2½in diameter boiler capable of accommodating water tubes in the vertical flue. Add to this a ceramic burner with the gas tank located between the frames in the rear bunker and that is the steam

generating side dealt with. Many models of a De Winton have the engine direct coupled to the front axle as per the prototype but really this was an excellent opportunity to incorporate gearing to provide the slow running required of this type of locomotive. The SVS geared oscillating engine fits neatly between the boiler and the dummy water tank and is geared 2:1 to the front axle.

The dummy water tank was made from 20mm x 40mm brass tube with the Goodall water filler valve located under the hinged filler cap. The frames are 8¼in long and the front and rear buffer beams 3¼in wide and the boiler is the standard SD1, 2½in diameter and 4in high unit set halfway into the frames. Several of these models have been produced and have proved to be very practical and easy to operate, the lack of external cab work giving clear access to the engine and boiler controls although it must be said the boiler water capacity is limited and requires careful attention to the water level. WN082 is shown as a front view and indicates that despite being oversize the locomotive looks correct against the track gauge and the following hopper trucks. The photographs of WN130 illustrate the classic De Winton layout with the model first photographed in as built condition in 2003 and then later in 2010, slightly scruffy but still doing the job it was built for. There have been several other De Winton models built reflecting the practical nature of these locomotives and two models have been constructed by Andy Cooper based on the same design.

A later model, WN174, was built with the curved bulge in the frames to allow the boiler

43. Photograph of a typical De Winton vertical boiler locomotive George Henry taken on the 30th June 1955. Although typical, in practice no two De Winton's locomotives were the same. Notice how in full size the engine was bolted to the side of the vertical boiler. The locomotive is marked in chalk as George Henry.

(Photo – K. P. Plant courtesy Andrew Neale collection (1))

44. (Left) Front view of an early De Winton illustrating that despite the model being oversize it looks well on the 32mm track and blends in well with the side tipper trucks.

(WN082 – Author's collection)

45. (Below right) Side view of a typical model showing the classic De Winton layout with the boiler dropping down into the frames to reduce the overall height. The gas tank fits neatly into the coalbunker and the dummy front tank includes the Goodall water filler valve under the filler cap.

(WN130-1 – Geoff Lumsdon)

46. (Above left) A later photograph of the same model in 2010, slightly scruffy, but still operating correctly after a lot of running including sustained operation at many an exhibition.

(WN130-2 – Dave Hill)

47. (Left) The De Winton Chaloner constructed this time with the frames curved to allow the boiler to fit through the frames as was often the case with the full size locomotives. Unfortunately with the model this prevents the ability to have a dual gauge facility. Notice how the lower arrangement of the boiler in the frames means that the ceramic burner tube would coincide with the rear axle. This tube has therefore had to be brought up through the footplate as can be seen in the photographs.

(WN174-1 – Author)

48. *(Left) The rather unusual De Winton Arthur arranged with the water tank next to the boiler and the engine free standing at the front end. The photograph illustrates the superb Anton 200 marine piston valve engine (9mm bore/8mm stroke), and the extra drive shaft located under the engine. With the full size locomotive the crankshaft of the engine occupied this position, driving as with the model via outside cranks and side rods to the leading axle.*

(WN155-1 – Mike Lax)

49. *One of two De Winton models built under licence by Andy Cooper to the same design as the previous locomotives.*

(De Winton – Andy Cooper)

to fit through the frames. In full size practice the coal fired boiler would drop through the frames to accommodate the firebox and ashpan but curving the plates in the De Winton kept the overall width down by allowing the outside cranks to be set further in, the coupling rods just clearing the 'boiler bulge'. With the model the disadvantage is in the loss of the dual gauge facility. The fire tube of the ceramic burner coincides with the rear axle and has to be turned up over. Trying to be more accurate to the prototype can have unforeseen consequences. WN156 illustrates a variation on the standard De Winton layout based on Arthur of 1890, built for the Pen-yr-Orsedd Quarry, Nantlle. In this design the water tank was fitted next to the boiler with the engine free standing at the front end. This location required a separate drive from the crankshaft of the engine to the leading axle using outside cranks and side rods. Arthur was probably the only locomotive with this layout. The engine used in this model was the

beautifully machined 'Anton 200' two-cylinder marine piston valve engine, which was supplied in kit form. Unlike the full size locomotive, the engine is geared to the extra drive shaft which is particularly required for a high speed over square engine (9mm bore /8mm stroke), designed for marine use. The engine is very compact and of the highest quality but is rather too fast for railway use, the model being capable of alarming speeds if not operated carefully.

A variation on the construction of the De Winton models occurred with WN221, which was built to a scale of 7/8in/ft and therefore appears in the chapter on this scale.

THE DE WINTON THAT WASN'T

Another marked variation from the standard De Winton appears on page 15 in the book Encyclopaedia of Narrow Gauge Railways by Thomas Middlemass, which showed a vertical boiler locomotive named Violet of most unusual appearance that, according to this book, operated at the Penryhn Quarries. This locomotive named Violet was one of three types supplied for 'main line' use and had outside horizontal cylinders and inside valve gear operating through a rocking shaft. Further research indicates that the three 'main line' locomotives, namely Violet, Hilda and Edward Sholto were indeed built by De Winton but these were more conventional locomotives with horizontal boilers and photographs of Edward Sholto and Hilda appear in the latest book De Winton of Caernarfon by Alfred Fisher, David Fisher & Dr Gwynfor Pierce Jones. There is certainly no mention of the Violet on which this model is based and therefore without further information the builder and operator of this locomotive must remain uncertain.

That said the model WN136, is based on the photograph but unlike the prototype is fitted with dummy cylinders and valve gear. The motive power is the SVS oscillating engine

50. (Above left) Vertical boiler locomotive Violet. Based only on a photograph that appeared in the book Encyclopaedia of Narrow Gauge Railways, this was described as one of three similar locomotives supplied to the Penryhn Quarries in 1876 for main line use. This would appear to be incorrect as these three locomotives were more conventional and were fitted with horizontal boilers. The photograph showed a vertical boiler but unlike the later De Winton the locomotives was fitted with outside horizontal cylinders and inside valve gear. This valve gear operated an outside rod to the valve chest using a rocking shaft. The drive engine with the model is the SVS geared engine hidden in the large water tank.
(WN136-1 – Geoff Lumsdon)

51. (Above right) The model shown in the brass, with the dummy outside valve operating rod visible under the running boards. The groove in the water tank top is to operate the forward/reverse lever of the engine. Notice the dummy volute axle springs above the running board whereas the vertical boiler De Winton locomotives had the axles directly fitted to the frames without any springing.
(WN136-2 – Geoff Lumsdon)

52. (Middle right) The underside of the model in the brass, showing the operation of the dummy valve gear from an eccentric on the rear axle. The engine drive is just visible under the dummy water tank. At the centre of the locomotive the boiler mounting plate has two sets of 6ba screws. The cross frame ones hold the ceramic burner and the diagonal ones the boiler. The centre screw is part of the burner and holds the central pillar on which the ceramic element is held.
(WN136-3 – Geoff Lumsdon)

53. (Below right) Comparison of the model of a standard De Winton locomotive against the vertical boiler WN136
(WN130-136 – Geoff Lumsdon)

54. (Above left) Photograph of a derelict Lumpy Tom reproduced by kind permission of Mr R. M. Sinclair. This interesting picture shows the nameplate on the front of the boiler and the number 33 above.

(Lumpy Tom – R.M. Sinclair collection)

55. (Above right) A Lumpy Tom locomotive photographed in the brass. The 'Boxer' type SVS engine can be seen mounted under the horizontal part of the 'T' boiler and just visible is the output spur gear, which connects to the larger spur

gear on the front axle. The cylindrical container alongside the engine is the water separator fitted in the exhaust steam pipe before it reaches the smokebox. Notice how the horizontal part of the boiler barrel includes the smokebox and the mounting of the chimney. The smokebox front is a separate brass disc located as can be seen by two 8ba screws through the copper tube. The gas tank is located between the frames in the rear bunker and attached at the base onto brass angles fitted at the bottom of the frames.

(Lumpy Tom – Geoff Lumsdon)

56. (Above) The finished Lumpy Tom model, WN149, which the nameplate indicates was the seventh one produced, and which for this particular model has included the addition of an auxiliary water tender of the same design as that of the Hohenzollern locomotive. The basic locomotive has been embellished with a small front footplate with side handrail stanchions.

(WN149-1 – Author)

57. (Right) Opposite side view of the same locomotive. Notice how the rear buffer beam includes a pin to attach a chain enabling the engine to operate without the tender. This is required when the locomotive is re-gauged for 45mm since the auxiliary tender is limited to 32mm only. The oval plate on the rear panel of the bunker was copied from the John Frazer plate seen on the smokebox front in the archive photograph supplied and reproduced by kind permission of Mr R M Sinclair. The displacement lubricator can be seen inside the right hand side panel and the Goodall water filler is located within the rear bunker alongside the gas tank

(WN149-2 – Author)

located in the false water tank. An eccentric on the front axle operates the rocking shaft but is obviously not in correct time to the cylinders. Whatever the origin of the full size locomotive this is an attractive locomotive to those who enjoy the unusual and a second model, WN245 has been produced.

LUMPY TOM

One of the most unusual locomotives in this section on industrial locomotives was based on two photographs that appeared in the publication Industrial Railway Record No159 (December 1999) and related to a contractor's locomotive of most unusual appearance. The second photograph was captioned 'Lumpy Tom at the King George Reservoir contract driven by B. C. Carter on 22nd May 1913'. The builder of this locomotive is unknown but according to the plate on the smokebox front, John Frazer & Son of Millwall, London, constructed the 'T' boiler. This plate is clearly seen on the reproduced photograph. The engine, possibly originally a winch engine, drove via chains and sprockets to the front axle and by side rods to the rear axle. A plate with the number 33 was attached to the top of the smokebox front. Further research by Dave Holroyde produced correspondence in The Industrial Locomotive No77 in an article by Frank Jones which mentioned home produced narrow gauge locomotives used by Charles Wall who was the contractor for the King George reservoir in the Lea Valley between 1908 and 1913.

One of the engines was called Lumpy Tom, a 0-4-0WT for 2ft 4in gauge. Following on from this article more information appeared including a reference to a 'No33' which was a chain driven 0-4-0 with a vertical boiler and horizontal smoke box and bearing the John Frazer & Son works plate. Further correspondence indicated that Charles Wall had six narrow gauge locomotives of 2ft 4in gauge including: Lumpy Tom, an 0-4-0T with 4½ x 6in cylinders built at the Globe Works, scrapped. Incidentally, the firm of John Frazer & Son Ltd, Millwall Boiler Works, London E14, were described as tank and boilermakers and plate metal workers. This was a substantial works whose main business was marine work, and although they would have been capable of building such a locomotive it is more probable that they may simply have supplied the boiler.

This information was sufficient to produce a model, WN78 of 1999. The open cab and side panels are pure conjecture as we will probably never know if any such structure was provided

and considering the date is highly unlikely. The model has a gas fired centre flue boiler with the vertical barrel central on the wheelbase, the weight of the oscillating engine at the front being balanced by the large gas tank in the rear bunker. The 'boxer' SVS engine drives through 2:1 spur gears to the front axle. The horizontal part of the boiler provides the steaming efficiency of the centre flue horizontal boiler with the vertical part giving a good head of water and a long gauge glass. The same boiler was used on the SLM trams and a slightly longer version on the 'T' boiler Shays. The boiler also has the advantage of being least affected by gradients. More than ten of these models have been produced over the years with the only alteration being to move the rather unsightly displacement lubricator to within the left hand side panel. WN149 was built with a suitable 4 wheel tender as used on the Hohenzollern locomotive. Despite the small 3in wheelbase the model is a very steady runner at the speeds expected of a geared locomotive.

REFERENCES:

Sentinel locomotives:
- Sentinel Patent Locomotives and Concrete Cases by The Sentinel Wagon Works Ltd.
- Narrow Gauge and Industrial Railway Modelling Review No 25. Article by Andrew Neale on Sentinel Convertible Locomotives.
- Narrow Gauge and Industrial Railway Modelling Review No73. Article by Peter Foley on Sentinel Industrial Locomotives based on S6895 of 1927.

Clayton locomotives & De Winton locomotives:
- Vertical Boiler Locomotives and Railmotors Built in Great Britain by the late Roland A S Abbot.
- De Winton of Caernarvon by Alfred Fisher, David Fisher and Dr Gwynfor Pierce Jones.

Robey Locomotives:
- Some Notes on Robey Locomotives – 1&2 by Frank Jux. The Industrial Locomotive Vol. 5, No 50 & 51, Summer/Autumn 1988.
- Some Early Robey Steam Engines by P J M Southworth.

Balmforth locomotives:
- The Narrow Gauge No 129. Article by Bill Corser and Peter Holmes titled Peelings Foundry and the Balmforth Coffeepots.

Lumpy Tom:
- Industrial Railway Record 159. Article by R M Sinclair including two photographs.
- The Industrial Locomotive No 77. Article by the late Frank Jones, which resulted in further correspondence in IL78, IL79 and notes by Michael Cook (IL not known).

FESTINIOG AND WELSH HIGHLAND RAILWAYS

FFESTINIOG RAILWAY ORIGINS

The Ffestiniog Railway is the most celebrated preserved line in Wales. Prior to the railway the towns of Porthmadog and Blaenau Ffestiniog did not exist, and this part of the country was a remote mountain area whose inhabitants scraped a meagre living from poor farmland that gave little promise of any industrial wealth. Slate was already being mined on the northern side of Snowdonia at the Penrhyn Quarry, near Bangor, but development on the southern side required a man of vision and wealth. Such a man was William Alexander Madocks (1773-1828), whose Anglo-Welsh family background, money and zeal for social change was to transform this area. His third scheme of land reclamation involved building the Cob, a mile long embankment designed to cut off the sea estuary of the River Glaslyn which was completed in 1811.

The deviation of the river through sluice gates at its northern end scoured out a natural harbour, which Madocks realised could be exploited by providing a port for the infant slate industry being developed around Rhiwbryfdir, north-west of the present day Blaenau Ffestiniog. The next step was to provide a better means of transport for the slate from the quarries, which originally had relied on packhorse and cart using indifferent tracks. The slate was transported to the now named Port Madoc, opened in 1824. It was after the death of William Madocks in 1828 that a scheme was put forward to finance and build the 13-mile Ffestiniog Railway from the sea at Port Madoc to the slate quarries at Blaenau Ffestiniog, some 700ft above sea level.

It was to James Spooner that the task of surveying and constructing the railway fell. The engineering work was immense and it took three years to complete with the official opening taking place on the 20th April 1836. Along the route the 1ft 11½in gauge track threaded its way high up on valley hillsides or crossed ravines on narrow stone embankments and in some cases cut through solid rock. The route included two tunnels, one of which was 730yd long. With a continuous ruling gradient of 1 in 82 the line could be operated with loaded trains down to the sea by gravity with the empty trucks returned by horse. Uphill each horse could haul eight empty slate wagons and one horsebox, called a dandy, which was used to transport the horse on the downhill gravity fed direction. By the 1850s the line was reaching full capacity and thoughts were turning to the possibility of replacing the horses using steam locomotives to haul the slate wagons with the possible additional benefit of carrying passengers.

THE GEORGE ENGLAND LOCOMOTIVES

However at this time it was not accepted that steam locomotives would be capable of hauling the required 35-ton load for 13 miles at an average speed of 10mph on such a narrow gauge. The specification for these locomotives was produced by C M Holland and the order placed with George England & Co of Hatcham Ironworks, New Cross, London. The first two were delivered in 1863 to a design agreed by Holland and England, but both locomotives were found to prime badly due to the boilers having been supplied without domes. This embarrassing situation was resolved by adding domes to the original locomotives and incorporating this modification to the remaining two under construction. The Ffestiniog Railway thus had four 8-ton 0-4-0 engines, The Princess, Mountaineer, Prince and Palmerston, each capable of hauling 30 tons up the line at 13mph. In 1867 the original locomotives were

1. (Above left) One of the small George England locomotives, easily identified by the marine-type coupling/connecting rods and spoked wheels. By the length of the nameplate it is probably Prince.
((13) Andrew Neale collection)

2. (Below left) Welsh Pony, one of the large George England locomotives seen in the LMS exchange yard at Blaenau Ffestiniog c1930s. Notice the disc type wheels and normal coupling/connecting rods. The standard gauge track is just visible behind the locomotive – and look at the slate spoil heaps in the background!
((14) Andrew Neale collection)

joined by two further enlarged versions with a longer wheelbase increased from 4ft 6in to 5ft, a boiler of increased diameter, larger firebox and with an all-over saddle tank. With water capacity of 480 gallons and a weight of 10 tons they were the largest and heaviest machines that could run over the existing track and with their increased tractive power could haul 50 tons, equivalent to 70 empty wagons. The earlier locomotives, with the exception of Mountaineer which was scrapped in 1879, were all rebuilt over the years with larger boilers and all-over saddle tanks.

From the model point of view there are several problems associated with the George England locomotives and the small loading gauge of the Ffestiniog Railway. Quite simply they are small locomotives with an equally small boiler and, as with all such models, controlling the speed can be a problem. Solving the speed control by using a geared engine drive is made more difficult by the inside frames and short wheelbase. The solution was to build the locomotive to a scale of 17mm/ft and to use the dimensions of the larger engines, Welsh Pony and Little Giant, regardless of which of the George England locomotives was being modelled. Adopting a

wheelbase of 3.25in, the SVS geared engine was mounted as low as possible between the axles which required the lower part of what remained of the frames to be reinforced.

Above the engine and using the full height of the saddle tank it was possible to fit a 2¼in dia. by 4½in long plain centre flue boiler, which is a large boiler for such a small model. The smokebox is arranged to be separate from the boiler. It is supported at the front by an internal bracket with a large insulating washer to seal against the front of the boiler, followed by the front of the saddle tank and then the separate smokebox. The rear of the boiler only just enters the cab, leaving sufficient room for the boiler fittings and the modular gas tank. Due to the size of the saddle tank the SVS engine is well hidden and it is therefore not obvious that there is a geared drive, suspicion only being aroused by the prototypical slow and consistent running. The large diameter boiler ensures a good water capacity but has to be topped up using the Goodall valve located under the dummy saddle tank water filler in order to match the gas tank endurance of approximately 35 minutes. The hidden geared engine drive provides steady and consistent slow running, which coupled with a

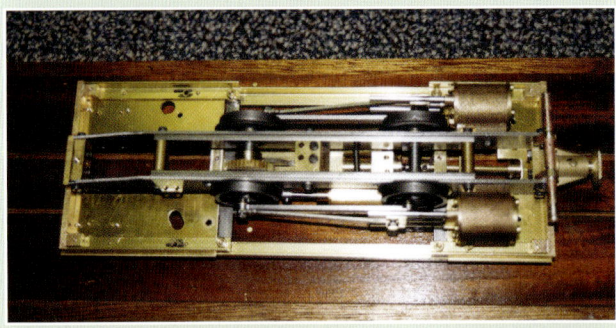

3. (Above left) The full-size Prince outside the old engine shed at Boston Lodge in 2009.

(Ffestiniog "Prince" – Geoff Lumsdon)

4. (Above right) WN131 The first model of the Ffestiniog George England locomotives, in this case Mountaineer. The wheels are of the correct spoked pattern but the coupling and connecting rods should be the marine type fitted to the four earlier small George England locomotives. From the photograph it cannot be seen that the engine is in fact geared, although the forward/reverse lever is visible in front of the smokebox. The gas tank is just visible in the rather small cab.

(WN131-1 – Geoff Lumsdon)

5. (Middle right) WN131 Underside of Mountaineer showing the dummy cylinders and the reinforcing straps running along the inside of the frames from the spacer at the rear of the cylinders to the spacer behind the rear wheel.

(WN131-3 – Geoff Lumsdon)

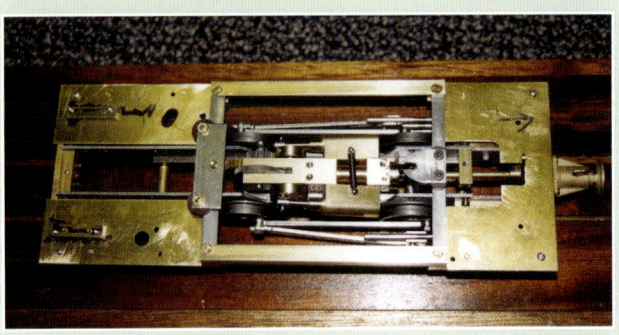

6. (Bottom right) WN131 Topside of the frame of Mountaineer showing the SVS engine shoehorned into the inside frames. The extension rod for the forward/reverse lever can be seen heading towards the front footplate. Notice how the oscillating cylinders are outside the frames and how close they are to the wheels.

(WN131-4 – Geoff Lumsdon)

correct rake of Ffestiniog carriages is not only prototypical but also a delight to watch. As for the scale of 17mm/ft this is hardly noticeable even when pulling the small Ffestiniog bug boxes.

WN131 was the first of many models of the George England locomotives and was named Mountaineer, taken from the only small England to be scrapped. The reason for this choice was that with such well documented and preserved locomotives it would be obvious that certain errors had been made. For instance the original four locomotives had marine type round rods with spoked wheels and the later large England's had disc wheels with conventional rods. There was also doubt about the colour. Naming WN131 after the scrapped Mountaineer would deflect some criticism from those more knowledgeable about such things.

WN135 Little Giant and WN140 Welsh Pony soon followed and there has been a steady construction of what must be one of the most practical and useful garden railway locomotives. The only disadvantage of the George England engines is the inside frames meaning that the model must be built to 32 or 45mm gauge. WN186 illustrates a variation of the large George England Little Giant with an open cab but unfortunately this arrangement does not hide the gas tank at the rear of the cab. This is a well-travelled locomotive and was used to officially open and run on the 16mm garden railway of the York City & District Society of Model Engineers on Easter Sunday 2011.

THE FFESTINIOG DOUBLE FAIRLIES

With traffic on the Ffestiniog Railway continuing to rise, along with possible competition from

7. (Above) WN135 Little Giant on the photographer's Netherton Moor garden railway hauling the correct Victorian rolling stock.

(WN135-1 – Geoff Munday)

8. (Above right) WN135 Left-hand side view of Little Giant beautifully lined by Lightline. The George England locomotives lend themselves to this professional lining due to the large number of panels and the triple lining of white/black/white. Although the coupling and connecting rods are correct for the large George England engines, the wheels should be of a disc pattern and not spoked. There is no hint of the oscillating engine hidden above the frames or of the large 2¼in boiler covered by the all-over saddle tank. The dummy water filler on top of the tank covers the Goodall type water-filling system with the boiler just below the tank top.

(WN135-2 – Geoff Munday)

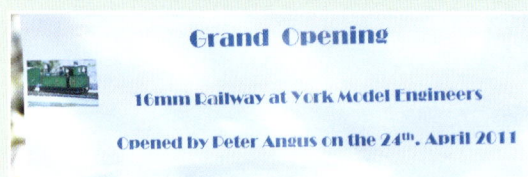

10. (Middle right) WN186 Little Giant with the open cab arrangement supplied by George England as their number 235 and based on photographs from the Ffestiniog Archives that have been published in several books/magazines. Unfortunately it has not been possible to reproduce one of these photographs in this book. The model has the usual double crosshead slide bars, which replaced the original single slide bars in 1869, and has steel disc wheels as fitted to the larger George England locomotives.

(WN186 -1 – Mike Lax)

11. (Below right) Little Giant breaks the tape on the occasion of the official opening of the York City and District Society of Model Engineers 16mm Garden Railway on Easter Sunday the 24th April 2011.

(WN186-3 – Paul Howard)

12. (Below) WN186 After officially opening the 16mm garden railway of the York City and District Society of Model Engineers, Little Giant takes the first official train around round the track with a set of Ffestiniog 4 wheel coaches loaned for the occasion by Geoff Munday.

(WN186-4 – Paul Howard from Tag)

other lines, authorisation was given in 1869 to double the track. However an alternative solution presented itself due to the efforts of Robert Francis Fairlie (1831-1885), who proposed an articulated form of engine which he patented in 1864. This would be the first narrow gauge example and would be capable of increasing the capacity of the line without the need to double or relay the track. The boiler was double ended and symmetrical with two separate fireboxes and a common water space. With the cab in the centre the fireman and driver occupied different sides of the firebox casing, water capacity was limited to side tanks and the bunker capacity to whatever space was available on the fireman's side.

As a means of providing a compact but powerful locomotive for short distance operation the double Fairlie had its advantages but as the size became larger so the water and fuel capacity was confined between the larger boiler and the loading gauge. There was also the problem of the complicated flexible steam connections to the swivelling power bogies. Nevertheless there were mountain railways with steep gradients and sharp curves where the inherent

qualities of flexibility, excellent riding at lower speeds and good adhesion proved their worth over many years. They were built by several manufacturers and operated in most parts of the world including 45 for the Transcaucasian Railway and some 50 for the Mexican Railways. The largest application of the Fairlie double boiler arrangement was the slightly altered Pechot-Bourdon locomotives built for the French military railways with over 300 being produced.

The first Ffestiniog Double Fairlie was ordered from George England & Co in 1868 and delivered in the following year. Named Little Wonder it was to be the last steam locomotive built by George England before the works became the Fairlie Engine and Carriage Works. For the first six months the locomotive underwent trials witnessed by engineers from several countries and under the watchful eyes of the railway press. The Fairlie proved capable of hauling more than twice the load of the large England 0-4-0 saddle tank engines at a greater speed and using less fuel. For the first time a 2ft gauge locomotive was able to negotiate curves of less than 120ft radius hauling 150 tons uphill at

13. Double Fairlie James Spooner on a train for Portmadoc in August 1913. It had been rebuilt five years earlier with a wagon-top boiler.

((22) Andrew Neale collection)

15. WN217 The third James Spooner locomotive and the second one constructed by Mike Lax. The single boiler has been extended with the centre flue containing water tubes to enhance the steaming in order to use the SVS engine with the larger 10mm cylinders.

(WN217-1 – Geoff Munday)

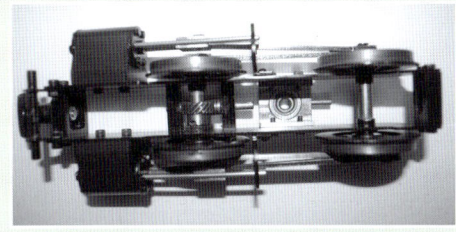

16. (Top left) The front bogie of this Double Fairlie uses a plain spherical bearing to provide all round movement which is limited by the close dimensions of the bearing housings. A further limitation is required on horizontal movement to protect the drive shaft during transport and in case of a derailment.

Double Fairlie front bogie – Mike Lax)

17. (Left) The rear bogie of the Double Fairlie with the large plain disc bearing sandwiched between the side bearings of the bogie frame. This bearing gives horizontal movement and a small degree of longitudinal movement whilst retaining the lateral relationship between the bogie and the main frame. The pin at the inner end of the bogie is part of the arrangement to limit the horizontal travel and thus prevent damage to the drive shaft. All of these limitations protect the underside of the main frame from the articulated bogie. Part of the crossed helical drive to the bogie can also be seen, although the alignment of the gears has not been completed.

(Double Fairlie rear bogie – Mike Lax)

18. (Right) WN239 – The fireman's side of the fourth Double Fairlie model, again built by Mike Lax to the original design. In this case the model has been named David Lloyd George on one side and the Welsh equivalent Dafydd Lloyd George on the other with the nameplates correctly to the left whichever side is viewed. This model was radio controlled on the steam regulator and the forward/reverse controls. Notice how all of these models have been lined by Lightline, a very easily justified extra that certainly enhances the looks of these attractive engines. (Geoff Munday)

(WN239-2 – Geoff Munday)

19. (Below right) WN239 – Who could resist a second photograph of David Lloyd George, seen this time from the driver's side, identified by the tool boxes on the side tanks? The fireman's side is distinguished by the coal bunkers in the side tank.

(WN239-3 – Geoff Munday)

20 miles per hour. The success of Little Wonder led the Ffestiniog Railway to order a further Double Fairlie from the Avonside Engine Company of Bristol (Works Nos. 929/930). The second locomotive, named James Spooner, was a modified version of Little Wonder and was to be the prototype for the later Double Fairlies. As built in 1872, James Spooner had a parallel boiler which was replaced in 1889 but a further rebuild of 1908 adopted the more familiar wagon-top boiler associated with the later Fairlies. Both Fairlies gave good service with Little Wonder being scrapped in 1882 after 13 years of hard work whilst James Spooner carried on until 1932 after two rebuilds.

Despite considerable interest in the Ffestiniog locomotives, models of the Double Fairlie are very few and it is not difficult to understand why. Along with the usual problems of the flexible steam connections there is the added complication of a double-ended boiler with two fireboxes and two burners. Many of these models have been started but not finished, or on completion have failed to live up to their owners' expectations or in some cases failed to operate at all. Another point to consider is the rather large size wheels which on the full size locomotive were 2ft 8in diameter equating to just under 43mm in 16mm scale. Couple this with the free running of an articulated locomotive and there is a recipe for high speed that makes it essential to fit radio control.

There is another problem with those large diameter wheels caused by the top of the wheels coming up inside the main frame. Now in full size practice the bogie movement can be contained within the frames, the sharpest curve on the Ffestiniog occurring at Tyler's curve at 2½ chains (equivalent to 8ft 6ins in 16mm), but for a garden railway environment with curves down to 3ft 6in or even less the wheels would come into contact with the main frame.

With all these problems to consider it is not surprising that the first model to be built waited until WN189, well down the works list. Since then there have been several more Double Fairlie models constructed to the same basic design but modified and built by Mike Lax. Whatever the problems, the sight of one of these locomotives pulling a correct set of rolling stock round a curved section of track, steam coming from both chimneys, is a wonderful sight, justifying the considerable effort required to construct these difficult models.

The object in building WN189 was to give the appearance of the Double Fairlie yet simplify the mechanical side. Instead of four direct drive cylinders, an SVS geared oscillating engine (Boxer type with double output shafts) was concealed below the dummy firebox with carden shafts down to a crossed helical open gearbox of 1½:1 on the outer axle of each bogie. This is the same method used on other articulated shaft drive models and though expensive in terms of the universal joints is very reliable. To enable the bogie to swing sufficiently for a minimum radius of 3ft 6in the wheel size was reduced to 36mm tread diameter which gives adequate clearance to the underside of the frames. Fortunately, the valve gear is inside the frames on the full size locomotive so that only dummy cylinders and associated running gear are required. To simplify the boiler arrangements the model was based on James Spooner of 1889 with the Nielson parallel boiler and all-over cab. The complicated double boiler was replaced by a plain centre flue boiler on one end of the locomotive only. The opposite side is a dummy shell with the gas tank located under it and across the frame. Inside the cab a dummy firebox cover connects the two 'boilers'. The water gauge and steam regulator are arranged to be clear of the firebox, the water gauge being a Roundhouse Engineering side-mounted type.

All this effort produced a spectacular model, as can be seen from the photographs, which captured the spirit of the Ffestiniog Double Fairlie and when matched with the correct rolling stock looked quite outstanding. However in reality this was a double engine with a single power system and therefore limited to moderate loads on a reasonably level track. Later models built by Mike have increased the single boiler length and include water tubes within the centre flue along with an up-rated SVS engine with 10mm bore cylinders. WN217 illustrates one of the later locomotives that was exported to and now operates in America.

THE SINGLE FAIRLIE – 'A JOY TO WATCH'

Designed by George Percival Spooner the first Single Fairlies were built for the North Wales Narrow Gauge Railway in 1875. Soon after in 1876 the Ffestiniog Railway received its own Single Fairlie from the Vulcan Foundry and named it Taliesin after the Head Bard of Urien Rheged who died about A.D.570. The intention was to replace the large George England locomotives, Little Giant and Welsh Pony, on the lighter trains. With a 0-4-4 wheel layout the engine looked similar to a conventional tank locomotive but was mounted on two bogies and was effectively half a double engine fitted with a cab, bunker and trailing bogie. The boiler was larger than the previous NWNGR locomotives and so too were the wheels and cylinders. It was a very successful locomotive running well over 20,000 miles a year initially and had covered over half a million miles before it was withdrawn in 1932.

The original design featured an inside framed bogie and straight sided cab but due to the tendency of the locomotive to roll it was possible for the upper corners of the cab to be in contact with the bridges and tunnels. In response its profile was altered to reduce the width of the upper cab and by 1877 the stability was improved by replacing the trailing bogie with an outside-framed unit. The semi-open cab was eventually replaced with an enclosed cab. An interesting point with all 0-4-4 locomotives involves the distribution of weight, which tends to make for unstable running when operating bunker first. The locomotive is naturally stable when running chimney first but relies on the trailing bogie to maintain stability when operating in the reverse direction with most of the weight distribution on the driving wheels. Side play on the trailing bogie makes the situation more pronounced and for example the 0-4-4 narrow gauge Forney locomotives of the Maine were turned to run chimney first every trip. The Single Fairlie locomotive on the other hand had the trailing bogie on a fixed pivot making it easier to control the movement

20. (Above left) Engraving of the Single Fairlie Taliesin, showing the inside framed rear non-powered bogie that was quickly replaced with an outside framed version due to excessive rolling.

((15) Andrew Neale collection – Engraving Taliesin)

21. (Above right) Taliesin with outside framed rear bogie but still retaining the half-cab arrangement.

((16) Andrew Neale collection – "Taliesin")

22. (Left) The replica Taliesin built at Boston Lodge Works in 1999 and seen at Porthmadog station in 2008.

(Taliesin-May 2008 – Geoff Munday)

of the engine. With the model this instability can be improved by using a heavy rear frame of 0.125in steel from which the forward support of the boiler is cantilevered out towards the front. The heavy steel plate also supports the rear bogie pivot.

Single Fairlies never enjoyed the success of the double version and were only produced in quantity for the New Zealand Government Railways by the Avonside Engine Company, who supplied 18 of the 0-6-4 R class in 1878-9 and a further seven of the similar S class in 1880-1. However, in North America the Single Fairlie type enjoyed more success in the form of the Mason Bogie built by the Mason Machine Works, Taunton in California. The first appeared in 1871 with the company producing over 140 engines ranging from small 0-4-4 to the larger 2-8-6 until the works

ceased locomotive production in 1890. A small number of Mason Bogies were constructed by ALCO between 1903 and 1914. They did not offer any power advantage over an equivalent rigid framed engine yet had the complication of flexible steam connections and power bogie pivots. The double engine had twice the power and far superior riding qualities. Despite these limitations the Single Fairlie remains one of the most attractive locomotives and the flexibility, particularly in model form, is a joy to watch. So here are the details of the Single Fairlie models.

SINGLE FAIRLIE TALIESIN

The advantages of articulation had already been appreciated with the construction of the Garratt Piracicaba, WN3, when it was decided to construct the first Single Fairlie. It

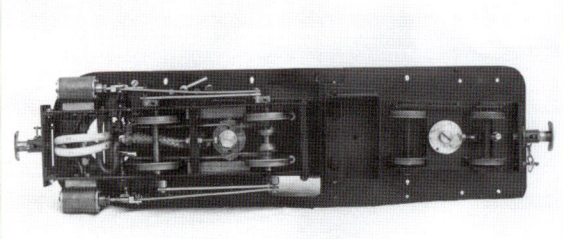

23. (Above top) WN004 – Single Fairlie Patricia constructed in 1984 using a Roundhouse Engineering 0-4-0 chassis as the basis for the power bogie. This is an early Roundhouse product with inside slip eccentric valve gear operating the outside cylinder steam valve via a rocking arm. At a time when many garden railway locomotives used methylated spirit fired pot boilers, this model was fitted with a centre flue gas fired boiler that also included a water gauge.

(WN004-1 – N D Kirkbride)

24. (Above) WN004 – Early model of the Single Fairlie from the left hand side. The gas tank was located in the rear of the left hand side tank along with the displacement lubricator at the front. This arrangement allowed the rear bunker to be used to house the radio control, provision for which was then far more difficult than at present due to the size of the receiver, batteries and particularly the servo . Unlike modern higher frequency radio control the aerial was long and was very much influenced by surrounding metalwork.

(WN004-2 – N D Kirkbride)

25. (Above) WN004 The underside of Patricia showing the articulated front power bogie and the rear four-wheel non-powered unit. Notice how the pivot on the power bogie is set back from the centre of the wheelbase. This offsets the weight of the cylinders at the front against the distribution of the weight of the main locomotive. Here there is even weight on each axle otherwise the bogie would be front heavy. The pivot can be seen to be a large disc for the horizontal movement with side bearings for limited vertical movement. Two stops are visible at the back of the rear wheels to limit the horizontal movement and thus protect the flexible pipes if the locomotive was to derail. The high-pressure inlet flexible steam pipe is made up of thick wall silicon tube reinforced with stainless steel braid clamped at each end. The two front pipes are the exhaust steam from the cylinders and require only the basic silicon tube. A simple pin type bearing serves the rear bogie which is mounted on a rubber bush to provide limited vertical movement.

(WN004-4 – N D Kirkbride)

26. (Below) WN132 – Model of the Single Fairlie Taliesin using a hidden geared engine drive. The forward/reverse lever of the SVS engine can be seen under the front of the cab, with the drive being via a carden shaft to the outer axle of the power bogie. The cylinders on the bogie are dummy. The gas tank is located in the rear bunker.

(WN132-1 Taliesin – Geoff Lumsdon)

was based on the Ffestiniog Railway Taliesin with its four-wheel power bogie and could, with certain artistic licence, use the available Roundhouse Engineering outside framed slip eccentric chassis. Built in 1984, at a time when garden railways were in their infancy and somewhat basic, WN4 Patricia was found to have a remarkable ability to hold the track. The use of a heavy steel plate rear frame improved the balance of the model and ensured that it could operate reliably in either direction. At a time when most models were simple 0-4-0s and derailments were par for the course this locomotive could enjoy an entire day's running without any mishap. The downside was the free running which tended to give a lively performance even with the small wheels of the Roundhouse Engineering chassis.

The next Single Fairlie was WN132, again based on Taliesin but using the hidden geared technology of an SVS engine located in the dummy firebox area with carden shaft drive to 2:1 crossed helical gears on the outer axle of the power bogie. The power bogies of the Single and Double Fairlie are identical and use the same 36mm wheels. The correct wheel diameter for the Ffestiniog Fairlies should be 43mm @ 16mm/ft, equivalent to 2ft 8in. However, the wheel diameter of the models was reduced to provide greater flexibility to the power bogies. A plain centre flue boiler with poker type burner supplied the steam and the gas tank was located conveniently in the bunker. The front power bogie has the expected limited horizontal movement along with longitudinal vertical play but remains rigid to the body in the lateral plain. To allow for twist in the track the trailing bogie has the horizontal movement bearing encased in a rubber bush to give a very limited longitudinal and lateral vertical movement. The geared drive ensures a steady and limited speed and the articulation of the Fairlie locomotive negotiates the curves and track irregularities with ease, whilst the heavy rear frame gives stable running in both directions. As with all articulated locomotives the movement of the bogies is controlled by stops thereby preventing the bogies from coming into contact with the main frames. Horizontal limits prevent the drive shafts from damage from the inner ends of the bogie frames and by careful arrangement of the drive the locomotive can negotiate curves of 3ft 6in radius.

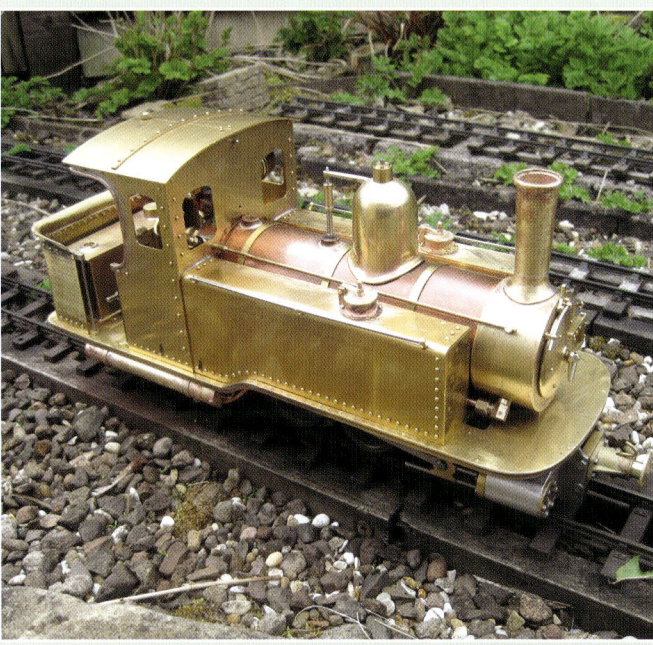

29. (Above right) – WN240 'In the brass' view of Moel Tyfan. This model uses a hidden SVS engine located in the dummy firebox area with a carden shaft drive to the leading axle of the front power bogie. The shaft transmits the drive to the axle using 1½:1 crossed helical gears. The union at the left hand side of the smokebox is for the exhaust pipe from the engine.

(WN240-4 – Author)

27. (Top left) Single Fairlie 0-6-4T Moel Tryfan at Dinas Junction.

((9) Andrew Neale collection)

28. (Above left) Snowdon Ranger at Dinas in 1909.

((4) Photograph by late KACR Nunn, courtesy of Andrew Neale collection)

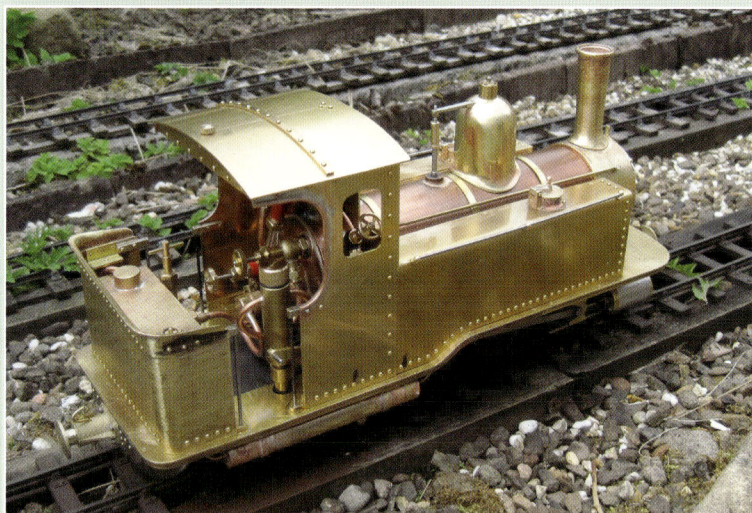

30. (Left) WN240 The cab and bunker of Moel Tryfan. The gas tank is located in the rear bunker with the floor mounted gas regulator in front. The lever at the right hand side of the cab entrance is the forward/reverse control and the small valve visible through the side window is the water level/blow off valve. Just inside the entrance can be seen the heavy steel plate forming the rear frame. This additional weight improves the balance of the locomotive when running in reverse.

(WN240-5 – Author)

31. (Above) WN240 Moel Tryfan running on Clive Shergold's garden railway at Middlesbrough.

(WN240-1 – Paul Humphries)

MOEL TRYFAN AND SNOWDON RANGER

The next Single Fairlie models were based on the first of the George Percival Spooner designed locomotives, Moel Tryfan and Snowdon Ranger, built by the Vulcan Foundry in 1875 for the North Wales Narrow Gauge Railway. G. P. Spooner had originally intended his Single Fairlies to be of 0-4-4T wheel arrangement but the weight restrictions on the light track of the NWNGR required an axle limit of 4½ tons. The power bogie had therefore to be stretched to the 0-6-4T wheel arrangement. Both designs were very similar but the power bogie could not use the same inside suspension of the FR locomotive due to the centre axle, so the sprung bearers were mounted outboard of the wheels giving a much stiffer resistance to roll. The 0-6-4T Single Fairlies were therefore able to retain the inside framed trailing bogie whereas that of Taliesin had to be changed to an outside framed arrangement.

The models WN141 and 240 followed the same drive system used on the previous Single Fairlie and both were named Moel Tryfan. For the same reasons as the previous Fairlies the driving wheels were retained at 36mm. The SVS engine occupies the dummy firebox area with the added advantage that the air receiver located under the right hand side cab footplate very effectively conceals not only the engine but also the forward/reverse lever mechanism. The gas tank occupies the rear bunker and consists of three vertical one inch square section brass tubes soldered together to give a tank 3in x 1in x 1½in high.

GOWRIE

This was not the end for the Single Fairlie models as there was still one more locomotive – the unique Hunslet Engine Company Gowrie. As with Moel Tryfan and Snowdon Ranger the wheel arrangement was 0-6-4 but it was a totally

32. (Left) WN240 – Close up view of the Single Fairlie Moel Tryfan. The dummy water filler covers the Goodall water filler valve. Notice that this Single Fairlie unlike Taliesin retains the inside framed rear trailing bogie.

(WN240-2 Paul Humphreys)

33. (Below left) Single Fairlie Gowrie at South Snowdon in 1909.

((2) Late KACR Nunn-courtesy Andrew Neale collection)

34. (Below right) Hunslet Works photograph of the Single Fairlie Gowrie.

((3) Andrew Neale collection)

35. (Left) WN173 – Finished model of the Gowrie based on the locomotive built by Hunslet Engine Works in 1908. The model has been lined by Lightline. Notice how the boiler is cantilevered out from the main frame. Under the smokebox can be seen the two steam pipes leading to and from the cylinders. One of the problems with this type of locomotive is the long steam pipes made worse by the six-coupled bogie which moves the pivot further away from the cylinders. To reduce the displacement of the flexible steam they must be routed as close to the pivot points as possible and in this case pass behind the pivot in a U shape. Passing in front would reduce the length of the steam pipes but increase the sideways displacement.

(WN173-1 –Geoff Munday)

36. (Right) WN173 – Three-quarter rear side view of Gowrie. The servo operating rod to the steam regulator can be seen in the cab opening. The rear bunker easily covers the gas tank and also houses the radio control receiver and batteries.

(WN173-2 – Geoff Munday)

different outline that was built by Hunslet in 1908 as their Works No 979. Gone was the neat inside valve gear of the previous Single Fairlie designs to be replaced with Walschaerts valve gear. The boiler was left to stick out front, without the curved running boards typical of the other Fairlies, resulting in a strange looking beast that seamed all rear and no front. Unlike the previous locomotives that had an active and long life this Hunslet Single Fairlie was not an outstanding success. There were problems with the flexible steam joints leaking and the rather long steam pipes caused loss of heat and a lack of flexibility. With dwindling fortunes the NWNGR took the opportunity to get rid of their hapless and basically redundant locomotive to the Ministry of Munitions in 1916 during the First World War. By 1918 the locomotive was again up for sale and may have done some work before being scrapped by 1930.

The model on the other hand lends itself to using the Roundhouse cylinders and their Walschaerts valve gear but requires radio control due to the free running of the Single Fairlie. The boiler is also rather long and thin being 1¾in diameter with an overall length including the smokebox of 9½in. To ensure that steam is picked up cleanly there is a large rear boiler turret in the cab with the steam regulator well above the top of the barrel. The safety valve is fitted to this turret and exhausts through a hole in the roof. Despite the long steam pipes and the long and small diameter boiler, the model performs very well and as with all articulated Fairlie locomotives is free running.

37. (Left) Linda at Porthmadog during its early days on the Ffestiniog Railway. Although running with a tender, the locomotive does not have the pony truck that was fitted in 1969.

((10) Penrhyn Hunslet Linda – Andrew Neale collection)

38. (Below) General Arrangement drawing of Hunslet Engine Company Order No 15420.

(Leeds Museums and Galleries – Armley Mills)

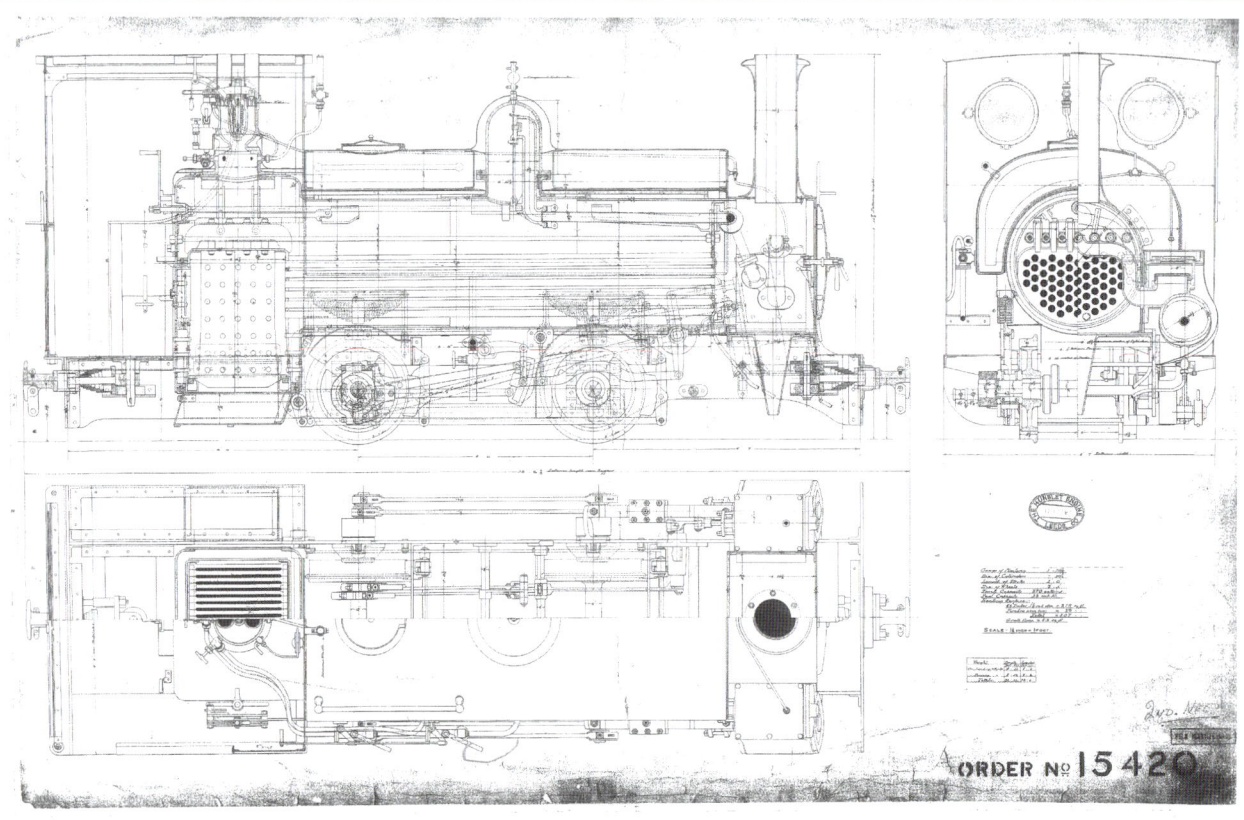

ORDER No 15420

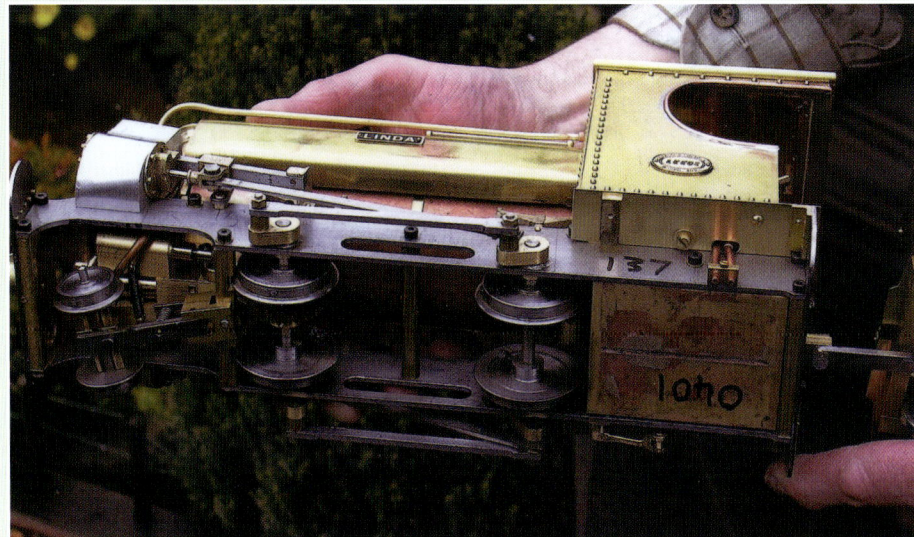

39. (Left) WN137 – The underside of the model of Linda showing how the SVS geared engine has been installed above the pony truck but under the boiler, the same method as used on the Hohenzollern 2-4-0 locomotive. Since the full size locomotive had inside valve gear it was only necessary to provide dummy cylinders and motion work. The gas tank can also be seen located between the frames behind the rear axle. It is the same type as used on the Sentinel and Robey locomotives.
(WN137-1 – Geoff Lumsdon)

40. (Below left) WN137 – Looking down on Linda with the model as yet unpainted. Notice how the cab is full of boiler fittings with little room for the turret of the Sentinel type gas tank. For the water level and blow-off system it was necessary to take a banjo fitting of the boiler with a pipe running to the left and down to a floor mounted valve in the bottom left of the cab. There is not much room to fit an engine driver in the cab.
(WN137-2 – Geoff Lumsdon)

THE PENRHYN HUNSLETS

The Penrhyn Quarries at Bethesda pioneered the concept of a railway to the sea in 1801, but it was 1876 before they followed the Ffestiniog Railway by converting to steam traction. Prior to 1801 only small quantities of slate could be conveyed from quarry to port on the backs of horses. The building of the two-foot gauge Penrhyn Tramway changed all that and made it feasible for large scale quarrying since much heavier loads could be transported along it to the port using horse power. This remained satisfactory until 1847 when the decision was taken to re-site the railway with easier gradients. The first engines came from the Union Works of De Winton & Co at Caernarvon and are illustrated in the chapter on industrial locomotives. Following these vertical boiler engines the quarry switched in 1882 to more conventional locomotives from Hunslet Engine

Works with power and weight variations to meet specific duties. For the main line to the port three large saddle tanks, Charles, Linda and Blanche, were delivered in 1882/3 and worked the 6½ mile line up until closure in 1962. Less than one month after closure, Linda was hired by the Ffestiniog Railway and was eventually bought by them along with her sister Blanche in 1963.

Whereas their performance was satisfactory on the Penrhyn Railway, the short wheelbase and large overhang made them too lively for the speeds required on their new line. Also the saddle tank and bunker capacity was totally inadequate for operation on the Ffestiniog. To deal with the water and fuel limitations Linda was fitted with an unused George England tender that also helped to steady the rear end of the engine. Modifications to Blanche soon followed but this time with a cab tender.

41. (Above) WN137 – The finished model of Linda. There is very little indication that the power is a geared SVS engine under the smoke box, except for the forward/reverse lever at the front. The displacement lubricator is just visible inside the cab with the filler part of the gas tank behind it. The tender is virtually the same as that used on the George England models.

(WN137-3 – Geoff Lumsdon)

42. (Left) WN137 – Front view of Linda showing how compact this locomotive is with an overall width of 3 ¾ in which would not have been possible if the locomotive was built with a dual gauge facility.

(WN137-4 – Geoff Lumsdon)

Further improvements included the fitting of a pony truck to Linda in 1969 and to Blanche in 1972 with the object of steadying the front end. The models of the two locomotives are based on the later versions as running on the Ffestiniog Railway.

The longest running production of live steam models based on the Hunslet Engine Works must be those of the Finescale Engineering Company, proprietor Tony Sant, with their Alice, Port and Large Quarry versions of the industrial/quarry locomotives. Many more of these excellent models have been produced over at least 20 years by other manufacturers, especially popular being the larger Hunslets such as Cackler and of course Charles, Linda and Blanche.

One of the earliest models was that of Lilla manufactured by Robyn Gosling to the very highest engineering standards. A chassis from one of these models was used on the first Garratt WN3 but exhibited the usual characteristics of direct drive cylinders and required radio control and also brakes. Even the Large Quarry locomotives were relatively small at 5ft 7in wide and a fraction less than 8ft high or, in 16mm terms, 89mm (3½ in) wide and 128mm high. Add to this a wheelbase of 5ft on a chassis of 16ft 7in and it can be seen that a model of these wonderful locomotives is not without difficulty and would give a lively performance at anything above slow speed.

The idea of building a model using a geared drive to give slow consistent running without

43. (Above left) WN168 – This model of Linda in the dark blue/black livery was based on a photograph of the full size locomotive next to the water tank at Porthmadog. It is a particularly attractive but short lived colour scheme used between overhauls in 1990/1 and 1994/5. The model is seen in steam at Bouth Station on the Forest Field Railway on a particularly damp day in June 2012. It is a tribute to the cameraman and the builder of the layout background that at first sight this could be a photograph of the full-size locomotive.

(WN168-1 – Ian Midgley)

44. (Top right) WN178 – An alternative to Linda was the sister locomotive Blanche (Hunslet Engine Co No 589 of 1893), purchased by the Ffestiniog Railway from Penrhyn Quarries in 1963. This model differs from those of Linda in that it is fitted with the cab-tender that has been retained with Blanche. The difference with the full-size locomotives was in the cylinder outline due to receiving new cylinders with outside admission piston valves during overhaul in 1972.

(WN178-1 – Geoff Munday)

45. (Above) WN178 – The Penryn Hunslet Blanche photographed by Geoff Munday on his Netherton Moor L. R. The model is finished in green with black edging.

(WN178-2 – Geoff Munday)

resort to radio control remained on the back burner until the advent of the Hohenzollern models. Now here was a locomotive with the same 2-4-0 wheel arrangement, slightly shorter, with a width even with the dual gauge facility of just over 3in and most of all an excellent performance on a track with gradients (limited by wheel slip on greasy track). Linda/Blanche could be built to a similar layout on a 10.375in long frame and by abandoning the dual gauge facility the width could be reduced to 3.75in. As with the Hohenzollern the SVS engine was located below the boiler and above the pony truck and driving to the front axle. Steam was generated by a 2in diameter plain centre flue boiler with a Finescale gas burner and a gas tank located between the frames. To improve the detail several castings, including the dummy cylinders, were kindly supplied by DJB Engineering.

The first of the Penrhyn Hunslets was WN137 and is illustrated finished in black livery and lined in red and light blue in the accompanying photographs. The method of mounting the hidden SVS engine can also be seen and is very similar to that used on the 2-4-0 Hohenzollern models. The second Linda, WN168, while mechanically the same, is finished in the very attractive dark blue/black livery with white lining. WN178 on the other hand was based on Blanche complete with the cab tender as fitted to the full size locomotive and finished in green/black with red lining. It is the only example of Blanche to be built. Further models of Linda have been built by Mike Lax.

ANATOMY OF A LOCOMOTIVE – THE BELL LOCOMOTIVE

The Bell locomotive is definitely an oddball and is virtually unknown despite the apparent success and interesting origins of the builder. The model is based on the only articulated version of several lightweight (20t and less) geared rigid framed locomotives produced by the Bell Locomotive Works, Inc of New York City. The designer was Harvey W Bell who in 1908 was the manager of the Stanley Steam Automobile Agency in Yonkers, New York. It was while visiting the Catskill Aqueduct construction site in Westchester County that he realised he could produce a more suitable contractor's locomotive than the gasoline engines then in use. So was born the Bell locomotive, which was to provide the sturdy workhorse for the next twelve years in the construction industry. However, as the locomotives were developed they started to take on the characteristics of the more conventional industrial engines whilst retaining the valuable automobile features of standard and interchangeable parts. One of these features was the use of a totally enclosed Stanley automobile engine with the cylinders, rods, valve-gear and gearwheels forming a single unit running in an oil bath. Roller bearings were applied to all moving parts other than the pistons and crossheads. The same engine was used regardless of gauge or size with the larger locomotives using two engines. This was a similar design feature to that of the Sentinel locomotives based on the Sentinel Wagon technology.

The boiler was of the horizontal fire-tube, 'water level' type (the water tubes went throughout the boiler and steam area), turned out by the Stanley Steam Car and had the outer shell wrapped in piano wire to give greater strength. These boilers could raise steam in only twenty minutes. A steam jet using the atomiser principle to lift the fuel to the burner operated the oil burner. Bell engines were used in plantations, quarries and clay pits and for all kinds of construction work throughout the United States, including the construction of the New York Subway. They were exported to Cuba, South America and the Philippines.

The model is based on the only articulated eight-wheel double bogie locomotive type, which had two geared engines, one on each truck with two 5in x 6in cylinders. Steam and hand brakes were fitted to all eight wheels. The locomotive was available in sizes from 10 to 25 tons but the only specification given was for the smallest at 20,000lbs weight for 24in gauge with an overall length of 14ft 11in over the buffer beams, a width of 4ft 6in and a truck wheelbase of 45in. This is a rather small locomotive so in order to use existing equipment the size of the model was increased to bring the length to 12in and a width of 3½in over the main frames. This also meant that the bogies of the Avonside articulated locomotive could be used with only slight modifications. The bogie or truck on the Bell locomotive was not fitted with a buffer beam, the buffing gear being attached to the main frame. Whereas the Bell locomotive had the drive engine on each truck, the model uses the tried and tested layout of the Avonside Articulated with the SVS engine located between the trucks and attached to the main frame. The large rear water tank houses a standard gas tank topped with a dummy fuel tank complete with fuel level gauge. The short fat boiler is fitted with water tubes.

The Bell locomotive was certainly not the most attractive engine, even by industrial standards, but it was a genuine attempt to build a contractor's locomotive designed for purpose rather than a conventional design modified for industrial use. With its fully enclosed interchangeable engine geared to the axle, its fast steaming high-pressure boiler and the use of stock parts from the automobile industry, it pre-dated the similar approach of the Sentinel

1. The construction of the bogie can be seen in this photograph. The two trucks are a modified version of the Avonside articulated locomotive bogie but unlike the Avonside there is no requirement for buffer beams. In the case of the Bell locomotive they were attached to the main frames. Between the frames and central to the wheelbase is the rear bogie pivot consisting of a flat brass disc for horizontal movement pivoted at the side for limited vertical movement. These side bearings are attached to the bogie side frames and the horizontal brass disc bearing locates up against a flat frame plate of gauge plate. As with previous articulated locomotives the vertical movement is limited to the longitudinal axis only, thereby retaining the relationship between the rear bogie and the main frame. The vertical movement of the rear bogie is limited by a 6ba socket cap screw firmly attached to the bearing cross member and passing through the enlarged hole in the small round ended

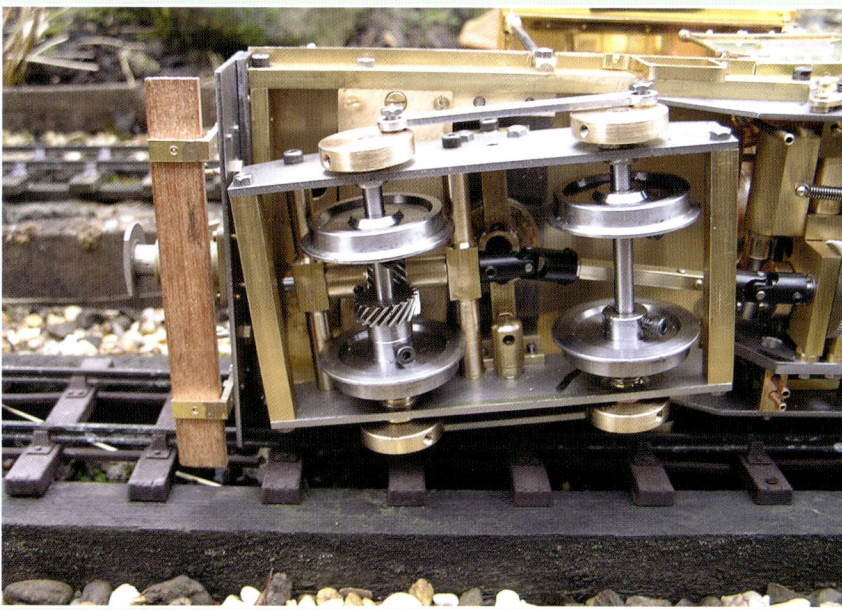

pillar attached to the bogie side frame – clearly visible in the photograph. Notice that since the model will have to be dismantled for painting, the crossed helical gear on the axle has not been aligned with the shaft gear. The wheels are dual gauge for 32mm and 45mm operation.

(WN198-7 – Author)

2. Here is the underside of the locomotive showing the drive shafts and the location of the SVS engine. This drive shaft arrangement is the standard for articulated models with carden shafts running from the engine over the inner axle of the bogie to crossed helical gears on the outer axle. Notice how the outer universal joint of the Carden shaft is located under the pivot in order to reduce sideways displacement when the engine negotiates curved track. Side rods then transmit power to the inner axle. Crossed helical gears are very efficient and the position of the bearing cross members can be accurately set up on the side frames using the digital readout on the milling machine. Unfortunately, due to the small width of this locomotive, the drive shafts are not quite in

line in the straight ahead position, as can be seen on the front bogie. Notice how the engine is as far to one side as possible with the forward/reverse lever neatly passed through the main frame reinforcing plate.

(WN198-6 – Author)

3. (Right) This picture illustrates the short fat boiler, the dummy water tank and oil tank. Typical of this type of model was the use of brass bar stock for the main frame, in this case 3/16in by 3/8in for the side and front/rear stretchers. The mainframe pivot plates are 2mm gauge plate which is used as a direct bearing surface for the front and rear horizontal disc bearing. The front bearing includes an extra pivot to provide full articulation but this movement is limited to about 1/16in at the wheels. In other words, the front bogie will tolerate twist and gradient to a maximum of 1/16in. over the wheelbase. On the other hand, the rear bogie will only tolerate inclination of the track but will maintain the same alignment with the main frame. The reinforcing plates on the main

frame have the added advantage of effectively hiding the SVS engine, since with the full size the locomotive the driving engines were located on each bogie.

(WN198-2 – Author)

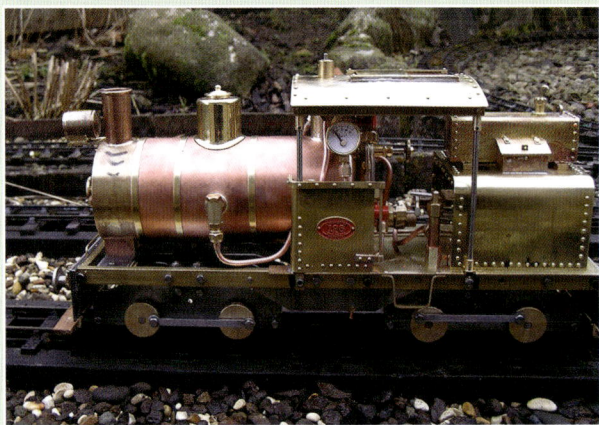

4. (Left) Opposite side view of the model in the brass in which there is no indication of the location of the SVS engine. The bogie frames and the main frame reinforcing plate effectively hide even the drive shafts. Notice the toolbox on top of the water tank, which covers the gas tank outlet banjo union.

(WN198-1 – Author)

5. (Below left) The locomotive finished in satin black with a simple white lining. The original locomotive did not have side panels to the cab but these were added to improve the rather basic industrial outline. The part open dummy water filler covers the gas tank filler valve and just above it is the imitation oil level gauge. The lettering was taken from the illustration of the locomotive in the <gearedsteam.com/bell/ double truck> website.

(WN198-4 – Author)

6. (Opposite) This front view of the locomotive illustrates the small width, the main frames being only 3½in wide. The square, inside domed attachments to the buffer beams are to locate poles used to push trucks on an adjacent track. Whether they were fitted to this locomotive is not known and in reality they would risk pushing the locomotive over. Still, it is a nice bit of detail.

(WN198-5 – Author)

Wagon Works in England. Unfortunately for both companies, they could not resist the relentless advance of the internal combustion engine spurred on by the technical advances brought about by the pressures of the First World War. The Bell Locomotive Works probably ceased production in the 1920s. The original illustration of the locomotive came from a reproduction of the companies Bulletin No. 134 published in the early 1920s.

REFERENCES:

From the Internet –

- Bell Geared Steam Locomotives Double Truck Eight Wheel.
- Bell Geared Steam Locomotives Geared Steam Locomotive Works.
- Bell Geared Steam Locomotives Components.

INTO THE WOODS

Wood has always been one of the most valuable materials for mankind whether for use in its basic form as a fuel, dressed wood for the construction and covering of buildings, the framework for machinery or as simple household items. Until the advent of iron and steel, huge quantities of timber were used in the construction of ships and boats along with road and agricultural transport. Having used up large quantities of timber in their own forests, European countries turned to their colonies with their vast resources of virtually virgin forest. Apart from timber for general use, there was also, within these forests, vast quantities of valuable exotic timber, if only it could be economically harvested.

It was not the felling of the trees as this was a fairly straightforward process, the problem arose when the timber had to be transported. Wood is both heavy and cumbersome and many of these exotic trees were of considerable size reaching in some cases a diameter in the order of 8ft. Once felled, the tree would be cleared of its branches and cut into reasonable lengths using hand saws but now came the problem of transporting to the sawmill and then from the sawmill as dressed timber to the main customer or shipping agents. Initially, timber would be cut close to a transport system such as a river allowing the whole logs to be floated to the sawmill and thence out to distribution. Soon this convenient situation was lost as the timber operation advanced into the forest and a means had to be found to move the logs over ground that was usually very wet and boggy. Initially, oxen were used but the said boggy ground required some sort of walkway for the

1. (Left) This is a small geared 4 wheeler New Zealand bush locomotive built by the Auckland engineering firm of Gibbon and Harris. They weighed about 6 tons with a two cylinder steam engine mounted under the smokebox driving to the front axle by spur gears. Side rods transmitted the power to the rear wheels. No two were exactly the same and the engines were probably from ships auxiliary engines and the wheels from NZR wagons. The model follows these general lines with appropriately a marine based engine, in this case the boxer version of the SVS engine geared to the front axle. This delightfully ugly locomotive in model form could have been improved by locating the displacement lubricator in the side bunker or at least by painting it black.

(WN 117-1 – George Ansell)

2. (Below left) This shows the opposite side view of the Gibbon & Harris locomotive. The gas tank of limited endurance is located under the rear of the boiler and above the inside frames. Gibbon and Harris built approximately five of these simple and inexpensive locomotives with an expected service life of 25 years but their small size made them redundant by the 1920's.

(WN 117-2 – George Ansell)

3. This photograph is a reminder of the Improved Meyer, Strathfarrer that appears in the chapter 'Early Days' illustrating a direct drive (on the full size locomotive) articulated bogie locomotive used in logging operations. Built by Andrew Barclay and described by them as an 'Improved Meyer', the model was based on a drawing of Works number 1956 of 1928 but fitted with the side tanks of Works number 1299 of 1913, the information being provided in the book Kitson Meyer Articulated Locomotives by Donald Dinns.

(WN042-2 – Peter Holland)

animals to gain a purchase on when they were pulling the heavy trunks, otherwise they would simply slide or sink into the soft ground. A solution was to use the discarded branches to form a firm path to the mill. Very quickly these routes became more sophisticated with raised walkways, gripping treads to assist the animals and a sledge arrangement on to which the timber was placed. This in turn was replaced by wheeled trucks running on longitudinal wooden rails which again were further developed to include replaceable capping. The stage was now set for the introduction of mechanically powered forest tramways. Not all logging operations followed this development, for there were also steam donkeys used to drag the logs through the forest, wooden flumes could be built on continuously falling ground to float logs and there were aerial ropeways, it all depended on the location and the natural circumstances of the forest. Either way the introduction of steam locomotives hauling logs through the forest was not without its own unique problems.

At first, small industrial locomotives of the 0-4-0 wheel arrangement were used but these engines were intended for reasonably well laid track on fairly flat and firm ground, not wooden tramways or light track laid on undulating ground. Their frames tended to be too stiff and in a logging environment the conventional frames worked little better than solid metal bars. Locomotives derailed and completely lost adhesion if the track varied even slightly from the dead level. Also their weight and inflexible wheelbase soon destroyed lightly laid track. The use of small direct drive 0-4-0 locomotives, often saddle tanks, was therefore confined to light trains on small operations where there was a short distance between the cutting site and the mill. The attraction of these industrial

type locomotives was their simple design, low cost, they were rugged to operate and straightforward to maintain. The development of locomotives to specifically deal with the demands of logging can be looked into from their use in New Zealand and the real home of logging locomotives, namely America.

THE NEW ZEALAND BUSH TRAM

From the simple 0-4-0 industrial saddle or side tank locomotive, the next development was to introduce gearing. This increased the power available at a corresponding loss of speed, which could be an advantage on severe curves and gradients and where rough track limited the speed anyway. The first horizontal boiler rigid geared engines to operate on bush tramways were a pair of 0-4-0T locomotives built by Robey & Co. of Lincoln, dispatched to the order of the National Mortgage and Agency Co. of New Zealand in 1879. They were Works number 5529 for owners John Murdock of Invercargill and Works number 5571 for McCallam & Co. An example of a Robey locomotive is shown in the chapter on industrial engines. However, the supply of engines was not limited to importing them from other countries, since the rigid geared 0-4-0 was also produced by the New Zealand firm of J. Johnston & Sons of Invercargill as their Johnston A and the firm of Gibbon & Harris.

GIBBON & HARRIS-WN117

It was the locomotives of Auckland engineering firm of Gibbon and Harris that was used as the subject of WN 117 and was built from the photograph appearing on page 133 in the book, The Era of the Bush Tram in New Zealand by

Paul Mahoney. They were small four wheeled locomotives weighing about 6 tons and driven by a twin cylinder engine mounted under the smokebox and above the frames. Spur gears then drove to the front axle and side rods to the rear axle. The boilers were obtained new from firms with boiler making capacity. Two of these simple and cheap locomotives were built between 1905 and 1907 for R. P. Gibbon's operations at Hikurangi and a further five for operations in the Northland and Auckland districts, but due to their small size were redundant by the mid 1920's. The model follows the basic design with a marine engine located below the smokebox and the boiler, the engine driving through spur gears to the front axle. Side rods then carried the drive to the rear axle. As with the full size locomotive, the boiler was raised to clear the engine allowing sufficient room to install a square ended gas tank under the remaining part of the boiler and into the cab. With inside frames and very small side coal bunkers there was no other location possible and the resultant gas tank was of limited capacity.

DIRECT DRIVE ARTICULATED LOCOMOTIVES

The loads hauled by these small locomotives could only be increased by using heavier, more powerful, engines but this would require extra wheels to keep within the maximum axle loading. Additional trailing or leading wheels could be used but this would reduce the effective adhesive weight. On the other hand adding driven wheels would increase the length of the fixed wheelbase. What was really required was a locomotive with increased power, more wheels with each axle driven, whilst retaining the ability to negotiate sharp bends and uneven track. This could only be achieved by articulation. The New Zealand bush tramways experimented with several imported double bogie articulated locomotives including the Duplex, Meyer and Mallet types. The Duplex was simply two 0-4-0 locomotives permanently coupled together to provide twice the power with only one crew. This Andrew Barclay, Sons & Co. locomotive, Works number 1130 of 1907), was successful but limited by the nature of the logging enterprise and also suffered from limited fuel capacity. The locomotive was eventually split into two separate units. Other types of articulated locomotive were tried on the New Zealand Tramways but the next locomotive from Andrew Barclay was of the Meyer type, although referred to as an Improved Meyer by the builders. It was Works number 1299, Joan, of 1913 and supplied to the Maymorn Estates Ltd, Upper Hutt. Unfortunately, the Maymorn Estates were over ambitious and closed in 1914 leaving this 23t locomotive to be used on various

lines, before resuming its career in the bush. The Meyer operated very successfully between 1924 and 1944 on the challenging Kanieri-Hokitika tram out of Hokitika which included a long 1 in 25 grade. The locomotive is illustrated by WN42, Strathfarrer, which is described in the chapter 'Early Days'.

However, the real requirement was for sufficiently powerful locomotives capable of negotiating uneven and often tightly curved track whilst at the same time having a low and well-spread axle weight. They would also require good adhesion on wet and slippery track and be capable of pulling and controlling their load on relatively steep inclines. Where these conditions existed, there was only one type of locomotive capable of satisfying these demands and that was the geared articulated locomotive. This type is usually associated with the American Shay, Heisler and Climax geared articulated locomotive, all of which were imported into New Zealand. However, New Zealand did have its own unique brands of multi axle geared engines and there are two examples in the works list.

A & G PRICE CLASS CB, WN017

The first example was WN17 based on the locomotives built by A & G Price of Thames, in particular their class Cb. The firm was established in 1868 by the brothers Alfred and George Price and steadily developed to become one of the largest and most successful engineering companies in the country. Price was the only private company to build a large number of locomotives for the government railway, supplying over the period 1904 to 1928 a total of 123 locomotives for mainline duties. In addition, they constructed 21 geared locomotives for the logging industry between 1912 and 1943. There were two types of locomotive classified as C & E with the C class divided into C, Ca, Cb and Cba. The C and Cb engines used bogies derived from the Climax locomotive but having inside frames, whereas the Ca and Cba bogies were derived from the Heisler. WN17 was based on the design and dimensions of the Cb locomotive Cb113 built in 1924, and delivered to the Tunnel Timber Company at Tapawae. This locomotive was designed to negotiate curves down to 50ft and surmount grades of 1 in 10. For simplicity, the model used outside frames and crossed helical gears, whereas the full size inside framed Climax bogie would have required a pair of skew bevel gears to transmit power from the lay shaft to each axle. In the Cb locomotive, the engine was a 50hp twin cylinder (7in bore by 8in stroke) launch type located at the rear of the cab with a spur gear drive to a lay shaft positioned below. Two speed

4. (Above) A very unusual model based on the A & G Price Cb113 Bush Locomotive of 1927. This right hand side view shows the lubricator just visible in the cab and directly attached to the Caton marine engine. The engine drives down to a gearbox located in front of the engine to provide a double ended output shaft for the carden shaft drive to the bogies. The output gear of the gearbox is just visible behind the lubricator drain valve. In full size practice, this gearbox gave two output ratios and a neutral position with the low ratio for gradients and the higher ratio for running on the flat. The drive is then transmitted to each axle by 2:1 crossed helical gears.

(WN017-1 – N D Kirkbride)

5. (Left) This is the same A & G Price locomotive from the left hand side. Notice the outside frame bogies built up from bar stock with the facility for dual gauge operation. The full size locomotive was fitted with inside frames for operation on 3ft 6in gauge. Chains can be seen attached to the bogie ends to limit movement should the truck de-rail. The rear bunker includes a water tank and hand force pump to top up the boiler. The lever behind the cab is the gas control valve.

(WN017-2 – N D Kirkbride)

6. (Below left) Photograph of the A&G Price locomotive on the West Lincolnshire Light Railway of Brian Hicks taken over twenty years since its construction in 1987 and proudly carrying the name of the owner, The Hicks Bay Timber Company.

(WN017-4 – Chris Henderson)

ranges were available from a pair of sliding spur gears on the crankshaft which engaged with a corresponding pair on the layshaft with the ratio being in high gear of 54:19 and in low 48:25. The overall ratio including the skew bevel gears was 3.85:1 and 5.75:1. For the model this was a bit unnecessary, so the drive was from the twin cylinder Caton marine engine to a splitter gearbox and thence via carden shafts to the bogies. The bogies themselves are built up from bar stock and fitted with dual gauge wheel sets. This requires the frames to be outside the wheels. The rear bunker of the model contained a water tank and hand force pump. A & G Price also produced a Climax B lookalike with Heisler type bogies called their 'E' class.

The history of Cb113 is interesting in that this locomotive is still in existence. Cb113 started as a request to A&G Price from Mr Edkin, Manager of the Tunnel Timber Company at Tapawae. The locomotive was delivered late in 1924 some 6 months after ordering at a quoted price of £1450. Employment of the locomotive was divided between logging in the bush on easy terrain to the cartage of milled timber from Tapawae to Porootarao, a generally level route of 3 miles followed by a final mile with gradients encountered of 1 in 12 and 1in 20. In 1932, the locomotive passed on to the Marton Sash and Door Company with an initial 5 miles of track which included grades of up to 1 in 14 and, following further development, included

7. (Above) The Johnston B geared articulated locomotive after lining by Geoff Munday showing the general arrangement of this very unusual engine. Notice how compact the model is, the large cab covering the vertical part of the T boiler and the large bunker housing the gas tank. The twin cylinder marine engine is mounted on the right hand side similar to the Shay and is slightly inclined to accommodate the engine base inside the frames and to move the drive over towards the centre. The cylinder in front of the engine is a water separator to reduce water condensate in the exhaust.

(WN040-2 – Geoff Munday)

8. (Right) Front end on view showing the offset boiler and side mounted slightly inclined engine. Unlike the Shay locomotive, the longitudinal main frames are symmetrical about the centre line of the bogie and locomotive, not offset as in the Shay. This leads to less confusion when dealing with the pivot points. It is easy to understand why this model is often referred to as a Johnston Shay.

(WN040-4 – N D Kirkbride)

a stretch of 1 in 11 for half a mile. After two further owners, the locomotive was out of use by 1956 and after 13 years was donated by Reese Brothers Ltd., to the Canterbury Branch of the New Zealand Railway and Locomotive Society at Ferrymead, Christchurch, where it was completely overhauled between 1969 and 1975.

J JOHNSTON & SONS CLASS B.

The final model of a geared articulated locomotive from New Zealand was based on the products of J. Johnston & Sons of Invercargill. Joseph F. Johnston and his sons, Bill, Jack and Joe were extensively involved in the timber industry and built at least 26 bush locomotives between 1896 and 1930 as well as steam log haulers, steam engines, boilers and machinery for sawmills. The first geared bush locomotives, the Johnston A, were simple 4 wheelers with the wheels driven by a central jackshaft which in turn were geared at 13:30 from a twin cylinder engine located between the frames under the smokebox. They weighed about 7 tons and would have operated with a

4 wheel tender. Johnston went on to develop a 16 wheeler with four 4 wheel bogies which could be used on existing tramways without extra strengthening since the weight on each axle was just over 1 ton. However, the subject of the next model, WN40, was the Johnston B. Now the side mounted engine and offset boiler will always be associated with the products of the Lima Locomotive Works of Lima, Ohio with their geared articulated Shay locomotives but it was not the only example of this layout. New Zealand had its very own example in the form of the Johnston B. Only two Johnston type Bs were known to have been built and there are no photographs of the locomotive. The model was built from a drawing registered by John Johnston with patent 27107 dated 30 December 1909, which was reproduced in the publication Locomotives International. It was a strange beast with an offset boiler and two vertical single cylinder engines mounted on the left hand side driving to a splitter gearbox in front of the cab, the output of which drove via universally jointed shafts to front and rear bogies using gears on each axle. At this stage it is best to look at the photograph of the model.

The layout is similar to the Shay but with the drive to the bogies along the centre line, leading to the model often described as a Johnston Shay.

WN40 follows the general lines of the drawing with a large cab and rear bunker. The boiler used was of the T type with a long 1¾ in dia. horizontal section, the main support for the boiler being the base of the vertical portion. Instead of two single cylinder engines, the model uses the Max II twin cylinder marine engine mounted at a slight inside angle to drive the gearbox. Gears carry the drive across to the central double-ended output shaft and then via carden shafts to the bogies. As with the full size locomotive, the drive is then to gears on each axle. As with most logging type locomotives, the buffing gear is attached to the frame rather than the bogies. WN40 is a light and very compact articulated locomotive and it is difficult to understand why so few full size engines were produced. It was certainly a lot simpler than the 16 wheel Johnston D with its 38 gears.

THE AMERICAN SHAY LOCOMOTIVE.

In any discussion on logging lines, the one locomotive that always comes to mind is the American Shay, although many of these locomotives were built for industrial, mining and civil engineering use. However, since Shays are usually associated with logging lines, they are included in this chapter. Virtually every Shay was built by the Lima Machine Works in Ohio. They all had the engine on the right hand side with the exception of four 10ton left hand Shays built for Sr. Octaviano b. Cabrera of San Luis, Mexico (C/N 757,758,826 and 827) and one unit originally built by Lima as C/N 2640 for the Marshall Butters Lumber Co. of L'anse, Michigan but purchased by the Ford Motor Co. and rebuilt with a symmetrical boiler.

The man responsible for the locomotive design was a Michigan logger by the name of Ephraim Shay. Throughout the 1870's, loggers all over the United States experimented with steam powered traction devices to find a way of hauling timber to the mill. As mentioned previously, the problem was not the availability of conventional locomotives but the conditions unique to logging that made these engines unsuitable. Shay was convinced that the answer lay in having a locomotive with the same characteristics as a loaded log car. This meant two trucks to negotiate tight curves and enough lateral and vertical movement for its wheels to remain in contact with the rails and provide maximum adhesion. From 1876 along

with his blacksmith, Shay worked on building his locomotive and was granted a patent in 1881 for his improved locomotive engine. Shay built a total of five locomotives excluding the prototype, but although the locomotives worked well the power transmission to the trucks was a source of trouble. Once the Patent had been received Shay then granted the Lima Machine Works the rights to manufacture his patent articulated locomotives under a licensing arrangement. Shay's original engine was rebuilt several times and was eventually shipped to the Lima Machine Works in 1880 where the problem of reliably transmitting the drive from the engine to the wheels was solved. The Lima Machine Works built their first true Shay in the same year for the Michigan logging company of M. J. Bond. The main aspect of the Shay design was the location of two power trucks under a rigid frame which also supported the boiler, cab and water/fuel bunker. With some exceptions the engine was mounted on the right hand side frame and transmitted power to the trucks using universal drive shafts and bevel gears and is best illustrated by the photographs of the models. The early Shays had vertical boilers but soon gave way to T and horizontal boilers. Shays were produced with two and three cylinder engines, normally two trucks but this could be extended for the larger Shays to three and even four trucks and weights from 10 to 150 tons. In 1945 the Lima Locomotive Works built their last Shay for the Western Maryland Railway Company as their No. 6, after producing over 2700, surely the most successful geared articulated locomotive.

Considering a model of a Shay locomotive there are two difficulties that require extra thought. Firstly, there is the matter of symmetry. The wheels, buffer beams and sides of the cab/bunker are spaced equally either side of the centre line of the track along with the important pivot point. The wheels however have a geared and non-geared side so that unless the non-geared side has a spacer fitted then the bogie, or more correctly the truck side frames will not be symmetrical about the track. Great care must therefore be taken to ensure that the pivot on the truck is symmetrical relative to the wheels and not necessarily the side frames. Be warned, you would not be the first to get it wrong. All this will be to no avail if the corresponding pivot on the main frame is not correctly located. Remember the buffer beams are symmetrical but not the main frame side members. To allow for the engine, the right hand side of the frame has to be set in-over which in turn requires the boiler location also to move to the left to give the characteristic lop sided appearance of the Shay. The next

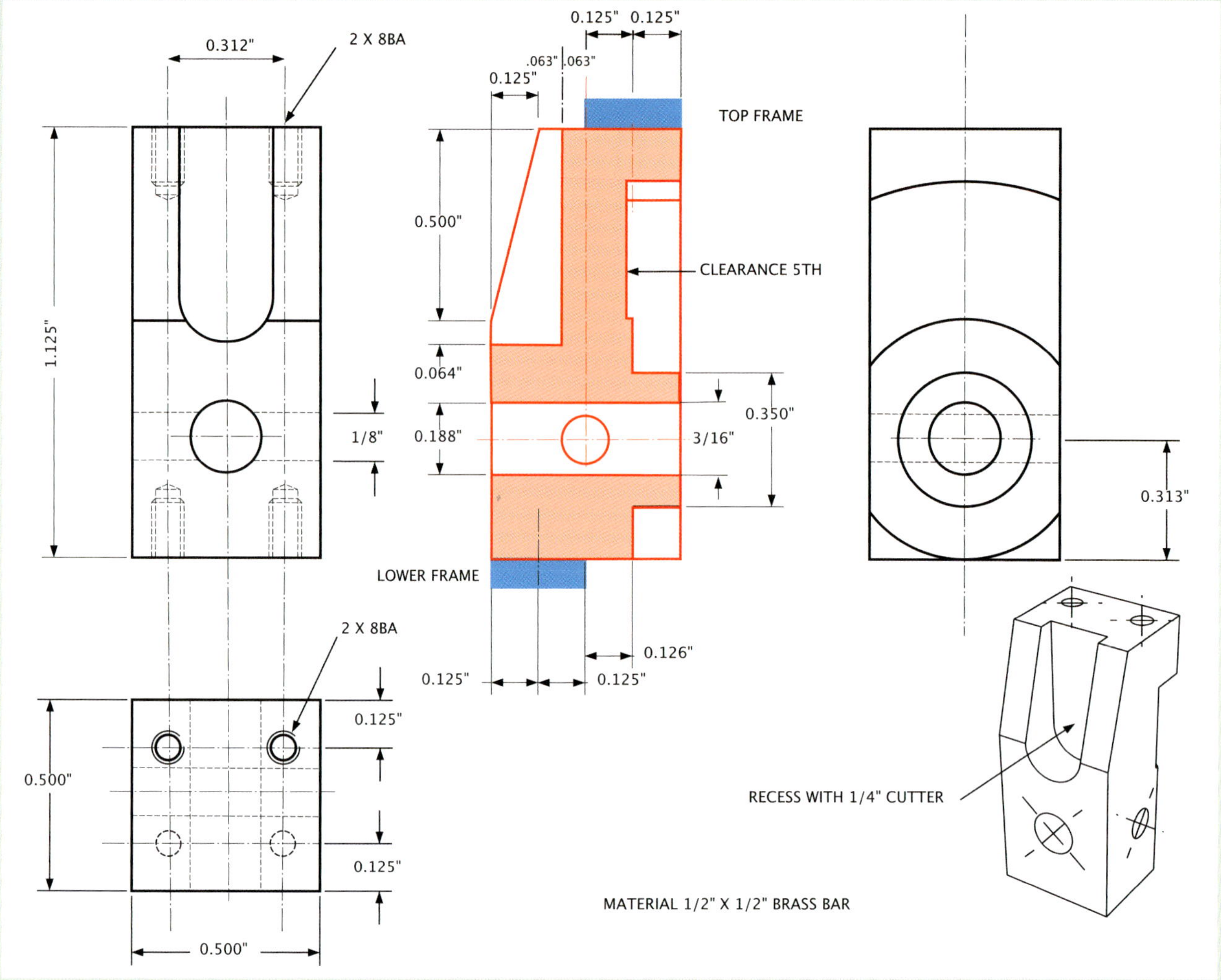

0.312"

2 X 8BA

1.125"

0.500"

1/8"

2 X 8BA

0.500"

0.125"

0.125"

0.500"

0.125" 0.125"

.063" .063"

0.125"

TOP FRAME

0.500"

CLEARANCE 5TH

0.064"

0.188"

0.350"

3/16"

LOWER FRAME

0.126"

0.125" 0.125"

0.313"

RECESS WITH 1/4" CUTTER

MATERIAL 1/2" X 1/2" BRASS BAR

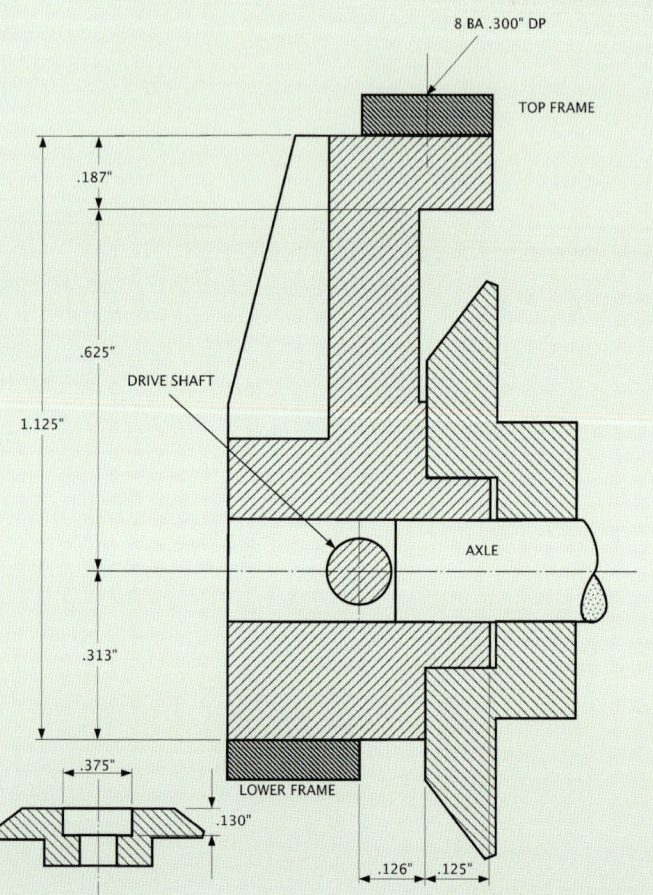

8 BA .300" DP

TOP FRAME

.187"

.625"

DRIVE SHAFT

1.125"

AXLE

.313"

.375"

LOWER FRAME

.130"

.126" .125"

9. (Above) Drawing of the full bearing showing how the bearing block is also used to accurately align the top and bottom frame members.

Another point to be noted is that for the locomotive to proceed the driving shaft bevel gears have to be on the same side of the axles, otherwise the trucks will pull in opposite directions. This is not recommended. Remember the stipulation that the drive shaft must be in line with the crankshaft of the engine. Most Shay locomotives were built for the larger narrow gauges such as 3ft or 3ft 6in with the engine vertical and in model form are more suitable for 45mm track. In the case of the 2ft gauge, it was necessary to incline the engine in-over to achieve the correct alignment with the drive shafts. This situation holds for a model designed to run on 32mm track with trucks designed for 32mm only. Alternatively, the trucks can be designed for 45mm but with allowance to move the wheels in-over for 32mm track. This arrangement is only possible if the axle mounted bevel gear is fixed to the axle independent of the adjacent wheel. Still want to build a Shay?

(Shay-2 – Author)

10. (Left) This diagram shows how the bearing for the axle has been increased by boring out a recess in the axle bevel gear. Without this recess there would be very little bearing surface to support the bevel gear end of the axle. This is particularly acute where the gear ratio is 3:1 due to the driving shaft being relatively closer to the front face of the axle bevel gear

(Shay-1 – Author)

11. (Right) Model of the A class Shay locomotive based on No.15, an 18-ton Shay built by Lima as number 2550 of 1912, one of seven supplied to the Ali Shan Forest Railway in Taiwan. This 2ft 6in line ran from Chiaya to Ali Shan, climbing 7600ft over a distance of 42 miles. Notice the Lima plates on the smokebox and Shay plates on the cab side. The builder's plate indicates that this model was built in 1997 and is photographed in 2010 on the Lincolnshire Light Railway of Brian Hicks.

(WN044-1 – Chris Henderson)

12. (Above) The Ali Shan No. 15 locomotive 2 cylinder Shay engine was built by Mike Beeson and is clearly seen in the photograph which illustrates how care has been taken to ensure the drive shafts are in line with the engine crankshaft. The drive shafts are short and as with all Shays limit the movement possible by the trucks. Covers are fitted over the driving bevel gears and the universal joints are similar to the full size units. Notice the side

springs located between the guides on the trucks and the bolster which is attached to the truck pivot. This spring arrangement allows a small amount of controlled movement between the truck and the main frame mounted horizontal pivot.

(WN044-2 – Chris Henderson)

problem involves the drive train and the bevel gears. The drive train has to be in line with the crankshaft of the engine or this will add to the displacement of the drive shafts on curves, a critical factor with the Shay. Unlike the Heisler layout described in the chapter on the Avonside Geared locomotive, the drive on the Shay is well out of the centre line of the wheels which leads to excessive displacement of the drive shafts in the longitudinal direction. This exaggerates the angular displacement when the drive is on the inside of the curve and also gives the maximum length allowed on the sliding shafts. Conversely, on the outer curve the sliding shafts must not disengage or reduce the sliding surface to an unacceptable level. Then there is the bevel drive which requires a bearing for the axle between the bevel gear and the longitudinal drive shaft. The maximum diameter of the axle bevel gear is set by the diameter of the driving wheels which then decides the diameter of the drive

shaft bevel gear. With a ratio of 2:1 this is not such a problem but if a ratio of 3:1 is required then it was found necessary to recess the face of the axle bevel gear. A drawing (Shay-1) of the bearing is shown which also illustrates the problem of providing enough bearing surface for the gear end of the axle. In this case the bevel gear has been recessed to provide this extra bearing surface. The drawing (Shay-2) shows how the top and bottom of the bearing block have been used to accurately locate the top and bottom truck frame members.

ALI SHAN FOREST RAILWAY

The first model Shay was WN44 based on No.15 of the Ali Shan Forest Railway. This 2 cylinder 18-ton Shay was built by Lima in 1912 as Works number 2550 and was one of seven supplied to this railway. Later a group of ten 28-ton 3 cylinder Shay locomotives were added

13. (Top) Kelly Island Lime and Transport Company No.31 2 truck A class Shay locomotive. Of particular interest is the adoption of the Maxwell Hemmens Max II marine piston valve engine arranged with the bedplate rotated back through 90°. The cylinder support side pillars have been removed and an extra reinforcing rib added between the trunk guides and the rotated bedplate. The universal joints are of a standard marine type rather than the correct Shay type. Note how the drive shaft bevel gears are in front of the axle on each truck or trouble will ensue. Advantage has been taken of the air receiver located on the running board to locate the gas tank.
(WN068-1 – Roger Pattie)

14. (Above left) Taken during construction, this photograph of the Michigan California No.2 Shay illustrates the alteration to the Maxwell Hemmens Max II marine engine to make it suitable for the Shay application. The bedplate has been disconnected and rotated through 90° and connected to the cylinder block by a webbed plate. To this plate has been attached a spacing block to bolt the engine to the frame side member.
(WN070-1 – Authors collection)

15. (Middle left) This is based on the Michigan California Lumber Company No.2 Shay built by Lima as their wn122 of 1884. The T boiler and generally old and wizened look, along with the cluttered appearance, give this model a lot of workmanlike character. The gas tank is disguised as the air receiver.
(WN070-2 – Roger Pattie)

16. (Below left) In this rear ¾ view it can be seen that although the axles are not sprung the truck is, allowing movement of the bogie relative to the main body. The springs are visible bearing up on the central cross bolster which is held between the vertical slides and the top cross member.
(WN070-3 – Roger Pattie)

to the roster. The 76cm Ali Shan Forest Railway ran from the Taiwan Government 3ft 6in gauge west coast main line at Chiaya (276 above sea level), via Chu Chi to Ali Shan at 2273m above sea level. The line was built by the Japanese Government in 1897 and included 50 tunnels and in the case of the Mount Tu Li spiral there were four complete loops with ten tunnels, the line emerging from the top spiral at 2267ft. For the operation of this difficult line, all of the engines were faced down hill with the locomotive leading the train downhill and pushing the train in reverse uphill. With the advent of the 28-ton Shays, the smaller 18-tonners worked the flatter section from Chiaya to Chu Chi and the logging spurs beyond Ali Shan.

The construction of the model coincided with the availability of a suitably correct Shay type engine built by Mike Beeson, with steam supplied from a gas fired plain centre flue boiler. The gas tank is arranged to mimic the large air receiver on the right hand footplate. The trucks are arranged for 32mm only, with the boss on the axle bevel gear retained but recessed on the gear side to increase the bearing surface at the end of the axle. The boss also moves the drive shaft further from the wheel, thereby increasing the width of the truck and improving the alignment of the shaft with the engine. This critical alignment of the drive shafts with the engine is clearly shown on the photographs.

KELLY ISLAND AND MICHIGAN CALIFORNIA A CLASS SHAYS

The next two Shay models used a twin cylinder marine piston valve engine produced by Maxwell Hemmens as their Max II engine. To imitate the 2cyl Shay type engine, the cylinder columns were removed and the bedplate turned through 90° with a brass reinforcing web fitted between the cylinders. The photograph of WN70 during construction illustrates this arrangement. Notice the offset frames with the pivots still on the main centre line. The T boiler is self supporting having two 3/16in stays through the vertical part of the boiler which terminate as 2ba studs outside the base to provide a suitable method of mounting. WN70, the T boiler Shay, was based on the Michigan California No.2 two cylinder 20 ton locomotive built in 1884 and supplied originally to the El Dorado Lumber Co. This delightful and wizened looking Shay is covered in detail in the book Pino Grande by R.S. Polkinghorn, an excellent book on American mountain logging. WN68 was based on the 2cyl

17. A Shay locomotive with a difference for this is a model of only four LEFT hand Shays built by Lima as their WN826 of 1903 for Sr. Octaviano B. Cabrera as their No.4, Pozos, and is a 10 ton, 2 truck Shay. The model was photographed in 2010 after ten years of service.
(WN075-1 – Andrew Cottenham)

19. (Above) Front view of the locomotive showing the rather unusual method of dropping the buffer beam using flat angled plates between the frame and the buffer beam. Again the gas tank is arranged to look like an air receiver located on the left hand running plate.

(WN075-3 – Andrew Cottenham)

20. (Right) Detail of the front truck of Pozos. Note the 3:1 bevel gears and how close the drive shaft is to the axle bevel gear face. Although the axles are not sprung, the truck is sprung relative to the locomotive body. The side springs are seen at the centre and press against the cross bolster which is located between the two vertical slide bars. The bolster carries the vertical pivot which is further controlled by a clearance hole in the top crossed plate seen bolted to the top of the bearings.

(WN075-5 – Andrew Cottenham)

A class Shay built for the Kelly Island Lime and Transport Co. as their No.31 using the drawing of No.26 (plan 1852).

Sr. Octaviano B Cabrera left hand Shay

Now take a look at the photographs of WN75 and look again. There is something odd about it and it is not the pipe and sheet metal cab, if you can call it a cab. No, the oddity here is the location of the engine and drive shafts on the left hand side. WN75 was based on Lima shop number 826 built in 1903 for Sr. Octaviano B. Cabrera , San Luis Potosi, Mexico. It was one of four identical 10-ton locomotives, numbers 757 and 758 built in 1902 and numbers 826

and 827 built one year later. The story goes that Cabrera was a British mining operation and the British engineers would naturally order a locomotive built to be operated from the left hand side. Notice also how the front buffer beam is dropped down from the main frame. The 2 cylinder Shay engine was supplied by Mike Chaney. The close up photograph of the front truck shows that the bevel gears are 3:1 ratio which forces the drive shaft closer to the face of the larger axle mounted bevel gear. To provide an adequate bearing surface for the end of the axle, it was necessary to recess the face of this large bevel gear to allow the bearing to pick up more of the axle. A drawing of this arrangement was shown previously.

STANDARD STEEL AND CASPARIS STONE COMPANY SHAYS

Unlike all the other model locomotives produced, these two Shay engines were constructed as a running chassis only. The reason was that they were required to have coal fired boilers, definitely a job for a specialist, in this case John Shaw. John fitted the boilers and the ancillary equipment as well as finishing the models. Another interesting aspect was the use of the correct Shay type engines which were supplied by Mike Chaney as extras on a batch of Shay locomotives destined for America. To complement the engines, the correct type of universal joints were fitted to the drive shafts and the trucks are the same as used on the previous locomotives. WN84 was based on the 20T 2cyl A class shay built for the Standard Steel Car Co., whereas WN85, again a 2cyl Shay was based on the Lima T boiler Shay C/N 782 of 1902 built for the Casparis Stone Company.

WN88 ACHILLES A 10 TON 2 TRUCK SHAY

At this point in the works programme, the SVS double acting oscillating engine was well established and thoughts turned to using it in a small Shay. There was already the Shay marketed by Tom Cooper using an oscillating engine but of particular interest was a delightful T boiler Shay built by Larry Lindsay, a New Zealander residing in Denver, Colorado. He built his first Shay in 1986 and in conjunction with Mike Bigger produced approximately twenty-two of these oscillating engine T boiler models. It was very similar to Achilles, a small 10ton - 2 truck 3ft gauge Shay built by Lima as Works number 341 of 1891, a photograph of which has appeared in several articles on Shays. From this photograph WN88 was constructed with the trucks arranged for 45mm gauge. The bevel gears were 2:1 to correspond to SVS engine reduction gearing of 4:1. One advantage of using this type of engine with the

21. (Above) Based on the two cylinder A class 20 ton Shay built for the Standard Steel Car Co. and shown on Lima Locomotive Works negative 186. The engine used on this model and WN85 is the correct Shay type engine produced by Mike Chaney.
(WN084 – Roger Pattie)

22. (Left) This T boiler Shay model is based on a photograph of wn782 of 1902 for the Casparis Stone Company, the full size locomotive named Ruth Casparis. As with WN84 this is a coal fired model with the boiler and ancillary equipment supplied, fitted and the model finished by John Shaw.
(WN085-1 – Roger Pattie)

23. (Above left) Side view of the model of Achilles, a diminutive 10 ton 2 truck Shay based on Lima works number C/N341 of 1891 and supplied to H. Kalbach & Company at Lebanon, Pennsylvania. Note also the correct Shay type universal joints.
(WN088-1 – Geoff Lumsdon)

24. (Left) It is unusual to see a photograph of the non engine side of a Shay locomotive so here is one of the model Shay, Achilles. Even the trucks look plain, especially in this case where the model truck frames are manufactured from flat gauge plate.
(WN088-2 – Geoff Lumsdon)

25. (Below) This view of Achilles taken alongside the locomotive illustrates how the SVS oscillating engine fits neatly alongside the frame. What is very important with any Shay locomotive is the alignment of the drive shafts relative to the engine and the trucks. From the photograph it can be seen that the drive system is almost in line along the length of the locomotive and lifts slightly to connect with the output shaft of the engine. The cylinder in front of the engine is a water separator in the steam exhaust line. With most locomotives the displacement lubricator can be hidden in the cab, a facility not available to the open awning of Achilles.
(WN088-3 – Geoff Lumsdon)

26. (Above) Shay model based on a photograph of Lima works number C/N1883 of 1907, a 10ton 2truck Shay supplied to the Yawata Iron Works, Yokohama, Japan. The oscillating engine fits very neatly into this small Shay and is very easy to mount on the bar main frames using the existing mounting holes and a small spacer.

(WN095-2 – Andrew Cottenham)

27. (Left) View alongside the model from the bunker end. The drive shafts are in good vertical alignment allowing the locomotive to negotiate 3ft radius curves. The flat plate truck side frames can be produced very accurately on the milling machine and are far less complicated than the built up type of the larger models. These trucks are also dual gauge.

(WN095-3 – Andrew Cottenham)

28. (Below left) View of the front truck showing the simplified plate frames and bearings along with the 2:1 bevel gears. Unlike the built up frames, the plate frame can be machined with great accuracy and along with the corresponding accurate bearings makes the assembly much easier. Notice the cut-out for the inside drive shaft bevel gear and the correct Shay type universal joints. Since the frames do not go beyond the wheels, the only frame stretchers are between the wheels, one large cross stretcher at the top and a spacer below.

(WN095-5 – Andrew Cottenham)

integral reduction gearbox is the increase in length of the drive shafts made possible since the engine gear output shaft is much shorter than the normal engine crankshaft. Further, the engine mounting holes bolt directly to the frames with a suitable spacer. For the smaller Shay this arrangement, despite the non-prototypical engine, provided a much simpler model with hopefully the charm of the original Larry Lindsey Shay, and several further models have been constructed.

YAWATA IRON WORKS 10 TON 2 TRUCK SHAY

Continuing on this theme WN 95 is fitted with the same SVS oscillating engine but with a horizontal boiler. Photograph WN95-6 illustrates how well the oscillating engine fits into the Shay model and does not look out of place, even when the locomotive is on the move. It was based on the 10 ton 2 truck Shay built by Lima in 1907 as works number C/N1883 for the Yawata Iron Works in Yokohama, Japan

29. *(Left) Close up view of the engine mounting. The disadvantage of using the SVS oscillating engine with integral 4:1 gearing is that the engine has to be mounted slightly higher to ensure that the output spur gear clears the track. This effects the horizontal drive shaft alignment and the photograph illustrates the slight lift of the shafts towards the engine from the trucks. Notice the reinforcing plate on the main frame behind the engine, the reinforcing being a common feature of all Shay locomotives. The reinforcing in the early Shay locomotives used a tie bar arrangement and later engines used a reinforcing plate to strengthen the main frame member that carried the engine.*

(WN095-6 – Andrew Cottenham)

30. *(Below) Engine side view of the vertical boiler model Shay based on C/N23 built by the Lima Machine Works in 1881. This was the only Shay model to use a geared ACS oscillating engine with twin cast cylinders of 8mm bore and approximately 10mm stroke. Originally designed for marine use with 8x8mm cylinders, the engine was changed for locomotive use by increasing the stroke and adding the 4:1 reduction gear. No further engines of this type were made and ACS Engineering ceased trading soon after. Notice how the engine has been lifted up so as to clear the output gear from the track. The trucks and drive shafts were supplied by Accucraft and re-gauged to 32mm. The wooden side planks are attached individually to the vertical stanchions and front reinforcing bars using 10ba screws. Likewise the bunker base, footplate and water tank horizontal planks are screwed to the main side frames.*

(WN162-1 – Paul Howard)

31. *(Above right) Engine side view again but showing the front of the locomotive. The gas tank can be seen in the rear bunker and could be hidden by adding dummy log fuel. Careful observation reveals that as with the horizontal locomotives the boiler and frames are offset to allow for the mounting of the engine. The displacement lubricator is located in front of the engine and the water filler in the front water tank covers the Goodall water filler valve.*

(WN162-2 – Paul Howard)

and named as their No 50. One of the features of this locomotive was the seemingly flat plate frame sides of the trucks. In reality they were probably cast sides but the photograph was not entirely clear. Consequently, the decision was made to use plate side frames for the trucks, which not only simplified the construction but allowed the introduction of CNC machining. Cut-outs were added to the frame sides which allowed the drive shaft to run close to the frame side and make it possible to use a simpler turned bush inserted into the frame to locate both the axle and the drive shaft. The cut-out in the frame allowed the smaller driven bevel to engage the axle bevel as illustrated. The frames are shown clearly on the photograph WN88-5. Incidentally, the Yawata Iron Company No50 model was built after Achilles and hence both locomotives benefit from the simpler flat plate truck frames.

A third set of these plate frames were used for another model of Achilles, WN145.

Vertical Boiler Shay – WN162

This interesting small vertical boiler Shay was based on Lima Locomotive Works C/N 23 completed on December 12th, 1881 and had an operating weight of 8 tons. The inspiration to build the model came from an article by Robert A.M Stephens in the magazine Outdoor Railroader August/September 1995 titled A History of the Shay, Part 1. This excellent article described the first experimental version of Ephraim Shay's geared locomotive in considerable detail, which included not only a side elevation but also detail drawings of the trucks and the peculiar engine arrangement where the engine was laid across the frame. This layout required an underslung drive shaft driven by spur gears from the engine, with an additional bevel drive to the truck drive shafts and which would make an interesting future project. In addition there was a photograph of a model of the later vertical boiler Shay, C/N 23, which included a side elevation drawing and

it was this locomotive that was to be the next model Shay, WN162.

The model was built using trucks supplied by Accucraft that were re-gauged to 32mm with a spare pair retained as supplied for operation on 45mm. Power came from a special version of a marine 8mmx10mm twin cylinder oscillating engine supplied by ACS Engineering, a company no longer trading. The engine used a similar arrangement to the SVS engine but had a shorter stroke with the cylinders machined from a casting. The boiler is the standard 2½in SD1 type fitted with a 47mm diameter ceramic burner. At least with this type of model there is no problem in finding a place to locate the gas tank which is installed in the rear bunker. A departure from normal practice was the fitting of a wooden footplate with the planks screwed to the main side frames by 10ba screws.

REFERENCES:
- The Era of the Bush Tram in New Zealand by Paul Mahoney.
- Kitson Meyer Articulated Locomotives by Donald Binns.
- Price of Thames – a review by Bob Stott.
- Bush Tram to the Mill. New Zealand Pictorial Record Series.
- Locomotives International No 12. Article by R.D. Grant titled "Johnston Logging Locomotives".

Shay Locomotives
- Pino Grande-Logging Locomotives of the Michigan-California Lumber Co. by R.S. Polkinghorn.
- Shay – modellers handbook series. Single Shot Gallery publishers.
- A History of the Shay, part 1. Article by Robert A. M. Stephens in Outdoor Railroader, Aug/Sept 1995.
- Baby Shays. Article by Allen J. Brewster in Model Railroader, September 1985.
- Shays'n Such. Article by James C. Mangels in Live Steam/January 1979 (includes the left hand Shay).

THE GARRATTS ARRIVE

The requirement to build articulated steam locomotives came about with the need to provide more power on railways where the limit in size had been reached for the conventional rigid framed engines. Railways built to a limited budget through often-difficult terrain, found that increased traffic soon outstripped the capacity of the line using their existing locomotives and rolling stock. The solution required longer trains pulled by more powerful engines. A simple way was to introduce double heading but this was never a preferred option, because it required two engine crews and there was the difficulty of the engines working together. On the other hand, providing more power from a locomotive meant increasing the size and weight. Such factors could be severely restricted by the capacity of the track and the minimum radius of the curves. The solution was to increase the number of driving axles but this would lead to an increase in the fixed wheelbase, which may not be possible due to the track curvature.

Alternatively, the weight could be transferred to a locomotive's carrying wheels but this would be offset by the loss of adhesion to the driving wheels. The only effective solution therefore, to provide more powerful locomotives on railways with lightly laid track and/or tight curves, was to provide some form of articulation that reduced the fixed wheelbase and spread the load of the engine. Now there were many ways of achieving this, including the example of the Avonside Geared Articulated locomotive already described in a previous chapter and several other articulated types, which are also illustrated in this book. However, the most successful fully articulated (as opposed to semi articulated locomotive such as the Mallet), was the design patented by Herbert William Garratt and developed by Beyer Peacock & Co.
His idea was sufficiently developed for a patent to be applied for and granted by 1907, but how he was able to interest Beyer Peacock in his design has not been recorded. The first Garratt locomotives were two small 0-4-0+0-4-0 units built for the North East Dundas Tramway in Tasmania. These were unique in having the cylinders fitted to the inner ends of the bogie and arranged for compound expansion. Compounding was repeated, with the solitary Burma Railways 2-8-0+0-8-2 built in 1926 (order 1119) but little advantage was gained and these three remained the only compound Garratt locomotives. Placing the cylinders on the inside of the bogies was only repeated on the Ferrocarril Austral Fueguino No 2 Garratt built by Tranex and its later sister locomotive No 5 built by Girdlestone and Associates.

It was with the second order for a locomotive for the Darjeeling Himalayan Railway, that Beyer Peacock realised there was potential in this new design and started actively to promote its advantages. By arranging the boiler to be slung between the power bogies and having the leading and trailing water/ bunker located on top of them, the design was quite different to any other articulated locomotives. This arrangement allows the weight of the engine to be spread over a greater distance, which made it possible for a more powerful locomotive to traverse lighter track or bridge structures.

Take for instance the Buthidaung-Maungdaw Tramway locomotives, the smallest Garratts built by Beyer Peacock with a tractive effort of 11,700 lbs at 90% boiler pressure on an axle weight of only four tons, and spread over a total wheelbase of 24ft 2in. Yet within this wheelbase, the power bogie wheelbase was only 4ft 10in. There were many other advantages of this design, which was enthusiastically promoted by Herbert W Garratt until his early death in 1913. The unique arrangement of the boiler in a separate cradle frame suspended between the engine units, allowed boilers to be designed for greater efficiency without the restrictions of wheels and frames. Garratt locomotives could thus have short fat boilers with optimum proportions of grate area, shape and volume of firebox, tube length and boiler diameter. The grate could also be enlarged to accommodate poor grade fuel. Entering a curve, the power units would take up their individual position on the track and the boiler would then form a cord to the curve. The weight of the boiler and cradle would therefore be inside the curve, resulting in locomotives to be renowned for their stability and steady running. This is even more apparent in model form on the tight curves of the average garden railway and also considering the higher (scale) speeds these models are often driven at. Enthusiasm for these locomotives is however tempered by the requirement for flexible steam connections to the bogies and the need to operate both sets of reversing gear. In full size practice, the flexible steam pipe connections utilised a metal-to-metal spherical ball joint with spring-loaded cover, self adjusting for wear and fitted with mechanical lubrication. This was one of the major successes, remaining basically unaltered over the production life of the locomotives. However, the length of the steam and exhaust pipes resulted in considerable expansion and contraction, which required progressive design and material alterations. The long and often tortuous routes taken by these pipes, was steadily improved to give long straight runs into expansion joints wherever possible and to give easier separation of the power units.

The next consideration with any articulated locomotive involves the pivot arrangement of the power bogies. In full size practice, the pivot bearings were of the flat cylindrical type incorporated in the bogie and mainframe stretchers. Vertical loads were taken care of by a single flat phosphor bronze plate secured to the lower part of the bearing. The steel upper part rested on this bearing and the weight of the boiler unit was sufficient to maintain contact. At either side, flat bearers not normally in contact, checked any excessive roll and the central keeper pin ensured that the pivots did not separate during excessive conditions. To allow for longitudinal tilting and lateral rolling, the bearings were provided with a running clearance that prevented any binding.

The first Garratt built by Beyer Peacock for the Tasmanian Government Railway as their class K, had these simpler flat disc bearings. Where extreme track conditions required it, the front pivot was of the hemispherical type to provide lateral tilting of the bogies relative to each other and was in effect a three-point suspension. The second and first true Garratt, designed for the Darjeeling Himalayan Railway, used a contoured front bearing which allowed the front bogie unit to take up a different alignment to that of the boiler frame and rear bogie. Pivot

design was to evolve over the development of the Garratt locomotive to reduce wear and maintenance costs, with the later bearings being self-adjusting with control springs, wedges and special oil feeds. Eventually, a design of self-adjusting bearing was developed with specially contoured mating faces, held permanently in contact by a wedge under the action of two vertical springs. This type of bearing removed the need for running clearances, thereby eliminating knock and ingress of dirt and consequent wear, whilst allowing for vertical displacement of the engine unit relative to the boiler frame. The Beyer Peacock self adjusting pivot proved to be one of the most important improvements in articulated locomotive design, as the wear was minimal and required little inspection.

There were other points to consider with the Garratt design that were also common to other articulated locomotives where the cylinders were mounted on the bogies. These were the operation of the forward/reverse mechanism and the brake linkage. Finally, there was the situation unique to the Garratt where the water tank was located in front of the smokebox involving its removal to replace of the boiler tubes. For the very small Garratt locomotives, the front tank could be removed and lifting eyes were fitted for this purpose. One early method was to provide a recess in the rear of the tank, but this was at the expense of water capacity and weight distribution. Three other methods developed over the years. One method being that the tank could be moved forward on built in rollers. Another was that the tank could be anchored to the frame at the front by two substantial pivots and the tank was raised on jacking screws. The final method was to fit a series of bulkhead doors across the inner end of the tank, which could be unbolted to give clearance for tube replacement.

FLEXIBLE STEAM PIPE AND BOGIE ARRANGEMENT ON THE MODEL GARRATT

In the case of a model, the problems are mainly in the articulation and the flexible steam pipes brought about by the more pronounced demands of tighter curves, track gradients and twists normally encountered on the typical garden railway. For instance, a full size smaller six-coupled Garratt, such as the SAR class NGG11, would be expected to negotiate 150ft radius curves (7ft 6in at 16mm scale). In model form, a minimum radius of 4ft 6in is required and some of the earlier Garratt models could negotiate the 2ft 6in curves of Mamod track. In addition, there is the important difference that full size locomotives are not picked up by a giant

PETER ANGUS – LOCOMOTIVE BUILDER

1. *The underside of a coal fired South African Garratt class NGG11 built by Mike Lax showing the pivot arrangement attached to the main frame. The rear bearing on the right has a large, plain, brass disc held up against the mainframe rear pivot plate to give horizontal movement. This plate is made of gauge-plate as it must be perfectly flat. Attached to the brass disc bearing is a cross member ready*

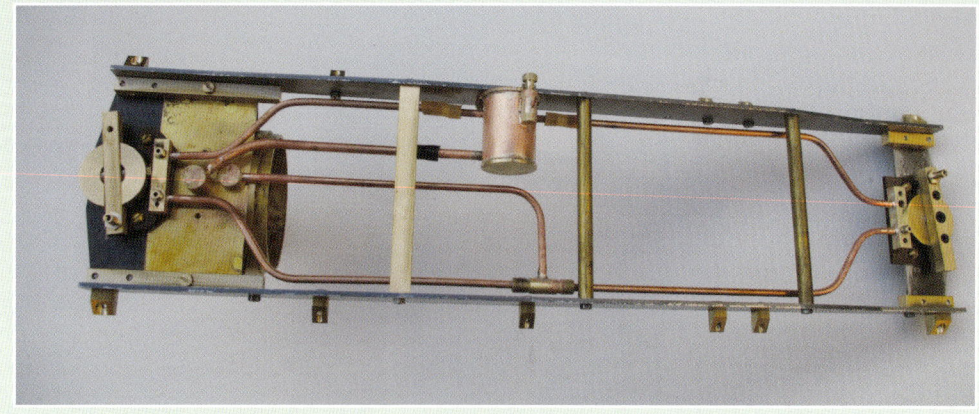

to be located on the rear bogie frame side pivots, thereby providing a small amount of vertical longitudinal displacement. At the left hand end of the main frame is the front bogie pivot. In this pivot the plain brass disc bearing is made deeper so that the cross-member can be pivoted to give lateral displacement. The tight fitting of this cross-member, with minimal clearance under the disc bearing, provides only a small lateral displacement. As with the rear bearing, the cross member locates in the bogie frame side pivots. The combination of the front and rear bearings effectively produces a three-point suspension system.

(WN251-1 NGG11 Frame pipes and pivots – Mike Lax)

2. *The pipe layout for this model emphasises the long pipe routes that are a feature of the Garratt locomotive. The inlet steam pipe starts from the rear of the smokebox having travelled through a hollow stay in the boiler from the steam regulator. In the case of a gas-fired model, this pipe would travel direct from the backhead-mounted regulator. In both cases the pipe splits at the mid or near mid-point*

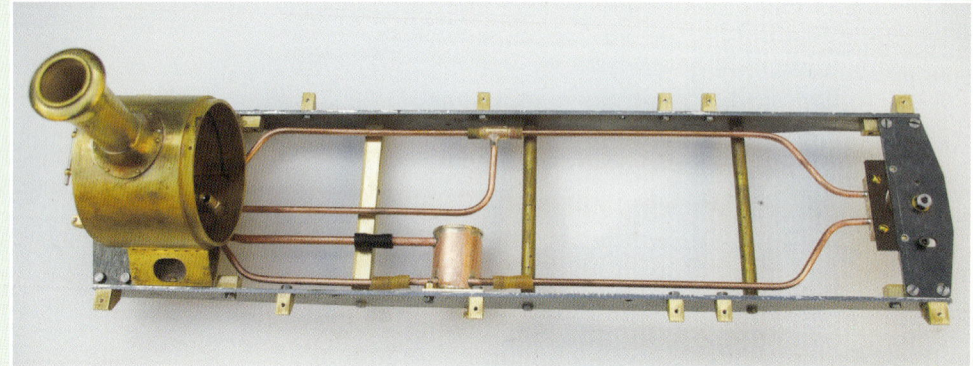

to equalise the steam flow to the front and rear bogies. Neither of the gas or coal fired locomotives use superheat and it will be noticed that the inlet steam pipes in the illustration retain the same diameter throughout. The inlet and exhaust pipes terminate on a manifold before connection to the flexible steam pipes. The exhaust pipes leave the manifold to come together at a water separator with drain valve, before exhausting into the smokebox blast pipe in the coal fired version or into the chimney for the gas fired locomotive.

(WN251-2 – NGG11 Pipe layout – Mike Lax)

hand and transported to other locations. The design of model pivots must make allowance for this excessive movement, including longitudinal and lateral displacement on the track, as well as the weight of bogie and boiler units during transport.

The type of pivot bearing adopted for the rear power unit, consists of a large, flat, brass disc pivoted at the sides to mate with side bearers attached to the frames. The disc with a central pin locates under the mainframe rear stretcher, which (for flatness), is usually gauge plate. The ¼in central pin is shouldered to bring the two surfaces together with minimal clearance and a 4BA nut and washer on top of the frame stretcher hold the whole bearing together. This allows the bogie horizontal movement and longitudinal tilting whilst maintaining the

lateral alignment of the boiler frame and rear bogie. Several variations have been tried on the front bogie to give the effect of a hemispherical bearing, thus allowing the front bogie to provide lateral and longitudinal displacement relative to the main frame.

The first methods used a small disc bearing with a pivoted cross stretcher, which in turn located on the bogie side frames as for the rear pivot. Other methods have used double ball self-aligning bearing or a plain spherical bearing. There are advantages and disadvantages to each but the former method has been used more often. Using this type of pivot design, some of the earlier Garratt models could negotiate Mamod track at 2ft 6in. After providing the model with articulation, it is vital to limit the movement to prevent damage to the flexible

3. Although this bogie is for the NGG11 Garratt, it is typical of the layout for the flexible pipe connection to the cylinders used on later models. The free ends of the flexible steam pipes will curve up vertically onto the mainframe-mounted manifold, this curvature allowing the flexibility required due to the movement of the bogie. The vertical termination of the flexible steam pipes to a manifold on the main frame, allows the pipes to be easily disconnected, if required, to separate the bogie from the locomotive. With the exception of the water pump and valve, the front and rear bogies of a coal-fired model Garratt locomotive are identical below the footplate level.

(WN251-3 – NGG11 rear bogie – Mike Lax)

4. This bogie for the SAR class NGG11 is easily identified as the front unit of a coal fired locomotive, due to the presence of the axle driven pump and fittings. Notice the by-pass valve mounted on the bogie side frame, the operating lever of which will appear just behind the water tank. This arrangement keeps the pipework to within the front bogie with only the high-pressure water feed having to travel back to the boiler. The boiler is topped up using a Goodall valve mounted on the main frame with a separate check valve. As can be seen in the photograph, the space between the rear wheels is tight and therefore the number of water feed pipes is critical, a situation made worse on 32mm gauge.

(WN251-5 – NGG11 front bogie – Mike Lax)

steam pipes or drive shafts. A simple pin and curved slot takes care of the horizontal limits. A long pin attached to the disc bearing, engaging with a hole in a pillar attached to the bogie side frame, takes care of the longitudinal movement. For the ball race and spherical bearing type, the limitation is built into the bearing housing. Only a very small displacement is required but it is essential for untroubled running on uneven track.

Photographs of the pivot arrangement, the layout of the steam pipes and the complications of the bogie and flexible steam pipes are few and far between. The opportunity has therefore been taken to illustrate these important features using a South African class NGG11 Garratt locomotive built recently by Mike Lax. It is based on the previous Garratt WN215,

which (apart from being coal-fired) is typical of the many Garratt locomotives described in this chapter. An illustration of the ball race type bearing is shown in the chapter on the Avonside Articulated locomotives.

SUCRERIE DE PIRACICABA AND PORTO FELIZ METRE GAUGE 0-4-0+0-4-0 GARRATT LOCOMOTIVES

The first Garratt to be built was WN 003 named Piricicaba and based on the metre gauge locomotives supplied by Société Anonyme de Sainte-Léonard for the Brazilian sugar plantations around Sao Paulo. These locomotives had side tanks that could be used to hide the firebox of the methylated spirits fired potboiler. Thick walled silicon tube provided the flexible steam connections. The inlet steam pipe was

5. (Top left) The first of a long line of model Garratt locomotives, Piracicaba was based on one of two identical locomotives built by St Léonard, this one being St. L. 2091 of 1927 for the metre gauge Sucrerie de Piracicaba, in the province of Sao Paulo, Brazil. With this model only the rear bogie is powered and its incredible free running resulted in the need for a disc brake to be fitted to one of the axles of the leading bogie, thereby reducing the risk of collisions. This model is externally gas fired with a simple potboiler and therefore requires the side tanks to cover the external firebox. Side tanks are very rare on a Garratt locomotive, the only examples being built by St. Léonard.

(WN003-1 – Authors collection)

6. (Left) In this side view, the model is not complete but illustrates well the general layout. The external gas burner can be clearly seen feeding into the external firebox. The rear bogie is powered using a Robyn Gosling Hunslet chassis, whereas the front one is a dummy although it uses parts from the same chassis. The flexible steam pipes to the rear bogie are just visible and are made up of silicon tube with a stainless steel stocking slid over. This contains the pressure for the inlet side, whereas the tubing on its own is sufficient for the exhaust steam.

(WN003-2 – N D Kirkbride)

7. (Below left) This photograph of Piracicaba was taken by Peter Dobson and appeared in his book Live Steam Model Locomotives Vol. 1 16mm Narrow Gauge of 1985. This book also includes photographs of Patricia, WN004, and Renishaw No2, WN005, all taken at the first Llanfair Garden Railway Show. Notice the radio control coiled aerial in the bunker amongst the stacked wood. The length of the aerial lead in these early models was always a problem, and one that has only now been solved with the introduction of 2.4G radio control.

(WN003-3 – Peter Dobson)

closely reinforced with a stainless steel braided stocking clipped at either end. To allow for the bogie movement, the flexible pipe followed a lazy U shape with location directly below the pivot. This simple arrangement worked very well, not only on this model but also on several other articulated locomotives until the supply of tubing and braid ran out.

The model was built using two GVT tram chassis provided by Robyn Gosling in his then workshop at Bellingham in Northumberland. However, to simplify the locomotive, only the rear chassis was powered with the front chassis dummy. The potboiler would not have powered four cylinders anyway. The only problem associated with this model was caused by the free running nature of the Garratt configuration. Even with radio control, closing the throttle still allowed the locomotive

to continue merrily on its way with minimal retardation and considerable threat to other track users. To correct this situation, it was found necessary to fit a servo-operated disc brake to one of the axles of the front bogie which gave adequate braking, and allowed peace to return to the garden railway.

The second Garratt locomotive was WN 26 named Sao Paulo, based on the same St. Léonard Brazilian sugar locomotives as WN003 but named after the Porto Feliz sugar company as Porto Feliz No 5 (St. Léonard 2108 of 1927). Unlike the previous model, the use of a mechanical drive from a hidden geared engine located on the main frame dispensed with the problem of flexible steam connections to the bogie. The source of power was the Maxwell Hemmens Caton marine piston valve engine located under the boiler in the position of the firebox. The difficulty in using this type of engine is that the crankshaft is close to the side frames and therefore it is necessary to move the drive over towards the centre line of the locomotive. This was achieved by a spur gear on the crankshaft driving an idler gear and then the double-ended output gear. The universal joint and drive shaft to the rear bogie then have to run between the engine trunk guide and the cylinder columns, due to the limited space under the boiler. Despite the difficulty of setting up the drive shafts, this mechanical system is very reliable and, apart from lubrication, requires minimal attention. On the other hand, the working cylinders of a true Garratt have to be replaced by dummy cylinders and valve gear. The geared engine arrangement does however provide the important additional benefit of slow consistent running and it can also reduce the minimum operating track radius.

The final Garratt locomotive based on the Brazilian sugar locomotives was WN46, Carla's Court. The same mechanical layout was used but the original Caton engine was no longer available, having been replaced by the CNC friendly Maxwell Hemmens Max II marine

piston valve type. A parallel stovepipe type chimney was fitted instead of the enormous spark-arresting unit of the full size locomotive.

BUTHIDAUNG-MAUNGDAW TRAMWAY 2FT 6IN GAUGE 0-6-0+0-6-0 GARRATT LOCOMOTIVES

WN32 was the fourth Garratt model to be built and it used the proven technology of a geared marine engine hidden in the area of the boiler firebox and carden shaft drive to the bogies. This would retain the unique look of a Garratt whilst providing a slow powerful model that would run consistently around the track without the need for radio control. The two Garratt locomotives of the 2ft 6in gauge Buthidaung Maungdaw Tramway, were not only very attractive and small but had the advantage that the motion was covered in, as per tramway practice, and would therefore not require dummy cylinders and valve gear. Only the reverse crank and eccentric rods were visible beyond the skirts and these could be easily provided terminating on a simple lever. These dinky engines were built by Beyer Peacock in 1913 as their Works number 5702/3 for the Arakan Flotilla Company, Burma

8. (Left) Sister locomotive to the previous one (St. Léonard 2091 of 1927) but supplied to the Sucriere de Porto Feliz, Brazil. Unlike the previous model the source of power is a geared Caton marine engine located under the cab in the region of what in full size would have been the firebox. The gas tank can be seen in the cab. The forward/reverse lever is just visible, appearing through the side skirt on the right hand side view with the displacement lubricator drain valve lever behind it.

WN026-1 – N D Kirkbride)

9. (Below left) In this view from the opposite side, the cylindrical gas tank located in the cab is more obvious, but is at least further away from the heat of the boiler than having it mounted inside one of the side tanks. The front tank has lifting rings used to remove the tank on the full size locomotive, thereby providing access to replace the boiler tubes.

(WN026-2 – N D Kirkbride)

10. (Above) Photograph of the final Brazilian sugar Garratt locomotive. This model has the conical chimney replaced by a simpler stovepipe chimney. At the time of construction, the original Caton marine engine was no longer available and therefore a hidden Maxwell Hemmens Max 11 unit with geared drive powers the model. Lightline carried out the lining on this locomotive.
(WN046-2 – Peter Holland)

11. (Left) A view showing the interior of the cab. The rather large displacement lubricator was supplied with the engine and the lever on the cab floor operates the forward/reverse on the engine.
(WN046-5 – Peter Holland)

and were the lightest and only tramway Garratt locomotives built by them. With an axle load of only four tons, they were only half a ton heavier than the smallest Garratt locomotives built by St. Léonard for the 600mm gauge Vicinaux du Mayumbe Railway and were the tenth and eleventh built by Beyer Peacock.

The area of Burma called the Arakan is located adjacent to the Indian border and next to the sea. At the beginning of the 20th century there was a move to provide a rail link between India and Burma, with three possible routes being considered, namely via the coast, the Manipur or the Hukong Valley. The coastal route was chosen as being financially viable and would link the capital of Arakan to the rest of Burma. Within the Arakan itself, there was an enormous annual inflow of field workers from the Chittagong district of Assam to harvest the rich rice fields, assist in the rice mills and to undertake ploughing and sowing the fields.

Many of these workers travelled by foot on tracks that converged near Maungdaw and then diverged again at Buthidaung. It was to cater for this traffic that the Arakan Flotilla Co. formed the Buthidaung–Maungdaw Tramway Co in 1913. The route of the line would be a section of the proposed Indo-Burma Connecting Railway but would be built to the narrow gauge of 2ft 6in. After several alterations, (the original gauge was to be 2ft), the materials were ordered in 1911 and construction started in 1912. Despite financial and construction problems, the line was opened on February 15th 1919. Unfortunately, the railway did not live up to expectations and the company went into liquidation, with the line closing on 1st April 1926. That could have been the end of the story but the track bed, now a road, was bitterly fought over during the Second World War and was effectively the 'Stop' line of the Japanese advance through Burma. The fate of the locomotives is not known.

12. *(Top) Works photograph of Beyer Peacock wn5702 of 1913 supplied to the Arakan Flotilla Company for the 2ft 6in gauge Buthidaug-Maungdaw Tramway Company Ltd.*

(CD1231 IMG00093 (11-C-38) – MOSI, Manchester)

13. *(Above right) Model of Buthidaung of the Buthidaung-Maungdaw Tramway, which was the lightest and smallest Garratt locomotive built by Beyer Peacock. There is little indication that this locomotive is actually gear driven from a Caton marine engine located under the boiler in the area that would be the firebox. Notice the dummy oil lubricator on the rear running board, (there is the same arrangement on the front unit), with working levers driven from the coupling rod.*

(WN032-1. N D Kirkbride)

14. *(Right) This is a wonderful black & white photograph of the 0-6-0+0-6-0 tramway Garratt Buthidaung. Careful scrutiny of the photograph sees the base of the gas tank just visible below the main frames at the point where the re-railing jack is fitted. In the bottom right hand corner of the dummy firebox is the forward reverse lever, with the exhaust port of the cylinder just below the firebox.*

(WN032-2 – Ken Johnson)

15. (Above) All is revealed with this photograph of Buthidaung on a mirror to show the underside. The Caton Marine engine can be seen lying across the frame with the crankshaft close to the nearside frame. The spur gear drive in front of the engine brings the output drive shafts to a point midway between the frames and into such a position where the drive can be split forward and backwards. The forward carden shaft is straightforward but the rear carden shaft has to run between the engine trunk guide and the cylinder column. Between the frames the base of the gas tank is visible with what appears to be a test label attached to it. Above this part of the frame, the gas filler valve and its turret are seen alongside the boiler. The connecting and eccentric rods disappear behind the motion covers to a swinging lever to provide the impression of a working system.

(WN032-4 – Ken Johnson)

16. (Top right) The second of the Buthidaung Maungdaw tramway Garratt locomotives named Trevithick. It was built to celebrate the momentous milestone of the 100th issue of GardenRail magazine. The name Trevithick, was taken from the famous Cornish engineer Richard Trevithick. The model uses the SVS geared engine located in the dummy firebox area, instead of the Caton marine engine, which by this time was no longer available.

(WN119-1 – Geoff Lumsdon)

17. (Right) The side skirts fitted to this tramway locomotive means that dummy cylinders and valve gear were not required, leaving only the reverse crank, eccentric rod and the connecting rod to be fitted. The length of the cab has been slightly increased to accommodate the vertical gas tank in the rear of the cab. The huge working headlight on the front tank was obtained from Finescale Engineering, having been supplied for a proposed model of this Garratt which unfortunately was never produced. The full size locomotive was fitted with a belly tank mounted between the main frames and in later models of Garratt locomotives where this was a feature, such as the Darjeeling Himalayan class D, this arrangement could be used to mount the gas tank.

(WN119-2 – Geoff Lumsdon)

18. (Below right) WN148, the third Buthidaung-Maungdaw Tramway Garratt locomotive built along the same lines as the previous model but in this case named Maungdaw.

(WN148-1 – Geoff Lumsdon)

The first of the tramway Garratt locomotives was WN32, taking the name Buthidaung from the first of the full size locomotives, (Beyer Peacock Works number 5702), with the correct lettered and shaped nameplate on the side of the cab. To provide the power, the Maxwell Hemmens two cylinder Caton marine engine was fitted across the main frames in the position of the dummy firebox. From the crankshaft and mounted on the engine bedplate, a spur gear drive brought the double output shaft towards the centre of the locomotive main frames, the rear drive passing between the cylinder columns and the trunk guide. The drive to the bogies followed previous practice for articulated engines. The spoked wheels were cast iron, supplied by Walsall Model Industries, to suit their square end 32mm coarse scale axles. The gas tank is located across the frames under the boiler with the gas filler alongside the left hand side of the boiler. This attractive model was finished in maroon, the colour of the prototype being unknown. On the model, the only disadvantage came from the use of inside frames, which precluded a dual gauge facility.

Two further models of this type of Garratt locomotive were built but using the SVS oscillating engine, as the previous marine piston valve engine was no longer available.

WN119 was built to celebrate the 100th issue of GardenRail magazine. It was named Trevithick and finished in two-tone grey with black. Finally WN148 was named Maungdaw, taken from the second Beyer Peacock locomotive Works number 5703.

CHEMINS DE FER VICINAUX DU MAYUMBE 0-4-0+0-4-0 CLASS E GARRATT LOCOMOTIVES

The first model, WN009, was based on the solitary E class Garratt locomotive supplied to the 600mm gauge Chemins de Fer Vicinaux du Mayumbe. This railway was unique in using mainly Garratt locomotives, (it is not known what the class D was). They were all supplied between 1911 and 1927 by the Société Anonyme de Sainte-Léonard of Liege in Belgium. Beyer Peacock licensed the Garratt design to the Baldwin Locomotive Works, Messrs Henschel & Sohn of Cassel, Germany and St. Léonard. There were four classes of locomotive, namely the four A class, eleven enlarged class B, four class C and finally the solitary class E. The class A were the smallest Garratt locomotives ever built at 23.15 tons in service. They developed 9000lbs tractive effort and had the distinction of being the first Garratt locomotives to be introduced to Africa. Following on from the class A, the class

19. (Left) Marguerite, the first of the Chemin de Fer Vicinaux du Mayumbe Garratt locomotives. Only the rear bogie is powered and the flexible steam pipe to the cylinders can be seen inside the cab at the rear. This pipe consisted of thick walled white silicon tube reinforced by a stainless steel braid laid over the pipe. To prevent the braid from unravelling, the ends were clamped with a brass clip, one of which can be seen in the photograph. For the exhaust steam only the silicon tube itself was required.

(WN009-1 – N D Kirkbride)

20. (Below left) This is Marguerite with a short train on the wood bridge at Whitley Bay. The left hand side tank hides the gas tank, the gas valve and tank end just visible in the picture. The headlamps are working units with the rechargeable cells located in the front tank. Notice the charging socket and the three way switch, (front-off and charging-rear), visible in the recess in the front tank.

(WN009-2 – N D Kirkbride)

21. (Above) An interesting posed view of WN034, the model of the Chemin de Fer Vicinaux du Mayumbe class E Garratt locomotive built in 1927 by Société Anonyme de St. Léonard of Liege, Belgium. These Garratt locomotives were the most narrow gauge in appearance, with their outside plate frames, crank webs extended to form balance weights and of course their small size. This photograph must have been taken soon after the model was built as the nameplate had not been fitted and the paintwork was unmarked.

(WN034-1 – N.D.Kirkbride)

22. (Left) View of the Caton engine as used on the Mayumbe Garratt. The engine lies across the frame in the area of the firebox, which requires the drive to be transferred to a more central position. This is achieved using spur gears with the gear frame attached to the engine bedplate. The final spur gear provides a double output to the carden-shafts and thence to the bogies. Notice how the rear drive shaft has to fit between the cylinder columns and the trunk guide. The engine is attached to the locomotive main frame on one side only, using two high tensile 6ba socket cap screws.

(Caton Engine-Garratt – Brian Clarke)

23. (Below left) This model of the Mayumbe Garratt, Christina, must be one of the most travelled and is seen here on the garden railway of the late Neville Mason on the Isle of Man.

(WN034-2 – John Messenger)

B included the unusual feature of side tanks, which was continued for the remaining classes. As further experience was gained, the class C added wood rails to the rear bunker. Finally, the solitary class E included wood rails to the side tanks, by which time the weight had increased to 29 tons. The only other Garratt locomotives to include side tanks were the Brazilian sugar Garratts. It is interesting to note that none of the Mayumbe Garratt locomotives had the U shaped recess in the rear of the front tank,

which in full size practice included lifting eyes to make removal of the tank easier.

As with WN003, the first Garratt model, WN009, had only one powered bogie. Experience had shown that this could easily lead to slipping either on greasy track or with heavier loads and so the rear bogie was ingeniously connected to the front bogie by a geared shaft between the two inner axles. This arrangement had two advantages. Firstly, it gave better adhesion with

24. (Top left) WN034 climbing towards the first of several horseshoe curves as the 32mm gauge, 1 in 30 line, winds its way to the top of the garden of Brian Watt M.B.E. at North Kessock near Inverness. Later that day the locomotive changed to 45mm to run on the lower line.
(WN034-3 – Late Brian Watt MBE)

25. (Top right) Mayumbe Garratt Christina, after running on the 32mm track of Brian Watt at North Kessock, spends the

afternoon on the lower 45mm track. The 32mm gauge line is seen in the background. To add to the portfolio, Christina has also operated on the Isle of Mull and in Holland at a railway exhibition at Utrecht.
(WN034-4 – Late Brian Watt MBE)

26. (Above) Christina on the 5ft high bridge of the author's 'Rothbury and Hillside' line in Rothbury in 2008.
(WN034-5 – Author)

all four axles driven and secondly, the geared drive acted as a brake on free running, providing a more docile operation that meant that radio control was not considered necessary. Named Marguerite, the model had a plain centre flue boiler with gas firing, the gas tank being located in the left hand side tank. The flexible steam feed to the rear bogie used the silicon tube reinforced with a stainless steel outer braid, which in over twenty years has only been replaced once.

For the second of the Mayumbe Garratt models, based again on the 1927 solitary E class, the locomotive was powered by a hidden Caton marine engine placed in the position that in the full size locomotive would have been the boiler firebox. Spur gears then transferred the drive to the centre of the locomotive, then via carden shafts to the outer axle of each bogie. Connection to the axle was then by 2:1 crossed helical gears. This method means that dummy cylinders and valvegear have to be produced.

27. (Above) RHS side view of the model based on the Ferrocarril Austral Fueguino No 2 Garratt locomotive Nora. The original locomotive, Nora, was in turn based on the Tasmanian K1 built by Beyer Peacock in 1909 for the North East Dundas Tramway, but built to a smaller scale and a gauge of 500mm. The model uses a geared drive from a 'Boxer' type SVS engine and the forward/reverse lever is visible protruding through the dummy firebox side. This is the only immediate indication that the locomotive has a hidden engine/geared drive system.

(WN138-1 – Geoff Lumsdon)

28. (Above left) Photograph of Nora taken from the booklet Argentine Adventure. A Railwayman at the end of the World by Chris Parrott and reproduced by kind permission of Cheona Publications. The was original Garratt locomotive designed and built in Argentina in 1994 for the Ferrocarril Austral Fueguino 500m gauge railway as their No 2 locomotive. Nora is thought to be the first steam locomotive to be manufactured in Argentina.

(FCAF No 2 Nora – Chris Parrott-Cheona Publications)

29. (Left) Side view of the FCAF No 2 showing the gas tank located at the rear of the cab. Again there is little evidence of the geared engine drive, which allows this diminutive Garratt to proceed at a sensible slow speed. The box like item on the top of the boiler, between the dome and the cab along with the down pipes, represents the external steam regulator and steam pipes to the cylinders.

(WN138-2 – Geoff Lumsdon)

30. (Below left) This photograph illustrates how neat this small Garratt is against the 32mm gauge track and yet the model has the facility for conversion to 45mm gauge. Although the original locomotive cab and front and rear tanks were of welded construction, the model has opted for a riveted version which looks much better. It all adds to the detail.

(WN138-3 – Geoff Lumsdon)

This extra work must be set against the removal of the flexible steam connections to the bogies and the value of slow consistent running that effectively removes the requirement for radio control. However, once all the parts are fitted, the mechanical drive is very reliable and apart from lubrication is maintenance free. The locomotive was WN34, named Christina and is certainly the most travelled of all the models, having visited garden railways on the Isle of Man, the Isle of Mull, North Kessock (beside Inverness) and exhibitions as far away as Ultrecht in Holland, as well as the usual venues such as Stoneleigh, Llanfair, Mersham etc.

FERROCARRIL AUSTRAL FUEGUINO 500MM GAUGE 0-4-0+0-4-0 GARRATT LOCOMOTIVE NORA/ING. L D PORTA

The last three hidden gear drive models were all based on the tiny Garratt locomotive of the 50cm gauge Ferrocarril Austral Fueguino in Tierra del Fuego, Argentina. The locomotive, FCAF No2 and named Nora was built in 1994 at Carupa, Buenos Aires Province as a scaled down version of K1, the first Garratt ever built and now running on the rebuilt Welsh Highland railway. The principal similarity with the prototype of 1909 was the 0-4-0 +0-4-0 wheel arrangement, the unusual position of the cylinders at the inner ends of the power

bogies and the general outline. However, the compound expansion of the original locomotive was replaced with simple expansion in the four cylinders and piston valves controlled the steam flow.

Before dealing with the locomotive, here is a brief history of the line. The Ferrocarril Austral Fueguino, (Southern Fuegan Railway in English), was reopened to passenger traffic on the 11th October 1994. The railway was originally opened in 1896 and operated to haul timber to the Prison of Ushuaia, where some 90 prisoners produced up to 700 logs per day, as the hard labour constituent of their sentences. The line closed in 1947 and remained derelict until an Argentine entrepreneur had the idea of reopening the 50cm gauge line as a tourist railway, giving an environmentally friendly means of access to within the boundary of the Tierra del Fuego National Park. The start of the line is 8km west of the port of Ushuaia at the Estacion Fin Del Mungo, (Station at the end of the World), and travels some 5.25km into the National Park, a nature reserve of restricted access to mass transport.

Two models have been built based on this Garratt locomotive, namely WN138 and WN201. The problem was scale. The original locomotive was built as a miniature of the K1. It was to

31. (Left) In 1991, the FCAF Garratt locomotive, Nora, was taken out of service for major alterations. This photograph shows the locomotive in its modified form and now re-named Ing. L. D. Porta, after the Argentinean steam engineer Livio Dante Porta. Notice how the boiler has been lifted by 450mm along with the increase in cab height (500mm). A taller tapered 'Lempor' type has replaced the original chimney and this, together with the various modifications has dramatically altered the appearance of the locomotive.
(FCAF No2 Ing – L D Porta – Martyn Bane)

32. (Left) This is the model shown in the brass before painting. The gas tank can be seen at the rear of the cab and despite the boiler having a rear steam turret the intrusion of the boiler into the cab has been kept to a minimum. Even so, there is only just enough room for the poker type gas burner. Just behind the front tank can be seen the mainframe and bogie pivot plates. Between these plates is a plain spherical bearing with the vertical movement limited by the close proximity of the plates. To the nearside of the pivot can be seen the 6ba socket cap screw attached to the bogie pivot plate and running in a slot in the mainframe pivot plate. Notice how complicated the front tank is with curved tops to the front and sides as well as the 'U' shaped cut-out in the rear of the tank.
(WN214-1 FCAF No 2 – Author)

33. (Top) This photograph is taken from the same angle but this time of the finished model. Notice the correct plates added to the cab sides and the front and rear tanks. The displacement lubricator is visible in the far side cab entrance. Again, the model has used riveted construction rather than the all welded construction of the original.

(WN214-2 FCAF No 2 – Author)

33A. (Above left) Enlargement of the previous photograph to show the correct builders and reconstruction plates.

(WN214-2 FCAF cab side – Author)

34. (Above right) Opposite side view, which due to heavy snow, had to be on a piece of track on top of a small carpet. The forward/reverse lever on the SVS engine can be seen in front of the cab, which indicates the location of the SVS engine across the frame. The original style of steam pipe from the regulator down to the frames has been retained, rather than the horrendous highly insulated pipes seen on the photograph of the full size locomotive.

(WN214-3 FCAF No 2 – Author)

run on 50cm gauge and if constructed to a scale of 16mm/ft, would have been very small indeed. The scale was therefore increased to bring the gauge up to the equivalent of 2ft or an increase of 24/20 (60cm/50cm). Even so, this is a very small Garratt with a length between the buffer beams just less than 17ins and a width of 4¼in. The drive arrangement followed the previous designs but using a larger bore SVS oscillating engine and a 1½:1 final drive to give an overall ratio of 6:1. To provide the extra steam required, the centre flue boiler was fitted with water tubes. The only major difference is the inclusion of rivets, whereas the original locomotive was of welded construction.

The development of tourism, with cruise ships stopping off at Ushuaia, put a growing strain on the facilities of the railway and it was becoming obvious that the steam locomotive fleet was not up to the demands of this increased traffic. Along with progressive improvements to the line and the stations, the No3 locomotive Camilla had modifications carried out in 1999 which resulted in lower fuel and water consumption allied to an increase in drawbar horsepower. The very basic nature of the Garratt locomotive Nora had resulted in problems from its introduction in 1994 with very low efficiency, mechanical failures due to manufacturing errors and unreliable and ineffective auxiliary equipment.

Locomotive No 2 was taken out of service in February 2001 following severe mechanical failure and boiler problems. The opportunity was taken to completely rebuild this locomotive to modern steam practice. These modifications included replacing the boiler with a spare unit mounted 450mm higher to provide extra firebox volume, as well as adding better insulation. The power units were extensively overhauled along with the steam circuit and exhaust system. The water capacity was increased and the cab redesigned to provide better crew comfort,

including the increase of the cab height by 500mm. It was out shopped on 11th December 2001 in bright red livery, re-designated class KM, and to mark the occasion of the 80th birthday of the Argentine locomotive engineer, Livio Dante Porta, was re-named Ing L.D. Porta, thus replacing its original name of Nora.

WN214 was based on this redesigned locomotive and is mechanically identical to the previous models. Again it was decided to include rivet type construction rather than imitate the welded

35. *(Above) Darjeeling Himalayan Railway class D based on Beyer Peacock Works number 5407 of 1910. The model is shown on Mike's line posing easily on the 4ft radius curve after the bridge. The minimum radius for the full size line was 90ft or 4ft 6in in 16mm scale.*

(WN180-2 – Mike Lax)

36. *(Left) Another view, this time approaching the bridge but notice how the front bogie has not only entered the curve but is also canted over in the wrong direction, illustrating the effectiveness of the articulation.*

(WN180-3 – Mike Lax)

37. *(Below left) This is the steam side of the Darjeeling D, showing the pipe layout and in particular the length of the steam circuit, which is always a problem with the Garratt layout. The Roundhouse Engineering twin flexible steam pipes can also be seen along with their location directly under the bogie pivot. With later Garratt locomotives, the flexible steam pipes locate on a manifold attached to the main frame, providing a more rigid anchor point and making it easier to separate the bogies from the boiler main frame. The cylinder on the exhaust line acts as a water separator to reduce the condensate ejected from the chimney. The gas tank is located between the main frames in the position of the under slung well tank of the full size locomotive.*

(WN180-3 – Mike Lax)

assembly of the modified prototype. The front water tank of this locomotive was particularly difficult to construct with the curved edges to the front and sides and to include the 'U' shaped cut-out at the rear. To improve the looks of the model, the heavily insulated steam pipes from the regulator down the sides of the boiler, were kept to the original diameter. Just look at the pipes on the photograph of Ing. L.D.Porta, they are rather dreadful. The plates on the cab side and the tank sides have been carefully reproduced from photographs of the full size engine.

A further brand new Garratt from South Africa was added to the locomotive fleet in 2006.

DARJEELING HIMALAYAN RAILWAY
0-4-0+0-4-0 CLASS D GARRATT LOCOMOTIVE

For the next Garratt locomotive models a return was made to direct cylinders as per the prototype. Roundhouse Engineering brought out their Forney model using the Single Fairlie type of articulation, which in turn required a flexible steam connection. This component along with their cylinders, valve gear, 33mm disc type wheels and No 24 axles and cranks formed the basics of the next model, WN180, based on the 2ft gauge Darjeeling Himalayan Railway class D. Built by Beyer Peacock in 1910 as Works number 5407, it was their second design of Garratt and the first to adopt the standard arrangement of simple expansion cylinders located on the outside of the bogies. This was a particularly difficult line with an average gradient of 1 in 30 and a ¾ mile stretch of 1 in 23 and over curves as sharp as 90ft. As could be expected with such a new design on such a difficult track, there were many problems and the locomotive, after much modification, was to see out its days on the lower hill section and finally on the plains section, in particular the Teesta Valley line. Despite this difficult start the locomotive was not withdrawn until 1954.

The model, WN180 was followed by WN172, 190 and 197, all to the same basic design. The 2½in diameter boiler had a 28mm centre flue with about ten water tubes laid in a spiral pattern and fired by a ceramic burner. Steam was taken from the dome to a backhead-mounted regulator without superheating, thence to the displacement lubricator in the cab. From the lubricator, the steam pipe ran around and under the boiler to a 'T' piece located at the midpoint of the main frame to ensure equal distribution to the bogies. This is an important point as the pipe arrangement can lead to unequal power at the bogies. Both pipes then terminate on a combined inlet and exhaust manifold from which the flexible pipes are attached. The two flexible pipes are then fed under the pivot to a fixed location point consisting of the steam inlet and exhaust pipes coming from the cylinder T pieces. The location of the flexible pipes below the pivot points and the route chosen are of particular importance to ensure the minimum of displacement of these joints on curves. Careful setting up of these flexible joints is rewarded with trouble free operation and long life. Other types of flexible pipe have been tried; including silicon tubing with a stainless steel stocking teased out along the pipe and held by clips as on WN's 3 and 9, but the tube will eventually fail. The flexible connections could imitate the ball and sliding joints of the full size locomotive but this has not been tried. Finally, the exhaust steam pipes pass to a small water separating tank with a drain valve with the exhaust from this tank going to the smokebox in a larger 3/16in pipe. The long steam pipes and remote cylinders produce more condensation than an ordinary locomotive and this tank is used to eject some of this water down towards the track.

Despite this locomotive being the earliest Garratt model with the full four cylinders, it has proved itself to be reliable and very easy to use. According to the well-known Garratt enthusiast Chris Moody, it is the most used locomotive on his Ttarrag Shed 'Garratt only' layout and is often used to introduce fellow modellers to Garratt operation.

THE 'SO CALLED' MODIFIED GARRATT

Whilst on the subject of the Darjeeling Garratt, an interesting variation from the basic arrangement was to place the cylinders on the main frame with a geared universal drive carden shaft drive to the two bogies. Since no such locomotives were actually built WN101 was based on the outline of the Darjeeling D class. In A E Durrant's book, Garratt Locomotives of the World, there is reference to the adoption of the Garratt principal for a proposed locomotive to operate on the Rimutaka incline in New Zealand. Three of these interesting and unconventional designs are shown but the one of particular relevance to WN101 was that proposed by the Vulcan Foundry in 1931. Here the cylinders are mounted on the main frame with drive shafts to two six wheel bogies arranged on the Garratt principal. The design removed the requirement for four cylinders along with the associated flexible steam joints and long steam pipes. The universal drive to the bogies could also include a suitable reduction gearbox to give greater

38. (Above) The Modified Garratt Manipuri, showing the general layout of this Garratt hybrid. Unlike the design proposed by the Vulcan Foundry, the cylinders were horizontal rather than inclined, making it much easier to mount them and also keep the inlet and exhaust pipes below the smokebox. The overall appearance is based on the Darjeeling Himalayan Railway D class, with only four-wheel bogies rather than the six wheel bogies of the Vulcan foundry proposal.

(WN101-5 – Geoff Lumsdon)

39. (Middle left) Close up view of the rear bogie of the Mike Lax Modified Garratt. The crossed helical gears of the drive to the outer axle are clearly visible. The meshing of the gears can be accurately set up from the machining of the bogie side frames, using the digital readout on the mill.

(WN270-4 – Mike Lax)

40. (Below left) The Modified Garratt Manipuri from the opposite side. The rear bunker of the Darjeeling lookalike provides a suitable location for the gas tank, which is just visible on this photograph.

(WN101-6 – Geoff Lumsdon)

and smoother torque to the driving wheels. The layout of the two inclined cylinders and splitter gearbox on the main frame was similar to that used on the Climax and the Price E type logging locomotives. Unfortunately these three designs remained as proposals only and no such locomotives were built for the Rimutaka incline.

The honour of producing the first model based on this design must go to Barry Milner with a 4+4 locomotive based on the outline of the NGG 16 and which he called a Modified Garratt. From his drawings, WN74 was built using an overall gear reduction of 3:1, producing a very powerful model but a little slow. This was followed by WN101, this time based on the outline of the Darjeeling 'D' class and fitted with an overall gear reduction of 2:1. This model used bevel gears for the transmission but the later engines have used crossed helical gears, as illustrated by the photographs of WN270 (built by Mike Lax) and showing the frames and bogies during construction.

This design has all the advantages of the Garratt articulated layout without the need for four cylinders and the associated flexible steam pipes and long steam pipe runs. If required, the bogies can be easily separated from the main

41. (Above) Works photograph of Beyer Peacock Works number 6629 of 1929, supplied to the 2ft 6in gauge Ceylon Government Railways as their solitary class H1. This locomotive had a total wheelbase of 35ft 9in and an overall length over the buffers of 41ft 5in (26in in 16mm scale). Each engine unit had a coupled wheelbase of 5ft 3in and a combined wheelbase of 10ft.
(CGR class H1, BP 6629 (17-B-61) – MOSI, Manchester)

42. (Top left) The first model of the Ceylon Government Railway class H1 gently lifts the safety valve as it stands during a quiet moment in New Chesterton yard on the South Arbury Railway in May 2007. This model has seen extensive use on the South Arbury Railway and is a regular runner on the portable layout 'Ttarrag Shed', where it may be operated by any of the regular Garratt drivers.
(WN205 – CGR class H1 – Chris Moody)

43. (Left) The second model based on the solitary Ceylon Government Railways class H1 narrow gauge Garratt. Of all the smaller Garratt locomotives this must be the most attractive and well balanced with its leading pony trucks, inclined cylinders and outside frames with balanced cranks. The radio control is fitted in the rear bunker with the servo leads to the steam regulator and front valve gear servo's using the coal chute to cross to the cab. Between the front tank and mainframe can be seen the lead to the front forward/reverse servo. This lead has been carried to the front of the main frame in a thin tubular brass conduit attached to the RHS frame side member. To protect the servo leads they are encased in plastic tube over the exposed areas. In amongst the dummy coal can be seen the charging socket for the batteries.
(WN206-1 – Author)

44. (Below left) The opposite side view of the same model illustrating the neat appearance of this Garratt with the rounded corners to the front tank. Notice the 'U' shaped recess in the front tank used in full size practice to access the boiler fire tubes without removing the tank. Just behind the front tank can be seen the servo operating rod for the lifting link on the valve gear. The oversize expansion links of the Roundhouse valve gear and the lifting arm and links can cause difficulties in this area.
(WN206-4 – Author)

frame i.e. during construction. It is unfortunate that no full size locomotives were built, as it would have given an interesting comparison with the conventional Garratt locomotive.

CEYLON GOVERNMENT RAILWAYS 2-4-0+0-4-2 CLASS H1 GARRATT LOCOMOTIVE

Next on the Garratt list was a model of the Ceylon Government Railways unique class H1 2-4-0+0-4-2 built by Beyer Peacock in 1929 as their Works number 6629. This locomotive must rank as one of the most attractive Garratt locomotives ever built with its inclined cylinders, outside cranks and front tank with rounded edges. Running on the 2ft 6in gauge line up the Kelani valley from the capital Columbo to Opanake, it was to remain the only narrow gauge example in Ceylon, although a 5ft 6in gauge Garratt had been supplied in 1927 to

be followed by a further eighteen in 1946. The 2ft 6in gauge had a route length of 106 miles and included the 19 mile long Uda-Pussella branch, which left at the junction at Nanu-Oya to Ragalla with a ruling gradient of 1in 24. A general arrangement drawing and a copy of the works photograph were obtained from the Beyer Peacock archives held at The Museum of Science and Engineering at Manchester but no further information on the locomotive could be found. Even the colour remains a mystery – which was a good excuse to finish WN205 and 206 in the beautiful LMS crimson lake lined with yellow.

SOUTH AFRICAN RAILWAYS 2-6-0+0-6-2 CLASS NGG11 GARRATT LOCOMOTIVE

The NGG11 class were developed for the 2ft gauge Avontuur and Stuartstown branches of the South African Railways. These three

45. (Top) Works photograph of Beyer Peacock Works number 5975 of 1919 supplied to the South African Railways as their number 51.
(NGG11 BP 5975 – (11-C-58) – MOSI, Manchester)

46. (Above) Full side view of the model of the South African Railways class NGG11 Garratt locomotive fitted with a coal fired boiler and axle driven water pump in the front bogie. This locomotive may not be as attractive as the class H1 but it certainly gives the impression of hidden power. At

first site the coal firing is not obvious but notice how the cab roof is on front mounted hinges to improve access to the inside of the cab. This is in addition to the open doorway access through the cab backsheet. Garratt locomotives are often seen as rather large for the average garden railway but hopefully this chapter has illustrated that the smaller narrow gauge engines featured can have a place even on quite modest railways.
(WN215-1 – Mike Lax)

47. A fine view of the coal fired model of the South African Railways class NGG11 Garratt No 55, WN215, under steam on the garden railway of Chris Moody at South Arbury.

(WN215-3 – Chris Moody)

machines were numbered NG51, NG52 and NG53 and were delivered in 1920 with NG51 sent to the Avontuur branch. However, once the two sister locomotives were erected at the Uitenhage workshops, all three were sent to the Stuartstown branch to take the place of the 4-6-2 tank engines then working the line. The Stuartstown line climbed 4400ft in 98 miles, with a ruling gradient of 1 in 33 and minimum curves of 150ft radius. The Garratt locomotives took these restrictions in their stride and were capable of hauling 150 ton loads.

A point to note is that in 16mm scale this minimum radius is equivalent to 7ft 6in and would be unacceptable to most garden railways. These Garratt locomotives weighed in at over 44 tons and spread their weight over a wheelbase of 39ft with a total length over the buffers of 44ft 7½in. These early 2ft gauge

Garratt locomotives were not superheated and had 'D' valves operated by Walschaerts valve gear. They were so successful that two further locomotives, numbered NG54 and NG55, were supplied by Beyer Peacock and erected in the SAR Durban workshops in 1925. Unlike the previous engines, the design was altered to include piston valves and superheaters. Fortunately, these two later locomotives still exist; with No 55 recently fully restored from a scrap condition by the Sandstone Heritage trust. The bulk of the restoration work was carried out at their Bloomfontain workshops.

For the model, WN215, not only was this the largest locomotive built so far, but was the first to be coal fired. This particular Garratt has the advantage of a low rear bunker providing better access to the rear of the cab, which was designed with a cut out door in the rear cab sheet. There are however particular problems with the introduction of coal firing to the previous Garratt designs. The steam pipes now have to be taken past the wide firebox of what is basically an extended 3½in gauge 'Tich' boiler and there is the addition of a cold water feed and bypass water pipes. All four have to occupy the limited area between the frames of the bogie, with the semi-universal pivot above and the rear axle below. The method is to prioritise the installation of the pipes. The most important pipe is the high pressure steam to the cylinders followed by the exhaust steam pipe, the two run alongside each other on either side of the centre line. The water pipes are not under pressure and bridge the gap between the main frame and the bogie using silicon tube, finding the best routes remaining. There is not much room for these pipes in a 16mm scale Garratt operating on 32mm track.

As mentioned the boiler is a 3½in gauge 'Tich' boiler with the barrel extended by 1¾in. Steam is picked up from the steam dome and brought to a boss on the backplate. The steam regulator is fitted into this boss and feeds steam to the lubricator and then to one of a pair of the hollow stays. From the smokebox end of the hollow stay the steam pipe enters the superheater firetube, and then returns on itself to emerge into the 'T' piece at the bottom of the smokebox. The steam is therefore split to the two bogies. The remaining hollow stay is used to convey steam to the blower jet in the smokebox. A final point to appreciate is that the full size locomotive was built to negotiate a minimum radius of 150ft, equivalent to 7ft 6in in 16mm scale, whereas WN215 can operate on a minimum radius of 4ft 6in, despite the multitude of pipes and the limited space available on 32mm gauge.

Building this coal fired Garratt was greatly assisted by the practical information supplied by John Britain whose coal fired Garratt locomotives are well known for their superb and powerful performance. However, the construction of a Garratt locomotive as an introduction to coal firing is not recommended. A far more sensible locomotive would have been the North British Burma Mines tender No 9 engine, which is described in a different chapter.

REFERENCES:

- Beyer Peacock Locomotive Builders to the World by R L Hills and D Patrick.
- Garratt Locomotives of the World by A E Durrant.
- The Anatomy of a Garratt by Peter Manning.
- Argentine Adventure – A Railwayman at the End of the World by Chris Parrott (Cheona Publications).
- The Narrow Gauge No 157. Article by Kelvin Parkes entitled The Arakan Light Railway. This is a definitive article on the Buthidaung Maungdaw Tramway including photographs and outline drawing of the Garratt locomotives.
- The Narrow Gauge No 79. Article by M Swift titled The Darjeeling-Himalayan Railway Garratt. A similar in depth article on the Darjeeling class D Garratt locomotive.
- Articulated Locomotives by Lionel Wiener. This is the definitive book on articulated locomotives of every possible type.

LOCOMOTIVES WORKS LIST

WORKS NO.	WHEEL ARRANGEMENT	NAME	DESCRIPTION	BASED ON LOCOMOTIVE BUILT BY	DATE BUILT	BUILT BY
1	0-6-0		Calidonia Chassis / Body Scrapped			PA
2	0-4-2	Juliet	0-4-0 Merlin Midas rebuilt	Freelance		PA
3	0-4-0+0-4-0	Piracicaba	Piracicaba Sugar Co Garratt	Saint-Leonard w/n 2108 of 1927		PA
4	0-4-4	Patricia	Ffestiniog Single Fairlie "Taliesin"	Vulcan Foundry w/n 791 of 1876		PA
5	4=4	Renishaw No.2	4cyl Avonside Geared Articulated	Avonside Engine Co w/n2059 of 1931	nnn-84	PA
6	0-4-0	Loxan	De Winton Type on R/H VB chassis	Freelance		PA
7	0-4-0	Goliath	Semi Tram on R/H VB chassis	Freelance		PA
8	0-4-0	Bulldog	Sentinel 80hp Industrial	Sentinel Waggon Works Ltd		PA
9	0-4-0+0-4-0	Marguerite	C de F Mayumbe class E Garratt	Saint-Leonard w/n2056 of 1926	nnn-85	PA
10	0-4-0	Atlas	Gosling chassis			
11	0-6-0	R.W.Rowley	Side Tank	Freelance		PA
12	0-4-0+0-4-0	Kakavos	Improved Meyer Articulated	Andrew Barclay w/n960 of 1903	nnn-86	PA
13						
14						
15	0-4-0	Bluebell	Overtype	Stephen Lewin Overtype		PA
16	0-6-0	Hercules	Fowler Plantation "Coolum"	John Fowler w/n 16036 of 1923		PA
17	4+4	Cb113	New Zealand Bush - A&G Price	A & G Price of Thames w/n 113 of 1924	nnn-87	PA
18	0-4-0	Glyn	Glyn Valley Tram	Beyer Peacock w/n 3500 of 1891	Mar-04	PA
19	0-4-0	Petal	Overtype	Stephen Lewin Overtype		PA
20	0-4-0	No.3	Overtype	Stephen Lewin Overtype	nnn-87	PA
21	0-6-0	Vulcan	Fowler Plantation with Tender	John Fowler w/n 16030/1 of		PA
22	0-4-0					
23	0-4-4	Colorado Star	Forney (radiating axle)	Matthias Nace Forney		PA
24	0-4-0	Sampson	Sentinel 80hp Industrial	Sentinel Waggon Works Ltd	nnn-88	
25	4+4	Renishaw No.4	4cyl Avonside Geared Articulated	Avonside Engine Co w/n 2059 of 1931	nnn-89	PA
26	0-4-0+0-4-0	Porto Feliz No.5	Garratt Brazilian sugar		nnn-89	PA
27	0-4-0	Sir Stephen	Freelance Tram			PA
28	0-4-0	Heracles ?	Overtype			PA
29	0-4-4	Evelyn A	SR&RL Forney			PA
30	0-4-0	Hannibal	Sentinel Industrial			PA
31	0-6-2	Christine	Otavi Railway Side tank	Arn. Jung w/n 708 of 1904		PA
32	0-6-0+0-6-0	Buthidaung	Buthidaung Maungdaw Garratt	Beyer Peacock w/n 5702 of 1913		PA
33	0-4-0	Sir Stephen	VB Tram	Freelance	nnn-90	PA
34	0-4-0+0-4-0	Christina	Garratt/Mayumbe Class E	Saint-Leonard w/n 2096 of 1927	nnn-90	PA
35						
36	2-6-0+tender	Maine Star	Tramway Cantareira	Baldwin wn37398 of 1911		PA
37	4+4	Ntinyana	2 Cyl. Avonside Geared Articulated	Avonside Engine Co w/n2055 of 1931	nnn-85	PA
38	0-6-2+tender		O & K Geared Plantation	Orenstein & Koppel wn8090 of 1916		PA
39	0-4-0		Surabaya Steam Tram	Beyer Peacock & Co Ltd		PA
40	4+4		Johnston B patent 27107	J. Johnston & Sons of Invercargill		PA
41	0-4-4	Bucyrus	Navarro Railroad "Dixie"	Bucyrus Foundry & Manufacturing Co.		PA
42	0-4-0+0-4-0	Strathfarrer	Kitson Meyer "Caledonia"	Andrew Barclay w/n 1956 of 1928		PA
43	0-4-0	Anaticula	Clayton 'C'	proposed by Clayton Waggon Works		PA
44	4+4	Ali-Shan No15	Ali-Shan Forest Railway 18T Shay	Lima Machine Works		PA
45	0-4-0	Goliath	V B De Winton Type	De Winton		PA
46	0-4-0+0-4-0	Carla's Court	Metre gauge Brazilian Sugar Garratt	St Leonard wn2091/2108 of 1927		PA
47	0-4-0	The Don	Vertical Boiler Contractors Engine	Balmforth Brothers		PA
48	0-4-0	Jasalda	Serajoedal Steam Tram	Beyer Peacock order 7875 of 1895		PA
49	0-4-0		Serajoedal Steam Tram	Beyer Peacock order 7875 of 1895		PA
50	4+4	Blackburn	4cyl Avonside Geared Articulated	Avonside Engine Co wn2059 of 1931	Apr-02	PA
51	0-4-0	No1	Alford & Sutton Wilkinson Tram	Black, Hawthorn & Co.		PA
52	0-4-0	No1	Alford & Sutton Wilkinson Tram	Black, Hawthorn & Co.		PA
53	0-4-0	Surabaya	Surabaya Steam Tram	Beyer Peacock & Co Ltd		PA
54	0-4-0	Lumpy Tom	Contractors Locomotive	Unknown-John Frazer & Co plate		PA
55						
56	0-4-0		Stehen Lewin Overtype	Stephen Lewin		
57	0-4-0	M.B.R.O No.21	Wilkinson Patent Vertical Boiler Tram	Beyer Peacock wn2377 of 1883		PA
58	0-4-0	Delilah	Stephen Lewin Overtype	Stephen Lewin		PA
59	0-4-0		Stephen Lewin Overtype	Stephen Lewin	Jun-05	PA
60	0-4-0	M.B.R.O No.22	Wilkinson Patent Vertical Boiler Tram	Beyer Peacock wn2378 of 1883		PA
61	0-4-0	M.B.R.O.No.23	Wilkinson Patent Vertical Boiler Tram	Beyer Peacock wn2379 of 1883	Aug-98	PA
62	0-4-0		MEG No46 Continental Steam Tram	Grafenstaden wn4805 of 1897		PA
63	0-4-0		Sentinel 80hp Industrial	Sentinel Waggon Works Ltd	Jul-02	PA
64			MEG No46 Continental Steam Tram	Grafenstaden wn4805 of 1897		PA
65	0-4-0	The Don	Vertical Boiler Contractors Engine	Balmforth Brothers		PA
66	0-4-0		MEG No46 Continental Steam Tram	Grafenstaden wn4805 of 1897		PA
67	0-4-0	Samson	Stephen Lewin Overtype	Stephen Lewin	Jun-99	PA
68	4+4	Kelly Island No31	2 Cylinder 'A' Shay	Lima Machine Works		PA
69			De Winton Type sold as scrapped			
70	4+4	Mich Cal No2	Michigan-California T boiler Shay	Lima Machine Works c/n 122 of 1884		PA
71	0-4-4	Patricia	Single Fairlie Taliesin	Vulcan Foundry w/n 791 of 1876		PA
72	0-4-0	Perla	Geared Saddle Tank	Robey & Co wn15776 of 1895	Jun-99	PA
73	0-4-0		Surabaya Steam Tram	Beyer Peacock & Co Ltd		PA
74	4+4	Firedrake	Modified Garratt	Freelance	nnn-00	PA
75	4+4	Pozos No4	Octaviano B. Cabrera left hand Shay	Lima Machine Works c/n 826 of 1903	Apr-00	PA
76	0-6-0	No57	RTM Continental Steam Tram	Orenstein & Koppel wn9194 of 1920	Feb-00	PA
77	0-4-0	Sir G Newness	Clayton 'C'	proposed by Clayton Waggon Works		PA
78	0-4-0	Lumpy Tom	Contractors Locomotive	Unknown-John Frazer & Co plate		PA
79	0-4-0	Surabaya	Surabaya Steam Tram	Beyer Peacock & Co Ltd	Sep-99	PA
80			Geared Plantation locomotive	Freelance		PA
81	0-4-0		VB Tram Freelance	Freelance	Aug-01	PA
82	0-4-0	Wilfred	De Winton type	De Winton	Feb-00	PA
83	0-4-0		Stephen Lewin Overtype	Stephen Lewin	Jun-00	PA
84	4+4	Chassis	A Class Shay Standard Steel	Lima machine Works	Mar-01	PA

WORKS NO.	WHEEL ARRANGEMENT	NAME	DESCRIPTION	BASED ON LOCOMOTIVE BUILT BY	DATE BUILT	BUILT BY
85	4+4	Chassis	A class Shay Casparis Stone Co	Lima Machine Works c/n 782 of 1902	Nov-00	PA
86	0-4-0	Lumpy Tom	Contractors locomotive	Unknown-John Frazer & Co plate	Apr-00	PA
87	0-4-0		Robey Geared Saddle Tank 15903	Robey & Co wn15903 of 1895/6	Jan-00	PA
88	4+4	Achilles	10T 2Truck 'T' Boiler Shay	Lima Machine Works c/n 341 of 1891	Mar-01	PA
89	0-4-2	Nadine	Hunslet "EVA" class	Hunslet Engine Co wn904 of 1906	Jul-00	PA
90	0-4-0		Stephen Lewin Overtype	Stephen Lewin	May-00	PA
91	0-4-0		De Winton type	De Winton		PA
92	0-4-0	The Don	Vertical Boiler Contractors Engine	Balmforth Brothers	Jan-01	PA
93	0-6-0	No.56	RTM Continental Steam Tram	Orenstein & Koppel wn9193 of 1920	Apr-01	PA
94	0-4-0	Graffenstaden	Continental Steam tram MEG 46	Grafenstaden wn4805 of 1897	nnn-01	PA
95	4+4	No.50	Yawata Iron Works 10T 2 Truck Shay	Lima Machine Works	Aug-00	PA
96	0-4-0		Stephen Lewin Overtype	Stephen Lewin	Jul-00	PA
97	2-4-0+T		German Military Locomotive	Hohenzollern fabr.nu.473 of 1888	Oct-01	PA
98	2-4-0+T		German Military Locomotive	Hohenzollern fabr.nu.473 of 1888	Nov-00	PA
99	0-4-0	Lumpy Tom	Contractors locomotive	Unknown-John Frazer & Co plate	May-01	PA
100	2-4-0.		Konigliche Eisenbahn Regiment	Hohenzollern fabr. nu. 483 of 1888	Mar-01	PA
101	4+4	Manipuri	Modified Garratt	Freelance	Jul-01	PA
102	0-4-0	Annie	Surabaya Steam Tram	Deyer Peacock & Co Ltd	Apr-01	PA
103	0-4-0		Robey Geared Saddle Tank	Robey & Co wn15903 of 1895/6	Sep-01	PA
104	2-4-0+T		Konigliche Eisenbahn Regiment	Hohenzollern fabr.nu.473 of 1888	Nov-03	PA
105	2-4-0+T	Sherara	Konigliche Eisenbahn Regiment	Hohenzollern fabr.nu.473 of 1888	Nov-1	PA
106	0-4-0	Bodkin	Stephen Lewin Overtype	Stephen Lewin	Jan-02	PA
107	0-4-0	Adrienne	Surabaya Steam Tram	Beyer Peacock & Co Ltd	Mar-02	PA
108	0-4-0	Meg	Surabaya Steam Tram	Beyer Peacock & Co Ltd	Mar-02	PA
109	0-4-0	Hector	Sentinel 80hp Industrial	Sentinel Waggon Works Ltd	May-02	PA
110	0-4-0	Silvolde	Continental Steam Tram GSTM 13	Machinefabriek "Breda" wn182 of 1900	Nov-02	PA
111	0-4-0		Continental Steam Tram NZHSTM-HL	SLM fabr. nr. 346-347 of 1883	Oct-02	PA
112	2-4-0+T		Konigliche Eisenbahn Regiment	Hohenzollern fabr.nu.473 of 1888	Jun-02	PA
113	None					
114	0-4-0		Sentinel 80hp Industrial	Sentinel Waggon Works Ltd	Mar-03	PA
115	0-4-0	Groningen	Continental Steam Tram DSM 25	Machinefabriek "Breda" wn236 of 1905	Jul-02	PA
116	0-4-0	St Etienne	Continental Steam Tram	SLM fabr. nr. 283 of 1882	Aug-02	PA
117	0-4-0	Challenger	New Zealand Bush Locomotive	Gibbon & Harris	Oct-02	PA
118	0-4-0	Kay	Plynlimon & Hafan Tram	J. Slee & Co	Nov-02	PA
119	0-6-0+0-6-0	Trevithick	Buthidaung Maungdaw Garratt	Beyer Peacock w/n 5702/3 of 1913	Jul-02	PA
120	0-4-4	Taliesin	Ffestiniog Single Fairlie "Taliesin"	Vulcan Foundry w/n 791 of 1876	Apr-02	PA
121	0-4-0		Continental Steam tram MEG 46	Grafenstaden wn4805 of 1897	May-03	PA
122	0-4-0	Victoria	Plynlimon & Hafan Tram	J. Slee & Co	Apr-03	PA
123	0-4-0	Lumpy Tom	Contractors Engine	Unknown-John Frazer & Co plate	Jul-03	PA
124	0-4-0		De Winton type	De Winton	Jul-03	PA
125	0-4-0	Puffin	Continental Steam tram MEG 46	Grafenstaden wn4805 of 1897	May-03	PA
126	0-4-0	Lumpy Tom	Contractors Engine	Unknown-John Frazer & Co plate	Oct-02	PA
127	0-4-0	Mirabella	Continental Steam Tram DSM 25	Machinefabriek "Breda" wn236 of 1905	Nov-02	PA
128	0-6-4	701	Bosnia Herzegovina Mountain Loco	Wiener Locomotiv Fabriks	Jan-04	PA
129	0-4-0		De Winton type	De Winton	Jul-03	PA
130	0-4-0		De Winton Type	De Winton	Oct-05	PA
131	0-4-0ST+T	Mountaineer	Ffestiniog George England (No3)	George England & Co wn199 of1863	Oct-03	PA
132	0-4-4	Taliesin	Ffestiniog Single Fairlie "Taliesin"	Vulcan Foundry w/n 791 of 1876	May-04	PA
133	0-4-0	Hummelo	Continental Steam Tram	Henshel &Sohn wn6014 of 1902	Apr-07	PA
134	0-4-0		De Winton type	De Winton	Apr-06	PA
135	0-4-0+T	Little Giant	Ffestiniog George England	George England & Co wn235 of1867	Jul-04	PA
136	0-4-0	Violet	Vertical Boiler Direct Drive	Unknown	Sep-03	PA
137	2-4-0T+T	Linda	Penrhyn/Ffestiniog Hunslet	Hunslet Engine Co wn590 of 1893	Feb-05	PA
138	0-4-0+0-4-0	FCAF No.2	Ferrocarril Austral Fueguino Garratt	Tranex Turismo S.A.	Jan-04	PA
139	0-4-0	Sir Theodore	Glyn Valley Tram	Beyer Peacock & Co Ltd wn2969 of 1888	Jul-03	PA
140	0-4-0+T	Welsh Pony	Ffestiniog George England (No5)	George England & Co wn234 of 1867	Nov-05	PA
141	0-6-4	Moel Tryfan	Welsh Highland Rly Single Fairlie	Vulcan Foundry w/n 738 of 1877	Jan-06	PA
142	0-4-0	Lumpy Tom 9	Contractors Engine	Unknown-John Frazer & Co plate	Dec-04	PA
143	0-4-0		Continental Steam Tram	SLM	Apr-05	PA
144	0-4-0		De Winton type	De Winton	Dec-03	PA
145	4+4	Achilles	10T 2Truck 'T' Boiler Shay	Lima Machine Works c/n341 of 1891	Jan-07	PA
146	0-4-0		Continental Steam Tram	SLM	Apr-05	MJL
147	0-4-0	MBRO No.24	Wilkinson Patent Vertical Boiler Tram	Beyer Peacock & Co wn2380 of 1867	Jul-04	PA
148	0-6-0+0-6-0	Maungdaw	Buthidaung Maungdaw Garratt	Beyer Peacock w/n 5703 of 1913	Apr-05	PA
149	0-4-0+T	Lumpy Tom No7	Contractors Engine	Unknown-John Frazer & Co plate	Dec-05	PA
150	4+4	Blackburn	4cyl Avonside Geared Articulated	Avonside Engine Co w/n 2059 of 1931	Mar-07	PA
151	0-4-0	Llanfair	De Winton type	De Winton	May-05	PA
152	0-4-0	Penmaen	Sentinel 80hp Railway type	Sentinel Waggon Works Ltd	Jan-04	PA
153	0-4-0	Glyn	Glyn Valley Tram	Beyer Peacock & Co wn3500 of 1892	Jun-04	PA
154	0-4-0	Glyn	Glyn Valley Tram	Beyer Peacock & Co wn3500 of 1892	Mar-06	PA
155	0-4-0	Arthur	De Winton type	De Winton "Arthur" of 1895	Aug-05	PA
156	2-4-0T+T	Linda	Penrhyn/Ffestiniog Hunslet	Hunslet Engine Co wn590 of 1893	Jul-05	MJL-1
157						
158	0-6-0	Dorman Long	Side Rod Sentinel	Sentinel Waggon Works Ltd X59	Jul-05	PA
159	0-4-0		De Winton type	De Winton	Apr-05	PA
160	0-4-0	Lumpy Tom No8	Contractors Engine	Unknown-John Frazer & Co plate	May-04	PA
161	0-4-0		De Winton type	De Winton	Jun-04	PA
162	4+4		Vertical Boiler SHAY	Lima Machine Works c/n 23 of 1881	Sep-07	PA
163	0-4-0	Glyn	Glyn Valley Tram	Beyer Peacock & Co wn3500 of 1892	May-06	MJL
164						
165	0-4-0	Anne	Freelance Tram as wn81	Freelance	Dec-04	PA
166	0-4-0	Troy	Stephen Lewin Overtype	Stephen Lewin	Oct-07	PA
167	0-4-0	Cleve	Bedburg-Hau Fireless Tram	Hohenzollern Fireless c1912	Dec-08	PA
168	0-4-0	Linda	Penryhn/Ffestiniog Hunslet	Hunslet Engine Co wn590 of 1893	Jun-05	PA

WORKS NO.	WHEEL ARRANGEMENT	NAME	DESCRIPTION	BASED ON LOCOMOTIVE BUILT BY	DATE BUILT	BUILT BY
169	0-4-0	Black Jack	Contractors Engine	Unknown–John Frazer & Co plate	Mar-05	MJL
170						
171	4+4	Khushal Khan	Modified Garratt	Freelance	Aug-06	PA
172	0-4-0+0-4-0	D.H.R. 31	Darjeeling Himalayan class D Garratt	Beyer Peacock & Co wn5407 of 1910	Aug-06	MJL
173	0-6-4	Gowrie	Hunslet Single Fairlie	Hunslet Engine Co wn979 of 1908	Sep-09	PA
174	0-4-0	Chaloner	De Winton type	De Winton	Dec-08	PA
175	0-4-0	Palmerston	Ffestiniog George England	George England & Co.	Nov-06	MJL
176	4+4	Renishaw No4	2cyl Avonside Geared Articulated	Avonside Engine Co wn2057 of 1931	Aug-09	MJL
177	0-4-0+0-4-0	James Spooner	Ffestiniog Double Fairlie	Avonside Engine Co. wn929/930 of 1872	Dec-07	MJL
178	2-4-0T+T	Blanche	Penryhn/Ffestiniog Hunslet	Hunslet Engine Co. wn589 of 1893	Aug-05	MJL
179	0-4-0	Glyn	Glyn Valley Tram	Beyer Peacock & Co. wn3500 of 1892	Apr-08	PA
180	0-4-0+0-4-0	D.H.R. 31	Darjeeling Himalayan class D Garratt	Beyer Peacock wn5407 of 1910	May-06	PA
181	2-4-0t+t	Linda	Penryhn/Ffestiniog Hunslet	Hunslet Engine Company wn590 of 1893	Oct-05	MJL
182	2-6-2T	1257	War Department Light Railway Loco.	Alco Cooke wn57148 and LR10003	Sep-05	PA
183	0-4-0+0-4-0T	James Spooner	Ffestiniog Double Fairlie	Avonside Engine Co. wn929/930 of 1872	Jun-05	MJL
184	o-4-0T	Prince	Ffestiniog George England	George England & Co.	Dec-05	MJL
185	0-4-0	Lumpy Tom	Contractors Locomotive	Unknown–John Frazer & Co plate		MJL
186	0-4-0T+T	Little Giant	Ffestiniog George England	George England & Co. wn235	Jun-05	MJL
187	2-4-0+T		Konigliche Eisenbahn Regiment	Hohenzollern fabr.nu.473 of 1888	Oct-09	PA
188	0-6-2T	Airdmillan	Australian Sugar Plantation Loco.	John Fowler & Co. wn20763 of 1935	Aug-07	PA
189	0-4-0+0-4-0T	James Spooner	Ffestiniog Double Fairlie	Avonside Engine Co. wn929/930 of 1872	Feb-07	PA
190	0-4-0+0-4-0	D.H.R. 31	Darjeeling Himalayan class D Garratt	Beyer Peacock wn5407 of 1910	Nov-07	MJL
191	0-4-0	Glyn	Glyn Valley Tram	Beyer Peacock & Co. wn3500 of 1892	Mar-06	MJL
192	2-4-0+0-4-2	C.G.R.	Ceylon Government Railways class H1	Beyer Peacock & Co. wn6629 of 1929	Aug-08	MJL
193	2-4-0T+T	Linda	Penryhn/Ffestiniog Hunslet	Hunslet Engine Company wn590 of 1893	Feb-06	MJL
194	2-4-0T+T	Stella	Penryhn/Ffestiniog Hunslet	Hunslet Engine Company wn590 of 1893	May-06	MJL
195	4-4-0+T	1621	North Eastern Railway class M1	W. Worsdell 4-4-0 built Gateshead 1893	Nov-06	PA/MJL
196	4+4	Wellington	Modified Garratt	Freelance based on WN101	May-07	MJL
197	0-4-0+0-4-0	D.H.R. 31	Darjeeling Himalayan class D Garratt	Beyer Peacock wn5407 of 1910	Nov-06	MJL
198	4+4	No. 1	Bell Geared Articulated Loco.	Bell Locomotive Works, Inc. Double Truck	Mar-09	PA
199	0-4-0+0-4-0	D.H.R. 31	Darjeeling Himalayan class D Garratt	Beyer Peacock wn5407 of 1910	Feb-07	MJL
200	4+4	Sezela No. 7	2cyl Avonside Geared Articulated	Avonside Engine Co. wn2058 of 1931	Sep-09	PA
201	0-4-0+0-4-0	FCAF No.2	Ferrocarril Austral Fueguino Garratt	Tranex Turismo S.A.	May-08	PA
202	0-4-0		SLM Steam Tramway locomotive	SLM fabr. nu. 306/346	Jun-06	MJL
203	0-4-0	Milti	Sentinel 80hp Convertable	Sentinel Waggon Works wn S6895	Dec-06	PA
204	0-4-0T+T	Prince	Ffestiniog George England	George England & Co. of 1863	Jun-08	MJL
205	2-4-0+0-4-2	C.G.R.	Ceylon Government Railways class H1	Beyer Peacock & Co. wn6629 of 1929	Apr-07	PA
206	2-4-0+0-4-2	C.G.R.	Ceylon Government Railways class H1	Beyer Peacock & Co. wn6629 of 1929	Mar-08	PA
207	None					
208	0-4-0	15	Samuel Geoghegan Guinness Brewery	Avonside Engine Co./W. Spence	Aug-08	PA
209	0-4-0	Lewin	Stephen Lewin Overtype	Stephen Lewin	Jan-08	PA
210	0-4-0T+T	Little Giant	Ffestiniog George England	George England & Co.wn235 of 1867		MJL
211	0-4-0	Winterthur	Continental Steam Tram SMAS No.1	SLM fabr. nu. 306 of 1882		MJL
212	0-4-0	Groningen	Continental Steam Tram	Machinfabriek "Breda" wn235 of 1905	Oct-09	MJL
213	None					
214	0-4-0+0-4-0	Ing. L.D. Porta	Ferrocarril Austral Fueguino Garratt	Tranex Turismo S.A.	Jan-10	PA
215	2-6-0+0-6-2	NG55	South African Railways NGG11 Garratt	Beyer Peacock wn6200 of 1925	Feb-09	PA
216	0-6-0+T	No9	Burma Mines Railway	North British Locomotive wn18672 of 1908	Jan-11	PA
217	0-4-0+0-4-0T	James Spooner	Ffestiniog Double Fairlie	Avonside Engine Co. wn929/930 of 1872	Dec-07	MJL
218	2-4-0+0-4-2	C.G.R.	Ceylon Government Railways class H1	Beyer Peacock & Co. wn6629 of 1929	Jan-09	MJL
219	0-4-0T+T	Prince	Ffestiniog George England	George England & Co. of 1863	Apr-09	MJL
220	None					
221	0-4-0		7/8 scale De Winton	De Winton & Company Limited	Jan-13	PA
222	0-4-0T+T	Welsh Pony	Ffestiniog George England	George England & Co.wn234 of 1867	Jun-08	MJL
223	0-4-0T+T	Little Giant	Ffestiniog George England	George England & Co.wn235 of 1867	Jun-08	MJL
224	4+4	Sezela No. 7	2cyl Avonside Geared Articulated	Avonside Engine Co. wn2058 of 1931	Oct-08	MJL
225	0-4-0T+T	Welsh Pony	Ffestiniog George England	George England & Co. wn234 of 1867	Apr-09	MJL
226	0-4-0+0-4-0	James Spooner	Ffestiniog Double Fairlie	Avonside Engine Co. wn929/930 of 1872	Jun-09	MJL
227	4+4	Ntinyana	2cyl Avonside Geared Articulated	Avonside Co. wn2055 of 1931	Jan-09	MJL
228	0-4-0T+T	Dillon Thomas	Ffestiniog George England	George England & Co.	Dec-09	MJL
229	0-4-0	Luther	Continental Steam tram MEG 46	Grafenstaden wn4805 of 1897	Dec-08	PA
230	0-4-0	Lewin	Stephen Lewin Overtype	Stephen Lewin	Apr-09	PA
231	0-4-0	Robey	Robey Geared Saddle Tank	Robey & Co. wn15903 of 1895/6	Mar-09	PA
232	None					
233	0-6-0	Ursula	Eaton Railway	Duffield Bank of 1916	Sep-10	PA
234	o-4-0+0-4-0	D.H.R. 31	Darjeeling Himalayan class D Garratt	Beyer Peacock & Co. wn5407 of 1910	Jun-05	MJL
235	0-4-0	Grace 55LR	Continental Steam Tram	Machinfabriek "Breda" wn235 of 1905	Sep-09	MJL
236	0-4-0	The Don	Vertical Boiler Contractors Engine	Balmforth Brothers	Dec-11	PA
237	0-4-0T+T	Bert Bateman	Ffestiniog George England	George England & Co.	Dec-09	MJL
238	0-4-0+0-4-0	D.H.R. 31	Darjeeling Himalayan class D Garratt	Beyer Peacock & Co. wn5407 of 1910	Apr-10	MJL
239	0-4-0+0-4-0	David Llyod Geo	Ffestiniog Double Fairlie	Avonside Engine Co. wn929/930 of 1872	Feb-10	MJL
240	0-6-4	Snowden Ranger	Welsh Highland Rly Single Fairlie	Vulcan Foundry wn739 of 1874/5	Aug-10	PA
241	0-4-0		Samuel Geoghegan Guinness Brewery	Avonside Engine Co./W.Spence		MJL
242	0-4-0	Groningen	Continental Steam Tram	Machinfabriek "Breda" wn235 of 1905	Jan-11	PA
243	0-4-0	Hops	Stephen Lewin Overtype	Stephen Lewin	Apr-10	MJL
244	0-4-0	Robey	Robey Geared Saddle Tank	Robey & Co. wn15903 of 1895/6	Jan-10	MJL
245	0-4-0	Violet	Vertical Boiler Direct Drive	Unknown	Nov-09	PA
246	None					
247	0-4-0	M.B.R.O No21	Wilkinson Patent Vertical Boiler Tram	Beyer Peacock & Co. wn2377 of 1883	Nov-10	MJL
248	0-6-0	SNV1060	Societe National Des C de F Vicinaux	Thiriau wn261 of 1920	Dec-10	MJL
249	0-4-0	Plettenberg	Plettenberg Klienbahn Tram	Henschel & Sohn wn11949 of 1913	Mar-11	PA
250	0-4-0	Jack	John Knowles (Wooden Box) & Co 18in	Hunslet Engine Co. wn684 of 1898	Feb-10	PA
251	2-6-0+0-6-2	No55	S.A.R. Class NGG11 Garratt (coal fired)	Beyer Peacock wn6200 of 1925	Apr-11	MJL
252	0-6-4	Moel Tryfan	Welsh Highland Rly Single Fairlie	Vulcan Foundry wn738 of 1877	Jan-09	PA

WORKS NO.	WHEEL ARRANGEMENT	NAME	DESCRIPTION	BASED ON LOCOMOTIVE BUILT BY	DATE BUILT	BUILT BY
253	2-6-2	Mountaineer	Ffestiniog ex War Dept Light Railway	American Locomotive Co. No57156 of 1916	Oct-11	MJL
254	0-4-0	Noah	Sentinel 80hp Convertable	Sentinel Waggon Works	Mar-13	PA
255	None					
256	2-6-0+0-6-2	No54	S.A.R class NGG11 Garratt	Beyer Peacock wn6199 of 1925	Sep-11	MJL
257	2-6-2	Mountaineer	Ffestiniog ex War Dept Light Railway	American Locomotive Co. No57156 of 1916	Nov-11	MJL
258	0-4-0	Esme	Sand Hutton L. R. Ex Deptford Depot	Hunslet Engine Co. wn1289 of 1917	Feb-12	PA
259	None					
260	0-4-0	Gwen	John Knowles (Wooden Box) & Co 18in	Hunslet Engine Co. wn1404 of 1920	Aug-13	PA
261	0-4-0+0-4-0	James Spooner	Ffestiniog Double Fairlie	Avonside Engine Co. wn929/930 of 1872	Aug-11	MJL
262	4+4	Barracuda	2cyl Avonside Geared Articulated	Avonside Engine Company	Mar-12	MJL
263	0-6-0	V.F.S. Co. No4	Vancouver-Fiji Sugar Co.	W. G. Bagnall Limited wn1825 of 1906	Oct-12	PA
264	0-4-0	Glyn	Glyn Valley Tram	Beyer Peacock & Co wn3500 of 1892	Apr-12	MJL
265	4+4	Ntinyana	2cyl Avonside Geared Articulated	Avonside Engine Company wn2055 of 1931	Mar-12	MJL
266	2-6-0+0-6-2		Future NGG11 Garratt			
267	0-4-0	Woolwich	18in gauge Woolwich Arsenal Railway	Avonside Engine Co wn1748 of 1916	Mar-14	PA
268	0-4-0+T	Welsh Pony	Ffestiniog George England	George England wn234 of 1867	Jun-12	PA
269	4+4	Sezela No. 7	2cyl Avonside Geared Articulated	Avonside Engine Company wn2058 of 1931	nnn-10	MJL
270	4+4	Holton	Modified Garratt	Freelance based on WN101	Jun-12	MJL
271	0-4-0T+T	Welsh Pony	Ffestiniog George England	George England & Co wn234 of 1867	Jul-13	PA
272	4+4	Ntinyana	2cyl Avonside Geared Articulated	Avonside Engine Company wn2055 of 1931	Feb-12	MJL
273	o-6-2	KF3	Kalighat-Falta Railway No3	W G Bagnall Limited wn2028 of 1916	Jul-13	PA
274	0-4-0	No9	Darjeeling Himalayan Railway classA	Sharp, Stewart & Co wn3016 of 1882	Sep-11	PA
275	0-4-2	Serapis	18in gauge Woolwich Arsenal Railway	W G Bagnall Limited wn711 of 1885	Dec-13	PA
276	0-4-0	Groningen	Continental Steam Tram	Machinefabriek "Breda" wn235 of 1905	Apr-13	MJL
277	0-4-0	Corris No3	Corris Railway No3	Hughes Locomotive &Tramway Engine Works	May-13	PA
278	0-4-0T+T					
279	0-4-0	Baby Sivok	Darjeeling Himalayan Railway	Possibly Orenstein & Koppel wn5130 of 1911	Feb-12	PA
280	0-4-0+0-4-0	James Spooner	Ffestiniog Double Fairlie	Avonside Engine Co. wn929/930 of 1872	May-13	MJL
281	0-4-0		Sentinel 80hp Industrial	Sentinel Wagon Works S6751 of 1926	Sep-10	PA
282	0-4-0	Groningen	Continental Steam Tram	Machinefabriek Breda fabr nu236 of 1905	Sep-12	MJL
283	0-4-0	Kathleen	Alexandra Slate Co.	Vulcan Foundry wn805 of 1876		PA
284	0-4-0	Ratgoed	Sentinel 80hp Industrial	Sentinel Waggon Works S6751 of 1926	May-13	MJL
285	0-4-0	Arquebus	18in gauge Woolwich Arsenal Railway	Manning Wardle wn1130 of 1889	Apr-12	PA
286	4+4	Traveller	2cyl Avonside Geared Articulated	Avonside Engine Works	Jan-13	PA
287	0-4-0	Baby Sivok	Darjeeling Himalayan Railway	Possibly Orenstein & Koppel wn5130 of 1911	Feb-13	MJL
288	0-4-0	MBRO No21	Wilkinson Patent Vertical Boiler Tram	Beyer Peacock wn2377 of 1883	Nov-10	MJL
289	0-4-0	Baby Sivok	Darjeeling Himalayan Railway	Possibly Orenstein & Koppel wn5130 of 1911	Jun-13	MJL
290	0-4-0T+T		Ffestiniog George England	George England and Company	Sep-13	MJL
291	2-4-0+T		Konigliche Eisenbahn Regiment	Hohenzollern fabr.nu.473 of 1888	Sep-11	PA
292	0-6-4	Gowrie	Hunslet Single Fairlie	Hunslet Engine Company wn979 of 1908	Jul-13	MJL
293	2-4-0+0-4-2	C.G.R	Ceylon Government Railways class H1	Beyer Peacock wn6629 of 1929	Jan-14	MJL
294	0-4-0	No3	Corris Railway No3	Hughes Locomotive &Tramway Engine Works	Mar-14	MJL
295	0-4-0+0-4-0	James Spooner	Ffestiniog Double Fairlie	Avonside Engine Co. wn929/930 of 1872		PA
296	0-4-0	No3	Corris Railway No3	Hughes Locomotive &Tramway Engine Works	Mar-14	MJL
297	0-6-4	Gowrie	Hunslet Single Fairlie	Hunslet Engine Co. wn979 of 1908	Mar-14	MJL
298	0-4-0	No9	Darjeeling Himalayan A class	Sharp, Stewart & Co wn3016 of 1882	Jun-14	MJL
299	0-4-0	No10	Darjeeling Himalayan A class	Sharp, Stweart & Co wn3017 of 1882	Jun-14	MJL
300	4+4	Ntinyana	Avonside Articulated Tank Locomotive	Avonside Engine Company wn2055 of 1931		PA

Key
PA   = Peter Angus
MJL = Mike Lax

NOTES